REPRODUCTIVE INJUSTICE

Reproductive Injustice

Racism, Pregnancy, and Premature Birth

Dána-Ain Davis

NEW YORK UNIVERSITY PRESS

New York

NEW YORK UNIVERSITY PRESS
New York
www.nyupress.org
© 2019 by New York University
All rights reserved

References to Internet websites (URLs) were accurate at the time of writing. Neither the author nor New York University Press is responsible for URLs that may have expired or changed since the manuscript was prepared.

Library of Congress Cataloging-in-Publication Data
Names: Davis, Dána-Ain, 1958– author.
Title: Reproductive injustice : racism, pregnancy, and premature birth / Dána-Ain Davis.
Description: New York : New York University Press, [2019] | Series: Anthropologies of American medicine: culture, power, and practice | Includes bibliographical references and index.
Identifiers: LCCN 2018037661| ISBN 9781479812271 (cl : alk. paper) | ISBN 9781479853571 (pb : alk. paper)
Subjects: LCSH: Reproductive health services—Social aspects—United States. | Discrimination in medical care—United States. | African American women—Medical care—United States. | Race discrimination—Health aspects—United States.
Classification: LCC RA564.86 .D38 2019 | DDC 362.1082—dc23
LC record available at https://lccn.loc.gov/2018037661

New York University Press books are printed on acid-free paper, and their binding materials are chosen for strength and durability. We strive to use environmentally responsible suppliers and materials to the greatest extent possible in publishing our books.
Manufactured in the United States of America
10 9 8 7 6 5
Also available as an ebook

CONTENTS

LIST OF TABLE AND ILLUSTRATIONS

This book is about race and medical racism, Black women, and premature Black infants. When I first set out to do this research, I thought the
focus was going to be solely on neonatal intensive care units (NICUs),
the specialized hospital units dedicated to providing extensive medical
attention to newborns who are premature or otherwise ill. But looking
at NICUs, I realized, also required looking at Black women's birthing
experiences. Black women have higher rates of premature births than
any other women in America, and these rates of prematurity go beyond
class. One might expect that lower-income and poor women would
have higher rates of premature birth because of lack of care or resources.
Yet among Black women, being middle- or upper-class provides little
protection from the precarity of prematurity, in ways that do not hold
true for women of other racial backgrounds. This book looks into the
dynamics of how this may be the case. Placing these differences in birth
outcomes into a historical context, the book shows how contemporary
ideas about reproduction and race have been influenced by ideas that
developed during the era of slavery.

This book had its origins in a party I attended to celebrate the forti-
eth birthday of a friend. The celebration was hosted by Eric Johannes,
a physician.[1] Copious amounts of good eats led to a lot of banter, and
a discussion ensued about the number of work-related obligations we
each had in the coming weeks, and the particulars of our respective professions. Eric joined in and announced that the following week he would
be flying to another state to be on call, a kind of work I was unaware
doctors did. I asked him to describe his job, to which he responded that
he worked in an NICU as a surgeon, providing specialized care for congenitally ill and/or premature newborns.

Intrigued, I began what became seven years of research on "neonatal
intensive care units" and "prematurity." Typing those words into a search
engine revealed an interminable stream of announcements about hospi-

tals breaking ground for new or expanding NICUs in Texas, Louisiana, Pennsylvania, and Illinois, among other places. Nearly every state had an NICU expansion story.

As I began to conceive of a study of these units, Eric Johannes, the surgeon who had hosted my friend's birthday party, agreed to be interviewed and arranged to give me a tour of the NICU at his hospital. I had initially intended to explore the meaning doctors and nurses gave to NICUs and had no intention of talking to parents of children who were or had been NICU patients. I worried that it might be too painful for them to relive such a crisis as dealing with their premature or sick child. Ultimately, I did end up interviewing parents, largely because of a fortuitous meeting followed by a discovery. It was that meeting and the subsequent discovery that opened up my research beyond my initial ideas, in the end leading to this book being about pregnancy, prematurity, race, and racism.

The fortuitous meeting occurred in the fall of 2014, after I gave a talk on NICUs at a university in Illinois. At the end of the talk, a young Black woman named Ashley approached me and said that she wanted to share the story of her pregnancy and premature birth with me.

Ashley's description of how she was treated during not one but two pregnancies raised a number of questions about the racial dimensions of prematurity and the technologies used to save premature infants born to Black women. Ashley felt that doctors had misdiagnosed issues that arose during her pregnancy and that racism had something to do with the care she received. I began to wonder what other women, especially women of color, thought and felt about giving birth prematurely, and what role they believed race and racism played in their pregnancy, their treatment, and the admission of their children into the NICU.

After hearing Ashley's story, I found myself remembering my own pregnancy, which I had not thought about in many years. Similar to Ashley, I had become pregnant when I was in college. In 1980, like Ashley, I too was single and working for hourly wages, at the Miya Gallery in Washington, DC. On the top floor of a beautiful brownstone, in the moderately renovated hot attic, I framed pictures. I also organized events, such as when Olabisi Olaniyi, the wife of the famous Yoruba modernist artist Prince Twins Seven Seven, exhibited her work at the gallery. Within my remembrance of my own birth story are many of the themes and threads about Black women, race, and prematurity that are the focus of this book.

My Birth Story

Being near-broke, which is not the same as being impoverished, forced me to identify resources that would facilitate the birth of the baby whom I wanted so badly. Although not a Seventh-day Adventist, I applied for and was admitted to a hospital-based clinic program for low-income women at the Seventh-day Adventist hospital in Takoma Park, Maryland. The arrangement required making monthly payments to cover the cost, which, I recall, was $700 based on a "normal," full-term vaginal delivery, or about $2,000 in 2018 dollars.

One morning in the spring of 1980, in my second trimester, I woke up bleeding. Scared, I made an appointment at the clinic. I had an ultrasound—the only one I received during my pregnancy. After consulting with the technician, the obstetrician, who was a white male, came into the examining room and told me it looked like I might be having twins and that one was a girl, which was "good because girl babies are strong." From the sound of his voice, which was foreboding, I assumed that I might lose the twins; after all, why would he say girl babies are strong? He asked what I did for a living, and I said I framed pictures and organized exhibits. He also asked a number of questions about my educational status, family background, and marital status. In retrospect, I do not think he was actually interested in me as a person. In fact, I thought his questions were condescending, in part because it seemed as if he was trying to find within my narrative a stereotypical thread about the young-looking twenty-two-year-old Black woman who sat before him. That is how I would characterize the doctor's questions—predicated on assumptions that my family or I were potentially pathological from his perspective. My perception was that he was judging me, based on ideas nourished by my race, my age, and the fact that I needed charity care. There was nothing in particular about what he said, but there was something about his tone and how he asked questions. I was just *uncertain* that he was *not* insinuating something based on his questions. Frankly, that interaction made me feel like I did not want to see him again, which was not a problem since in the clinic I rarely saw the same doctor twice.

His final warning to me was that I should be on bed rest for a month or I could lose the twins or go into premature labor.

After leaving the doctors' office, I went to see the social worker assigned to my case. What "assigned" really meant was that she wanted to ensure that I made my payments. At least, that was what I surmised. When I arrived at her office, we discussed what would happen if I had a premature birth, and the social worker informed me that my final payment would skyrocket. That was her primary focus—skyrocketing payments. I resented the entire conversation.

Prematurity is scary, and no one is really ever prepared. I have no recollection of ever being informed why I was bleeding, what it meant to have a premature infant, what the circumstances were that could precipitate such a turning point in my pregnancy, or the consequences either for me or for the babies. My fears were not centered on the possibility that a neonatal care unit was in my future—because at the time, I did not really know what that was. What concerned me more was losing the babies and the possibility of having to pay far more than I could afford for anything other than a vaginal birth. As it turned out, my ultrasound was misread and I did not have twins. Nor did I go into labor early. However, I did have a cesarean section (C-section), which increased my final payment by about $250. The hospital pestered me for several months until it was paid off.

My recollection of that event was precipitated by the interview with Ashley, and it made me feel as if our paths were similar. In some ways neither of us knew what was going on with our pregnancies, and neither of us had been told about the consequences of premature birth, either. Inspired by the similarities in our respective situations, the focus of this project centered on Black women's specific experiences with prematurity. The research was also driven by the fact that in US politics, as many scholars have pointed out, women have been largely erased from the issue of reproduction. Indeed, the politics of reproduction have generally centered on fetuses, newborns, and infants (L. M. Morgan and Michaels 1999). This book brings women—specifically Black women—to the center of inquiry on the social context of reproduction.

Rediscovery

Later, one winter night in 2015, I made a rediscovery that led me to focus on prematurity. In a search of historical references offering definitions of prematurity, I came across a document that, in 1948, defined prematurity as "a pregnancy that has ended at 37 weeks" (Dunham 1948, 1). Three pages later it stated that since gestation was only an estimate, a neonate—defined as a newborn less than twenty-eight days old—with a birth weight of five pounds and eight ounces or less, regardless of the estimated last period a woman reports, was premature. I recalled my mother mentioning that I had been born early by about a month. After searching for and finding my baby book, there it was: I had weighed five pounds and six ounces. So, according to the document's definition, I was considered premature.

Ashley and I, two Black women separated in age by more than three decades, had somewhat similar encounters. The circumstances of our pregnancies were similar, and both of us were apprehensive about the interactions we had with our medical providers. We were both women with some college education—I was to graduate in the fall of 1980, and my daughter was born in 1981—at the time of our pregnancies. Depending on one's definition, we would both be considered middle-class women. Class, of course, is a fuzzy category, as anthropologist Emily Martin has noted: those in the middle strata include both people in professions and those who possess access to resources that offer "greater autonomy, responsibility, mobility and prestige" (1987, 4). However, class is also raced in different ways, depending on gender. For instance, women who are working and middle-class are often understood to be white, whereas Black women are often viewed as being low-income or poor (Bettie 2014, 34).

Ashley and I had access to resources, and our class position intersected with race. From our respective perceptions, it was race that confounded our medical treatment and the care we received. So, while class was the presumptive factor that may have positively orchestrated our health care—as many believe is the right that comes with class—our race preempted the social capital that supposedly accompanies particular class benefits with regard to that care. We were two Black women.

There is also the fact that Ashley was just as likely to have a premature birth in 2008 as I was in 1981. That reality did not coalesce only around class; it was race that was the defining feature that made each of us twice as likely as white women to give birth prematurely (Centers for Disease Control and Prevention 2015). Race mattered for us because white women do not fit into the dominant narrative that moves across the American imaginary about who gives birth prematurely. It is Black women who hold that place, and it is Black women who are castigated for their reproduction.

Importantly, for both Ashley and me, in our medical care interactions neither of us was able to shake the feeling that some degree of racism had sabotaged a part of our prenatal care. We were not always quite certain *how* race and racism mediated the care we received during our pregnancies, but we knew it did. That is what this book is about: Black women's narratives of prenatal care, pregnancies, and prematurity and their understandings of the racism they experience as they strive to give birth to children who will thrive and to give voice to the ongoing legacy of racism in the way they are treated—a legacy now several hundred years old.

Being born prior to full term almost always leads to admission of a newborn to the NICU. So, the NICU became the conversational place of departure from which I learned about Black women's thoughts on prematurity. I wanted to hear their viewpoints regarding what contributes to premature birth and to experiences in the NICU. I was especially interested in how they and their infants were treated by doctors, nurses, and others involved in the care of their children.

This is a topic with which you probably have some familiarity. The popular press regularly reports on Black women's adverse birth outcomes. A search in the *New York Times* for the term "Black women premature birth" showed sixty-five results between 2007 and 2017.[2] Although you have probably read about Black women and infant mortality, Black women and low-birth-weight infants, and Black women whose babies are born too early, this book tells the contemporary story of pregnancy and premature birth against the backdrop of the legacy of slavery. It underscores the history of Black women's reproductive exploitation and reminds us that Black women have had to endure a medical structure that has historically not really viewed them as worth caring for—I mean *really* caring for.

I listened to women (and some men) share their stories. On the one hand, they spoke their truths about pregnancy, laboring, birthing,[3] and, for most of them, waiting for their newborns to be discharged from the NICU. On the other hand, their descriptions sometimes hint at, or boldly demonstrate, the gradations of racism in medical encounters. These gradations include cases where racism was not felt or perceived by Black women and men. For instance, whereas some women felt the derision of racism, others did not. Yet it is important to point out that even if the people with whom I spoke reported not having had to confront racism during their medical encounters, this does not mean racism is not operating within the medical system. One of the primary claims of this book is that in issues of reproduction and prematurity, race matters. Racism matters. This holds true even when there is no direct impact perceived by those receiving treatment. The data and statistics support— and plainly illustrate—this claim.

The geographer Ruth Wilson Gilmore (2007) usefully defines racism as the institutional and state-sanctioned practices that make particularly designated groups of people vulnerable to harmful outcomes and premature death. Others such as Omi and Winant (1986) have analyzed the ways in which racial groups are formed. Focusing on how race and racism are understood and felt by Black women in their medical encounters while pregnant and after their babies are born and enter the NICU, this book looks at experiences of racial inequality at the very start of life, and from the point of view of racialized childbearers—that is, Black mothers. At the heart of this book are an understanding and an analysis of how these women characterize their interactions with medical professionals regarding the care they received (or did not) during and after their pregnancies, and the ways that medical racism continues to contribute to differential life chances in the contemporary United States.

Medical racism refers to much more than the care that is rationed by the medical profession, as Dr. H. Jack Geiger (1996), one of the originators of the community health center model in the United States, has pointed out. Medical racism also includes the sometimes subtle and sometimes not-so-subtle ways in which the medical complex, in each of its parts, cumulatively dismisses, misdiagnoses, and undermines women's feelings and intuitions about their reproducing bodies and, more specifically, disproportionately undermines Black women's reproduction. This book, then, views medical racism as a problem that transcends individual doctors and medical professionals. It also views medical racism as compromising more than individual women. In exploring the meaning and interpretations women have of racism by analyzing their oral histories, here referred to as birth stories, this book examines medical racism and Black women's reproduction as a complex cultural system with deep historical roots.

As women shared their birth stories, their circumstances of conception, what their pregnancies were like, and how they felt during labor, birthing, and after, I was struck by how much of the content of their contemporary narratives resembled accounts of medical racism from centuries past. Thus, these women's accounts illuminate the ways in which historical structures and conceptions of race are inextricably tied up in contemporary medical understandings of prematurity and pregnancy in the twenty-first century, drawing our attention to the existence of a medical racism that continues to operate today, often similar to ideas and practices that originated during the era of slavery.

Introduction

How do you keep the Black female body present and how do
you own value for something that society won't give value to?
—Claudia Rankine (Cocozza 2015)

In 2008, Ashley Bey, a nineteen-year-old African American woman
from Illinois, was a college student when she became pregnant and then
delivered a little girl, Jamie, three months early.[1] We met after I gave a
talk in 2014 at a university in Illinois about my research on neonatal
intensive care units (NICUs). She brought both of her children, Jamie
and Justin, to the talk. Jamie sat on the side of the room coloring while
her mother rocked the carriage in which Justin was sleeping. An hour
later, at the end of the talk, Ashley tremulously made her way to the
front of the room where I was standing. I saw her from the corner of
my eye, but I was engaged in conversation with some of the faculty who
had attended. Ashley waited patiently. After I finished my conversation,
I turned and gestured for her to come closer. She appeared uncomfort-
able, so I made small talk and chatted with her daughter, which seemed
the best way to ease Ashley's discomfort. After a while, there were only
about two or three other people left in the room. As they conversed with
each other, Ashley looked at me and said in a hushed tone, "My daughter
and son were premature, and I would like to talk about it." In social science research, we hardly ever have people ask to be interviewed, but she
and I exchanged contact information. The plan was to let her take the
lead in contacting me. I suggested she call me when she was ready to talk
about the births of her children.

Ultimately, that conversation with Ashley would help to alter the
shape of this book. Her story, as we will see, exemplifies a common
problem. Black women are more likely than any other women in the
United States to experience premature births, and to have low-birth-
weight infants. This book, in part spurred by that fateful conversation

with Ashley, undertakes a historically grounded discussion of this phenomenon. Ashley's story is one of the many I collected during seven
years of research that have culminated in this book. I argue that some
pregnant Black women, like Ashley, experience medical encounters
reminiscent of racist medical practices and beliefs that have persisted
from the 1700s. My attempts to understand the historical roots of those
experiences took me to medical journals, historians' accounts, and other
sources ranging from the 1700s to the twenty-first century. Using the
afterlife of slavery framework as a critical lens to situate medical professionals' practices, this book explores how Black women's prenatal care,
labor, birth, and treatment in medical environments, are extensions of
eighteenth-, nineteenth-, and twentieth-century racial thinking. My
analysis shows that despite the determined efforts of medical personnel,
of the staff of agencies working to reduce adverse birth outcomes, and of
birthing and reproductive justice advocates, the power of race and racism cuts across the American class divide, producing racial disparities in
infant mortality and prematurity rates that call into question the efficacy
of the "technologies of saving" pursued by advocates of NICUs and the
health education campaigns used by public health proponents.

After the talk at which I met Ashley, I was driving to the airport and
heard a weather report on the radio: the waters of Lake Michigan were
surging. My palms felt as wet as the lake from anxiety, sweaty as I considered the implications of now including women in my research on
NICUs. How could I tell their stories about pregnancies and births in
ways that did not reproduce "ethnoporn," a term I use to describe sustained ethnographic descriptions of incidents weighted down by graphic
detail?[2] Concerns revolving around power dynamics and ethical relationships between researcher and informant have been taken up by feminist scholars for several decades, and these matters also preoccupied
me not only as a researcher but as a Black mother, and as a technically
premature birth myself (Stacey 1988; Oakley 2016).[3]

It was not so much that I feared an ethical dilemma about the research, although I wondered what feelings might emerge as a result
of women reliving the memories of their difficult pregnancies and the
births of their children. Rather, I wanted to be mindful of the choices I
made in sharing the women's experiences, of the analytical pitfalls and
incentives that sometimes accompany such research (González-Lopez

2011). For example, narrative data presented in talks and panel discussions, often with predominantly white audiences, sometimes introduce the risk of narrowly positioning Black women primarily as victims. Like literary scholar and author Roxane Gay (2017), who describes how her discussions of being raped might be the only thing that would make her memorable, I was concerned that women's accounts of adverse pregnancies would be the *only* way in which they might be remembered.

After consultation with some of the women who participated in the project, I determined that there was no way to anesthetize women's descriptions of pregnancies that ended up in premature birth. If the women were willing to disclose the trauma of their pregnancies, labors, and births, then I would not write *around* what happened or the feelings that surfaced. And, indeed, they were willing. Their narratives led me to see how Black women interpret their births and how some resisted the shroud of adverse outcomes. Many do this by finding comprehensive care and alternative birthing methods. Women shared their encounters, hoping that others might benefit. So, it is with great humility that I share their stories with you.

* * *

Two months after we met, Ashley called, and we agreed to connect in a phone interview a few weeks later. When we spoke that first time, hardly any niceties were exchanged; Ashley launched right into what happened during both of her pregnancies. The reason for the first premature birth, Ashley revealed, was that she had placenta previa, a condition in which a placenta partially or totally covers the opening in the mother's cervix. The placenta, which provides oxygen and nutrients to the developing embryo and removes waste products from its blood, is attached to the uterine wall, from which the umbilical cord arises. In most pregnancies, the placenta attaches at the top or side of the uterus, but in Ashley's case it was attached at the lower end of her uterus. Because placenta previa can cause severe bleeding before or during birth, care providers recommend that women who are diagnosed with this condition refrain from physical exertion for a portion of their pregnancy. Despite bed rest, it is still likely that these women will have to undergo a C-section.

Just after Ashley disclosed that she had given birth prematurely, there was a pause—she inhaled then exhaled. Her deep breath seemed to propel the energy she needed to continue her story. After the exhale, Ashley was calmer than before, as she described her pregnancy. After she found out she was pregnant, Ashley took a leave of absence from college, moved home with her parents, and began working at a part-time job. She also signed up for All Kids, an insurance program for low-income people, during her pregnancy.[4]

Ashley had an ultrasound during her first trimester, and everything seemed fine. But during her second trimester, Ashley began to sense that something was wrong; she just did not feel right. Her concern precipitated her request for an additional ultrasound, but she said her doctor told her, "No, we don't want to give you another ultrasound because we don't want to hurt the baby." During that same visit, Ashley asked the doctor again, and he responded that she did not need one. Ashely recalled, "After that, I was afraid. I thought I was going to have a miscarriage."

One weekend, when her parents were out of town, things took a turn for the worse. Ashley shared with me:

> It was early in the morning. I was confused, scared, and bleeding. I went to the hospital and they put me on magnesium for hypertension so I wouldn't have seizures.[5] I was at a teaching hospital. The nurses wanted to put in the IV. But I was swollen, my hands looked like I was a drug addict. . . . The people [at the hospital] were talking to me, but I did not hear what they were saying. I finally only understood [what was happening] because my grandmother and my aunt—who were both medical professionals—RNs—came later and explained what was going on with me.

It was at this point that Ashley's placenta previa had been diagnosed. In a brief departure from the story of her unexpected labor, Ashley then began to tell me about her aunt, who had been a midwife for ten or fifteen years. I think this was Ashley's version of taking a small break because when she resumed talking about the birth, she began talking rapidly:

> When I arrived at the hospital, they tried to keep me on bed rest most of the day. They had me on machines and kept a close watch. They were hoping that the bleeding would stop. But then Jamie's heart rate dropped

and they performed an emergency C-section. Jamie was born at twenty-six weeks and weighed one pound and eight ounces. She received a steroid shot to help with lung development, and then they took her to the incubator in the neonatal intensive care unit. I was in the hospital for about three days. Jamie was in the hospital from January 10 to March 6.

It is January 9, I thought to myself. At that moment, I realized we were having our conversation just one day before the anniversary of Jamie's arrival. Worried, I wondered if it was too difficult to continue the conversation. Should I offer to end it? I asked, but Ashley said she wanted to continue, although just after sharing with me the details of her admission to the emergency room, there was silence on the phone. I broke it. "Ashley, how did they treat you and Jamie in the NICU?" Ashley responded, stating, "They treated Jamie fine. The NICU care was good." Her response was not entirely accurate because later during our conversation, Ashley shared two disturbing incidents. First, on one of her daily visits Ashley arrived at the NICU to find that the tape used to hold down the nasal cannula inserted into Jamie's nose had been taken off. The removal of the tape had pulled off some of the skin from Jamie's upper lip. Ashley mentioned this to the nurse and requested they be more careful, which, Ashley felt, caused the nurse to be annoyed with her. The nurse's annoyance intimidated Ashley, which in turn, she said, made her feel that some harm or neglect might befall Jamie.

Then there was the time when a nurse, who had not seen Ashley, put her own photo over Jamie's isolette, or incubator. To Ashley, it was both infuriating and humiliating. It was infuriating because the nurse felt entitled to express her attachment to Jamie, which was disrespectful to Ashley, as Jamie's mother. At the same time, it was also humiliating because Ashley said she was afraid to confront the nurse, though she wanted to do so, but feared there might be some retaliation against Jamie.

I later asked the question again, trying to ascertain if Ashley thought she was treated differently because she received All Kids, since receiving Medicaid or assistance from any public insurance program often "is sufficient to establish that a woman is 'at social risk'" (Bridges 2011, 57). I also asked all women and the fathers whether they felt they and their children were treated differently due to race. Ashley responded, "I personally don't think they cared about me." Even though she had some college education, Ashely admitted that she lacked knowledge about prenatal issues. So, when she asked questions, she doubted herself a little bit. When the medical staff spoke they "spewed out words," which led to her feeling somewhat inept. Ashley believed that her care was compromised by the fact that she was young and the assumptions that the staff made about her education and economic status. These issues, combined with her race, led to medical professionals treating her dismissively. It did not matter if the medical professionals were Black or white, because Ashley's providers were both. One of the points here is that as a cultural system, medical racism can be enacted by people of any racial or ethnic background; what matters more is who is being acted upon, and who suffers the consequences.

It should not be difficult to see how Ashley might connect the medical staff's unwillingness to give her the second ultrasound, being dismissive of her concerns, and even the nurse taking the liberty of posting her own picture above Ashley's baby's isolette as manifestations of the intersection of race and class. Indeed, she surmised, "I think they looked at me as just another young Black girl receiving aid. And, that is why I did not get the second ultrasound. If I had, maybe they would have been able to catch the placenta previa."[6]

While this may not seem relevant to the discussion of Ashley's treatment, the point she made was that she had not received the appropriate care. She felt that her race combined with her age and the fact that she received assistance meant that the medical staff considered it unnecessary to treat her with respect or take the time to explain what was going on in a way she was able to comprehend. Ashley's summation suggests that when age and race intersect with type of insurance, that combination comes to stand in for one's class and one's ability to synthesize medical information, and these things together can influence how a person is treated. Preconceived ideas about Black women and public assistance certainly circulate in the popular realm and in the medical profession. Notably, receipt of public assistance is not necessarily indicative of a lack of education or lack of health knowledge. Nonetheless, poor women and women of color are often viewed with contempt by medical professionals and are seen as having "unruly bodies" (Bridges 2011, 16) and are easily disregarded.

What if the problem is age? It may seem easy to attribute Ashley's situation to her youth; she was, after all, just nineteen. One might presume that her age made her less capable of negotiating with medical providers. One might also conclude that access to resources and private insurance offer protections against racial stereotyping or mistreatment. But, as the stories in this book will show, the questions, concerns, and uncertainties Ashley had about her treatment by doctors were similar to what other Black women of all ages experienced as well.

* * *

As she spoke, Ashley tacked back and forth in time, recalling different incidents. Sometimes it was difficult to follow her narrative. Her storytelling method illustrated the anxiety Ashley felt because she sensed there was a problem with her pregnancy but was dismissed by the doctor when she suggested another ultrasound. She expressed confusion about why she was bleeding but not being fully informed by medical personnel what was happening to her body. What may have been useful was for Ashley to have support, someone to serve as a mediator between her and the medical professionals—a person to advocate for her and on her behalf, as well as to be a witness during her medical encounters. Although her grandmother and aunt could have served that purpose, they did not live nearby.

Ashley's story offers insight into the sometimes complicated relationship that Black women have with medical professionals with regard to reproduction, and specifically with regard to pregnancy and childbirth. She is one of the many African American women who have given birth prematurely in the United States and whose reproductive lives are often conveyed in terms of statistical data.[7] Black women are more likely to die in pregnancy or childbirth, at a rate of three to four times that of white women (Maron 2015); according to the March of Dimes (2011), Black women in the United States are two times more likely to give birth prematurely than any other group of women. Ashley's reproductive outcome is thus common among Black women who, regardless of class, have higher rates of premature births and low-birth-weight infants (Mullings and Wali 2001).

Among the range of health concerns Black women face during pregnancy, childbearing, and after birth are inadequate receipt of prenatal care, the prevalence of preterm birth, fetal mortality, restricted fetal growth, and maternal mortality. All these problems vary by maternal race/ethnicity (Bryant et al. 2010). Similar disparities exist among Native American women. Consider, for example, the work of sociologist Barbara Gurr (2015), whose scholarship is considered to be the first analysis of Native American women's reproductive health care. At the time Gurr conducted her research, she found that the infant mortality rate was 28 percent higher among Native women than for all other US groups combined. Legacies of racism, gender, and class inequities also help to explain some of the obstetric violence toward and neglectful maternal experiences of Mexican women (Dixon 2015; Smith-Oka 2013), although racial categories in Latin America are typically organized in relation to ancestry and socioeconomic status, and racism is articulated differently than in the United States.

This book explores how medical racism—that is, the ideas and practices that perpetuate racial hierarchies and compromise one's health or facilitate vulnerability to premature illness or death—influences medical encounters in the United States, particularly as it relates to Black women's reproduction. It argues that Black women's pregnancies and premature births are important sites of analysis to help us to understand medical racism.

Black women's poor reproductive outcomes are often seen as a woman's personal failure. For example, Black women's adverse birth outcomes are typically discussed in terms of what the women do, such as drinking alcohol, smoking, and having less than optimal eating habits that lead to obesity and hypertension (Florido 2014). In other instances, their low earnings or their age is the focus of blame (Shamus 2016). They may be seen to be at risk based on the presumption that they are "single," when in fact they have a partner—but are unmarried. Whatever the circumstance, Black women become wedged between embodying risk and being the targets of intervention.

Articles in the popular press tend to point out risk factors related to premature birth and birth outcomes by focusing on women who live under the most socioeconomically compromised circumstances: with poor prospects for employment and often facing health challenges such as diabetes and high blood pressure, along with other negative social determinants (see Braverman 2008). Combined, these characteristics make Black women the foci of behavioral and public health education interventions. To be sure, these are factors that should not be dismissed. But that was not Ashley's story line. Nor was it the story line of any other woman interviewed for this book.

What makes this book unique is that it centers on women whose social location—through their attainment of higher education and professional status—complicates common presumptions about who "carries" the risk factors leading to adverse birth outcomes. In this book, it is Black women—and those who are professional and college educated— who are central. Importantly, they too give birth prematurely at higher rates than white women with the least amount of education.[8]

Additionally, this book is distinctive because discussions of premature birth generally privilege the infant and treatments used to address issues of fetal viability or underdevelopment. Here the focus is on mothers, placing Black women at the center of an analysis of reproduction. This approach is acutely important because the rise of reproductive technology has tended to decenter or displace women. Because of the degree to which technology mediates reproduction, much of the research has made technology the object of reproductive investigation. For instance, many scholars view surrogacy as a form of assisted reproductive technology (ART) that reduces women to rentable wombs (Twine 2011). Other feminist scholars of reproduction have noted—with alarm—that the rise of fetal protections, fetal surgeries, and ARTs and the dismantling of support for access to reproductive health care has led to the diminished importance of women (Casper 1998; Petchesky 2003; Ross and Solinger 2017).

Finally, this book does what anthropologist Leith Mullings suggests in her important article "Interrogating Racism: Toward an Antiracist Anthropology" (2005a). It goes beyond discussions of the socially constructed nature of race and attends to how racism in *practice*, a fundamental element of the social structure, is captured in women's impression of medical encounters. It takes a different tack than sociologist John Hoberman's book *Black and Blue: The Origins and Consequences of Medical Racism* (2012). Whereas Hoberman describes what *doctors* think about racial difference and how those differences play out in treatment, this book excavates *women's* sense of racism during medical encounters. Consequently, this book is inspired by critical medical anthropology, which anthropologist Hans Baer defines as that which "aspires to merge theory and praxis in [a] desire to promote experiential health as opposed to the functional health associated with contemporary political economics around the world" (1990, 1011). Because it appraises experiences rather than extrapolating data in the way that epidemiology does, this book offers a critical voice to the medicalization of pregnancy (Scheper-Hughes and Lock 1987).

This book draws on ethnographic interviews with nearly fifty people, including professional Black women (and three fathers), as well as doctors, nurses, March of Dimes administrators, and birth justice advocates, with the goal of examining pregnancy, prematurity, and NICUs as sites through which medical racism can be understood. Those narratives place this project in the tradition of Black feminist thought in the United States, as this research focuses on Black women to understand everyday life. As used here, a Black feminist approach resists the erasure of Black women's lives and recognizes their experiences as sources of knowledge production. It takes seriously the credibility of Black women's interpretive lens and privileges their feelings and analysis of the world, in this case of medical encounters (Collins 1991; Mullings 2000). As Lorde (1984) and Anzaldúa (1987) remind us, the details of the everyday and the particularities of lay knowledge stimulate an understanding of and ability to dismantle power.

Feminist inquiry into reproduction in the United States has tended to focus on the development and/or consequences of reproductive technology (see, for example, Casper 1998; Rapp 1999; L. M. Morgan 2009). Some scholars have conducted provocative investigations of nation building through reproductive processes (see Andaya 2014; Kanaaneh 2002). Other feminist anthropologists have unpacked the confluence of reproduction and race or race-making, which has been particularly insightful. For example, anthropologist Elizabeth F. S. Roberts's (2012) ethnography of assisted reproduction in Ecuador reveals the relationship between science, religion, and race, emphasizing how race—whiteness in particular—is achieved through the types of medical care received. A second example is Daisy Deomampo's (2016) research on surrogacy in India. Delving into how race is formed through instruments of the state and medical practices, Deomampo shows how ideas of race are articulated in the transactional process of egg donation for surrogacy and further mediated through medical professionals and the state. Although race is increasingly at the center of reproductive scholarship, a limited number of anthropological texts explore reproduction and race in the United States—and too few lift up Black women's reproductive lives.

In addition to being grounded in a Black feminist approach, this book is rooted in a Black feminist praxis by virtue of its citational politics (Ahmed 2017; Bolles 2013). This is a politics that insists on replicating knowledge about the subject of reproduction, prenatal care, and giving birth—as much as possible—from the corpus of work developed by women of color in general and Black women in particular. So, while this work builds on the robust tradition of feminist anthropological scholarship that has placed reproduction at the center of social theory (Ginsburg and Rapp 1995; Colen 1995) and is ideologically, theoretically, and politically aligned with that work, I have also placed emphasis on citing women of color.

Four US-based feminist scholars of reproduction and medical anthropology have especially influenced this book. Legal scholar Dorothy Roberts; anthropologists Leith Mullings and Alaka Wali; and legal scholar and anthropologist Khiara Bridges have each shed light on the racial aspects of reproduction. Respectively, they explore how law and policy seek to interrupt Black women's reproduction, how low birth weight and infant mortality occur in the context of social stress and racism, and the political economy of reproduction.

In *Killing the Black Body: Race, Reproduction and the Meaning of Liberty* (1997), Dorothy E. Roberts considers the linkage between reproduction and racial inequality, drawing out how Black women's reproduction has been regulated, which in turn has shaped what reproductive liberty means in the United States. Using historical and legal documents, Roberts explains how racial inequality has sabotaged, indeed destroyed, the idea of reproductive liberty on the backs of Black women.

The rich analysis Leith Mullings and Alaka Wali provide in *Stress and Resilience: The Social Context of Reproduction in Central Harlem* (2001) is based on an investigation of factors that lead to Black women's higher rates of preterm birth and low-birth-weight infants. These scholars analyze a cross section of women's experiences to understand what kinds of stresses impact their reproduction (such as housing fragility, unemployment, and work-related stress). Mullings and Wali also identify the strategies that Black women deploy in the face of challenges related to their pregnancies and other forms of social reproduction.

More recently, in *Reproducing Race: An Ethnography of Pregnancy as a Site of Racialization* (2011), Khiara Bridges has explored the medical practices that racialize pregnant women living in New York City who are receiving Medicaid and use a public hospital for prenatal care. What Bridges describes in her analysis of women's medical interactions during pregnancy resonates with some of the incidents described by the women featured in this book. However, another group of women are also important in this book, namely, birth workers. Examining Black women's encounters of medical racism with medical professionals is another way of understanding biopolitics—the authoritative practice of intervention (Foucault 1997)—and can ultimately lead us to investigate how women resist that power.[9] Therefore, by exploring what it means for Black women's reproduction to be abridged or neglected by medical professionals, this book also investigates the role played by reproductive care providers and advocates. Thus, the book asks, what are the ways in which pregnancy, labor, birthing, and having a premature infant in the NICU intersect with articulations of medical racism, and what strategies are used to address these problems?

Importantly, the difference in rates of prematurity by race in the United States has held strong since the time of enslavement. Thus, it is also useful to ask, how can historical references help us to understand how Black women are cared for and treated during medical interactions today? What form does contestation against the power of medical professionals take in stemming the tide of premature births among Black women?

What of women who do not have encounters that are characterized as medical racism? Do they confound the questions posed here? This book does not shy away from examples of women who maintain they have not had to contend with the same sort of racist practices in their medical encounters that Ashley confronted. In fact, it attempts to depict a range of circumstances experienced by Black women who were pregnant and gave birth. Even when women have positive encounters, they are giving birth in an anti-Black society, one that has continued to treat Black people with disdain, and they are experiencing their pregnancies and labor in a time that is the afterlife of slavery.

In the Afterlife of Slavery

This book offers a critical analysis of Black women's pregnancy and premature birth, arguing that ideas about Black women that have historically circulated in the medical field must be understood as an extension of what Saidiya Hartman calls the afterlife of slavery. More specifically, prematurity, the most common cause of infant mortality, is an expression of this afterlife of slavery, interpretable through history. Hartman defines the afterlife of slavery this way:

> Slavery had established a measure of man and a ranking of life and worth that has yet to be undone. If slavery persists as an issue in the political life of Black America, it is not because of an antiquarian obsession with bygone days or the burden of a too long memory, but because Black lives are still imperiled and devalued by a racial calculus and a political arithmetic that were entrenched centuries ago. This is the afterlife of slavery—skewed life chances, limited access to health and education, premature death, incarceration, and impoverishment. I am the afterlife of slavery. (2007, 6)

I take Hartman's definition of the afterlife of slavery not only as an impetus to connect the past to present issues but also as a form of situatedness. She identifies her position as a Black professional woman who feels the reverberation of enslavement, thus elucidating the broad reach and impact of the afterlife of slavery. The afterlife of slavery is a critical framework that makes it possible to talk about the continuation of racism in the medical management of Black women's reproduction. The precarities of chattel slavery continue to impose on the conditions of Black life. Whereas reproduction has been invigorated by past racial hierarchies, the dystopian past is not *just* the past. The dystopian past inhabits present practices, including the practice of medicine.

Across a number of disciplines, rich scholarship explores antiblack racism through the afterlife of slavery concept to theorize how racial hierarchies have been and continue to be replenished.[10] Among the contributions this scholarship makes is offering a way to think about the continuity of white supremacy; it does not decouple Black people's contemporary lives from earlier periods, and it advances a critical methodology that facilitates a mode of inquiry that brings the past and present closer together. Cumulatively, this body of work offers a radical reading of current issues as they relate to historical sources.

Both racism and slavery in the United States have facilitated a reproductive dystopia in which almost all aspects of reproduction idealize whiteness. From breastfeeding to the fragility of uteruses, the pretense of perfection and importance has been legitimated through white womanhood (Schiebinger 2004). Additionally, in obstetric medicine, physicians have increasingly rebuffed women's sense about their bodies, relying less on patient narratives in diagnosing disease and more on physical examinations (Schwartz 2006, 129). These changes in medical practice have positioned women differentially: whereas white women's reproduction has been depicted in terms of chastity, enslaved women's reproduction was generally viewed as evidence of promiscuity and lasciviousness or as necessary for racial capital (J. L. Morgan 2004). As medicine garnered greater acceptance, slaveholders relied on physicians to determine women's reproductive status, harnessing medical treatment and diagnosis to the racial calculus identified by Hartman. The echoes of this racial calculus influenced the shift away from women's narrative and feelings in diagnosis, a shift detected in current medical interactions, as is evident in Black women's recollections of their birth experiences.

The afterlife of slavery, which makes connections between the present, the history of chattel slavery, and after slavery, draws from archival sources—broadly defined—that following Dorothy E. Roberts are "keyed specifically to our contemporary neoliberal and, it is implied, seemingly postracial reproductive landscape" (Weinbaum 2013, 50). Indeed, methodologically, this book stems from questions about what happens if ideas about the prenatal body, laboring, and birth outcomes are put into conversation with archival sources of transatlantic slavery and its afterlife. This book contends that Black women's higher rates of premature birth are an expression of the afterlife of slavery, interpretable through documents such as medical texts, reports, pamphlets, narratives, and historians' accounts of pregnancy and birthing.

Conceptually, the afterlife is not simply a consequential expression of inheritable trauma. In other words, I am not arguing that the afterlife of slavery has resulted in an epigenetic phenomenon (although it may). Instead, I argue that one way Black women's prenatal experience, pregnancy, and birthing can be understood is as an extension of tropes, practices, and beliefs that can be traced back to antebellum and postbellum periods. What we see is that racism is continuously recalibrated—a racism that is a reinterpretation of enduring processes of slavery. In many ways, positioning biopolitics in this way, shuttling between the present and the past, shows, as Hartman notes, that slavery's imprint is demonstrated in all sectors of society and has resonances in the contemporary moment.

My line of inquiry has some resonance with anthropologist Lisa Stevenson's (2014) work, which examines the colonial bureaucracy that focused on improving the lives of Inuit in the Canadian Arctic. Stevenson draws on historical records to examine the influence of approaches to addressing two epidemics, tuberculosis and suicide, and finds that the texture of care and saving is recalibrated. Care, which Stevenson argues is a product of colonialism, is a liberal instantiation of the state's interest in making citizens live. However, the liberal instantiation of the state's approach to facilitating life, and presumably well-being, I argue, is much less stable and less valued relative to Black women.

Decolonized Methodology

One of the most important research principles I embrace as a feminist ethnographer is to connect my work to broader movements. In this case I wondered, "How might this project speak to or be informed by a reproductive justice framework?" Reproductive justice exists when all people have the economic, social, and political power and resources to make healthy decisions about their lives. It includes the right to have or not have children and focuses on personal bodily autonomy and living in safe and sustainable communities (Ross and Solinger 2017).

Taking up Indigenous education scholar Linda Tuhiwai Smith's (2012) observation that many researchers and academics *assume* that our research will be beneficial, I intentionally sought out a community of people active in the reproductive justice movement to help me do more than deconstruct prematurity. I wanted the research to be useful. Participatory-action research seemed to be one logical methodological approach; however, I saw no obvious *action* in which people could participate as a result of my inquiry. One early attempt to collaborate with a reproductive justice organization in Louisiana, where I conducted my first NICU observation, did not pan out. Initial interest waxed and then waned because the organization had to mobilize against proposed legislation mandating that abortion providers be affiliated with a hospital. At the time, organizing against the nationwide attack on access to reproductive services took precedence over doing work with a researcher.

Still committed to actualizing some form of feminist practice and choosing to be held accountable beyond the institutional review board, I invited a group of reproductive justice workers to join a reproductive justice interlocutor team. This was a team of people working in various realms of reproductive justice who were in dialogue with me from the beginning of the project. The four women who agreed to be part of this research endeavor are Toni Bond-Leonard, Andrea Queeley, Lynn Roberts, and Andrea B. Williams.

Toni Bond-Leonard is the cofounder and former president of Black Women for Reproductive Justice. When we met, Toni was board president of the National Network of Abortion Funds (NNAF), and I worked with her on NNAF's strategic plan. Toni has two decades of experience in reproductive activism and has parlayed that expertise into a set of concerns centered on theology. She was also one of the women who created the term "reproductive justice" and has been active in the reproductive justice movement for more than twenty years. Toni helped me think through the ethical positioning of decentering the NICU.

Andrea Queeley is both an activist and a scholar, whose work examines African diasporic subject formation, migration, and the negotiation of globalized structural inequalities. Andrea worked with me to shape the theoretical direction this work eventually took.

Lynn Roberts is often referred to as the "godmother" of the reproductive justice movement. One of the original members of SisterSong—a women of color reproductive justice collective[11]—her research lies in the areas of adolescent and women's health, violence prevention, community organizing and development, and health disparities. Lynn and I met regularly and discussed the interviews and emergent analyses.

Finally, Andrea B. Williams is a lawyer who manages the ReConnect project, a leadership training program for formerly incarcerated women at the Correctional Association of New York (CA). Before joining the CA, she was public policy coordinator at the HIV Law Project, where she managed the Center for Women's Organizing, an advocacy training program for women living with HIV and AIDS. Working with formerly incarcerated women to advocate for change, the CA has worked to redress the shackling of pregnant incarcerated women when they go into labor. Andrea read several drafts of my work and provided innumerable sources that helped shape this project.

Some members of the team helped to frame interview questions, others read various drafts, and still others pointed me in the direction of resources. They also helped to discern how this work might be useful to the broader reproductive justice movement as it offers an analysis of a reproductive issue that had not, until recently, been center stage in the movement—birth justice. The greatest gift they bestowed was in allowing me to draw on their vast knowledge—the knowledge of four Black feminists doing, or concerned about, reproductive justice work.

In addition to these four interlocutors, forty-nine other people participated in this project. This included seventeen parents, fourteen of whom were mothers and three of whom were fathers. The questions to parents centered on the content of their interactions with medical professionals during their pregnancies, asking them to recall their birth stories and how race factored into their medical treatment and hospitalizations. Of the seventeen parents, all but three identified as Black. Two were Filipina, and one was white. Between them, the parents had seventeen children admitted to an NICU, although several parents had other children as well. Two of the infants had a congenital illness. Nine of the infants were born at or before twenty-eight weeks, making them very preterm. Five of the infants were born between thirty and thirty-seven weeks, making them moderate to late preterm, and three infants were born at term, or forty weeks' gestation.

Ten birth workers participated, including three midwives, three doulas, and four reproductive justice advocates. All of the birth workers but one identified as Black; the other worker was white. With this group, I was interested in how they viewed the issue of prematurity and the link between medical racism and adverse birth outcomes. Conversations also centered on the value they saw in returning to traditional childbirth as a strategy to arrest Black women's unfavorable birth outcomes.

Among the seventeen hospital-based medical personnel there were seven neonatologists or residents and one retired obstetrician, five of whom were white and three of whom were Black. Among the doctors three were men, three were women, and one was gender nonconforming. The obstetrician was a Black woman. Eight nurses participated (two were labor and delivery nurses, and the others were NICU nurses), as well as one hospital-based social worker. Of the nurses, four were Black and four were white; the social worker also was white.

I spent time with and interviewed five current or former administrators/executives from the March of Dimes, all but one of whom were white. The questions posed to both medical professionals and March of Dimes staff explored how they viewed NICU technology, what role they thought technology played in addressing premature births, and how they understood race with respect to premature birth.

The ways in which I came to meet the people interviewed varied. What some might say was opportunistic (Andaya 2014), I prefer to frame as serendipitous (Rivoal and Salazar 2013). In other words, unanticipated events opened up avenues for exploration and conversation with people who were not part of the original research project. As mentioned previously, originally I did not plan to interview parents. However, after Ashley initiated contact, I recruited other mothers on Facebook and through my social networks (convenience sampling) and was surprised when three fathers also agreed to be interviewed. Initially I thought the Facebook recruitment would lead me to people I already knew. As it turned out, I actually knew only five of the parents; all the others were unknown to me but made contact, wanting to be interviewed, and two were introduced by a mutual friend.

Attempts to broaden the range of parents to include those who had different degrees of access to resources and who were not professionals involved distributing flyers to mothers in an Early Intervention Program (EIP) housed at a New York City nonprofit organization. In New York, the EIP is administered by the New York State Department of Health through the Bureau of Early Intervention. According to the department's website, "The New York State EIP is part of the national Early Intervention Program for infants and toddlers with disabilities and their families. EIP was created by Congress in 1986 under the Individuals with Disabilities Education Act (IDEA)" (New York State Department of Health n.d.). To be eligible for services, children must be under three years of age and have a confirmed disability or developmental delay, as defined by the state, in one or more of the following areas: physical, cognitive, communication, social-emotional, and/or adaptive. Although I offered gift certificates as an incentive to be interviewed, no one from the EIP program contacted me. One might say that too was serendipity, since the project ultimately focused on professional Black women, who are generally overlooked in feminist reproductive scholarship.

Those who responded to my Facebook request were all professional women and men—some of whom introduced me to other people whose children had been born prematurely. Generally, I believe they responded more readily than those whose children were part of the EIP because their children were older. Children in the program are no more than three years of age, which is the maximum age to qualify for services. Of the parents who did contact me, their children ranged in age from seven months to thirty-five years. My guess is that those parents who did agree to be interviewed generally had more emotional distance from when their child had been born prematurely and thus found it easier to discuss.

Another example of serendipity was that three fathers wanted to discuss their children's premature birth. Even though this project is concerned with Black women's premature births and their opinions of NICUs, I did not limit participants to mothers, African Americans, or those whose children had been born prematurely. If parents wanted to discuss their pregnancy, labor, and birth, it seemed unnecessary, even callous, to reject them by constructing rules of engagement that upheld the falsity of an "ideal" research participant. All parents, except one lesbian who was married, were heterosexual. Two mothers used ART to achieve conception. All the parents had singletons who survived, except one parent who had a set of twins, one of whom did not survive. Parents lived in California, Florida, Illinois, the New York tristate area, North Carolina, Texas, or Washington, DC, although that is not necessarily where their children were born.

Among medical professionals, snowball sampling was the primary recruitment tool. One physician introduced me to another, and so on. Dr. Johannes, the first neonatologist I met, introduced me to the chief of his unit, who in turn introduced me to another neonatologist on his staff. Later meetings with neonatologists were facilitated by convenience sampling, with two colleagues putting me in touch with neonatologists they knew. The same sampling processes occurred with nurses and the social worker.

The project took on new dimensions after I made a cold call simply to obtain information about the public health approach to premature birth, a serendipitous event. I found myself in dialogue with administrators at the March of Dimes, interviewing them over the course of a year at their offices in New York and Washington, DC, and via phone. Consequently, I broadened the scope of the project to examine how the largest nonprofit organization in the United States dedicated to addressing premature birth thinks through and addresses the racial disparity associated with prematurity.

Another unexpected turn in the project was the result of registering for a birthing justice conference. Serendipity led to meeting and interviewing birth justice workers. When I arrived, doulas, midwives, mothers, fathers, public health providers (some of whom were men), and advocates had gathered to discuss the importance of demedicalizing birth and linking reproduction to broader social issues such as criminalization and policing. From this conference, it immediately became clear that some birthing projects and radical birth workers were in fact critiquing the organization of medicine and how it perpetuates reproductive racial inequalities. I participated in doula meet-up groups and trainings for doulas and birth workers of color in New York and Washington, DC. The birth workers interviewed were from Florida, Georgia, New Jersey, New York, and New Mexico. At the end of the research, I entered a doula training program and supported my first client just four weeks after completing my training. As a reproductive justice advocate and activist working toward the abolition of medical racism in the care that many Black women receive, becoming a doula has been an important aspect of this research.

I must admit, though, that having interviewed this large number of people does not mean I have reached the highest level of knowledge about pregnancy, prematurity, and race. Nor have I exhausted the interpretive possibilities of women's experiences with medical racism. There are always more stories to hear, more NICUs to visit, and more documents to read. There is always more to know. But I hope what has been learned underscores that we need to care and do more to increase the birth options that Black women can access.

Deterritorialized Ethnographic Inquiry

Traditional ethnographic research has been place-based, but I take the view that feminist ethnographic inquiry can transcend parochial methods of participant observation in one locale with one group. An alternative to more traditional ethnographic inquiry is deterritorialized ethnographic inquiry, which centers on an issue, not a place (Wies and Haldane 2015). As described earlier, at the beginning of the research I tried to work with a reproductive justice group. Then, in the middle of the project I attempted to locate a "site" at one NICU and was approved. Research at that hospital never got off the ground, however, due to major renovations, making it impossible to conduct observations. In the end, given what some of the doctors and nurses shared, it was best not to have been at only one site because the multiple locations afforded medical staff anonymity, particularly for personnel of color who were often the only Black doctor or nurse at a hospital. Rather than being anchored to one NICU, ethnographic observations took place at various hospitals. Attending nurses' meetings afforded me an opportunity to see how labor and birth and neonatal nursing responsibilities were delegated. I interviewed all the neonatologists and the obstetrician in person and interviewed nurses on the phone and in person. These specialists lived and worked in Florida, Louisiana, Minnesota, the New York tristate area, New England, and Ohio. NICUs can benefit from anthropological research, "helping people recognize other interpretations of a space and experiences that might otherwise be overlooked" (Downey and Dumit 1997, 3).

Neonatologists and nurses took me on guided tours of NICUs where I observed neonates in their incubators. These visits provided a first-hand view of how technology was grafted onto babies' bodies. They were sometimes challenging because every moment felt like a potential emergency that could be followed by a potential loss. It was disconcerting to think that death or a negative outcome, despite technological advancement, might await the neonates in the NICU.

Not knowing the potential consequence of a birth outcome is a crucial reason I chose not to recruit parents whose children were currently in an NICU as research participants. Their vulnerability was palpable; having previously worked at a battered women's shelter, I was leery of trying to disentangle the emotions of having a child in an NICU and talking about racism *at the time of crisis*. Indeed, I am convinced that talking to parents at that time would not have necessarily revealed any particularly illuminating insight into what racism felt like to them. In fact, how parents felt about and understood the racism they encountered may have been digested and expressed with greater clarity *because* time had passed. Additionally, centering the ethnographic work on a particular place was not necessary for uncovering Black women's accounts and recollections of their meetings with medical professionals. In the end, descriptions of those medical encounters that involved racism had similar expressions. In other words, regardless of place and time, narratives of racism were experienced in very similar ways by women of different ages and whether they were pregnant twenty years ago or eight months ago.

Interdisciplinary literatures informed the research and spoke to the many ways in which I believed I could learn the "secrets" of a subject—one with which I (and often the public) have little familiarity (Franklin 2013). To learn about prematurity and to get at its emotional vocabulary, I engaged with reproductive studies literature; science and technology studies; television shows such as *Boardwalk Empire*, which features an opening segment in which a man walks through a world's fair with infants on display in incubators; documentaries such as *Unnatural Causes* (Strain 2008); newspaper articles; fiction; and self-published books by mothers and fathers who chronicled what it was like having their children born prematurely and then admitted to the NICU (see, for example, Degl 2013; A. Stevenson 2010).

I also read books written for the siblings of NICU babies and manuals by doctors and nurses explaining prematurity and NICU care. Not one of the fifteen books was written for Black children or was about prematurely born Black infants. I conducted a search on Amazon for books about premature birth. Of the forty-five books with images of premature infants or parents, four had an image of a person who appeared to be other than white. I examined websites for hospitals that had NICU services. In sum, I just followed the "subject." Inspired by anthropologist Rayna Rapp's (1999) methodological strategy of following the "object" in her biotechnology research, which involved examining biotechnology in labs and hospitals and was linked to the recruitment of research participants, I followed the subject of pregnancy, prematurity, and racism that women experienced. I did so through observation, trainings, interviews, the collection of participant narratives, and an investigation of both primary and secondary archival sources.

For me, a Black feminist approach to ethnography has always meant putting Black women's voices front and center. Recollections and memory are fundamental to this project, which is why Black women's words are at the center of this book. Some of their memories of medical encounters produce important knowledge about the experience of medical racism. That knowledge provides an emotional literacy that may be difficult to capture through other methods.[12] It is through the braided research and analytical strategies, including face-to-face interaction, archival research, and "following the subject," that this ethnography gets at the meaning of people's experiences. In sharing Black women's stories from their perspective, and understanding at an intimate level how they negotiate the world and explain the things that happen to them, this book accomplishes what anthropological inquiry does best: calling attention to new issues and making connections between underexplored aspects of questions that cannot be adequately understood through broader strategies such as epidemiology or public health campaigns. Indeed, as I show, the processes that produce statistics and public health messages are deeply enmeshed with race. Through my research, I discovered that it was as important to understand the ways in which race infiltrates these practices as it was to expose the human toll that racial discourse takes upon Black women's lives. The statistics show starkly that Black women's bodies and babies are profoundly at risk. Thus, it is Black women's words that we must hear if we are to understand the meaning and impact of that risk.

And so, I repeat: women's own words are a legitimate source for knowledge production. How cruel and ironic that I even need to write that sentence. Across all of the research conducted, I simply wanted to learn from Black women if and how race and racism were manifest in their dealings with their doctors and nurses during prenatal care and while their children were in the NICU. What better evidence than their own words and experiences?

The Chapters

The analysis takes shape through the investigatory approaches as well as the structure of the book. Investigating pregnancy, prematurity, and race required looking at the issues from different angles. The dominant angle is rooted in Black feminist epistemology and centers women's medical interfaces during various stages of pregnancy and the birth process. Other angles include looking at NICU technology and prematurity from the perspective of medical professionals. I also needed to look at prematurity from another angle, from the interventionist, educational, and preventionist domains. Therefore, the book is divided into two parts. Part I engages the concept of the afterlife of slavery to analyze prenatal care, labor, birth, and NICU admission narratives in the context of the legacy of Black women's treatment at the hands of antebellum slave owners and doctors. Part II turn the lens toward the three different approaches that seek to address prematurity.

Part I consists of three chapters that center on Black women, most of whom are professionals and all of whom have attained higher levels of education. Organized around their narratives, the first three chapters make connections between women's encounters using archival and popular sources. Archival materials serve as both evidence and interpretive tools alongside other data collection strategies to show that race and racism in the United States are tethered to Black women's medical interactions as artifacts of slavery during their pregnancy and labor and while their infants received care in the NICU.

Chapter 1, "Premature Predicaments," begins with a passage from Harriet Jacobs's autobiographical narrative *Incidents in the Life of a Slave Girl* that signposts a series of questions about the definition and etiology (or causes) of prematurity. Race and racial science animated the discovery and definition of prematurity, which are described in the chapter. To demonstrate the persistence of premature births among Black women in the United States, I share four women's narratives of pregnancy and birthing, one each in the nineteenth and twentieth centuries, and two in the twenty-first century. The focus of their prenatal and pregnancy care sits at the intersection of race and the medical management of their reproduction.

The second chapter, "Into the NICU," opens the door to the space where premature infants are admitted. The dominant point here is that the NICU is a space with multiple meanings and interpretive possibilities. This chapter explores the meaning of the NICU and focuses on how the NICU has been interpreted by three parents and three neonatologists. Typically, the NICU is understood as a space that attends to a premature infant's incomplete development, but based on parents' descriptions, other dynamics emerge. Through their stories and based on discussions with neonatologists, we find out the circumstances under which racial dynamics do and do not percolate in the NICU. This chapter explores some of the undercurrents that take place in the NICU that go beyond saving premature and congenitally ill infants.

Chapter 3, "Pregnancy and Prematurity in the Afterlife of Slavery," offers a close reading of one woman's pregnancy and labor to illustrate the medical treatment she received during this time and after giving birth.[13] This chapter considers how medical practice and care are orchestrated against Black women's interests. Making interpretive connections between one woman's experience and primary sources from medical journals and historians' accounts, this chapter demonstrates that earlier ideas about Black women and infants and about medical racism have migrated to the present in the form of diagnostic lapses.

Segueing to the second part of the book, I offer an interlude by describing a birth in which I participated. Then, part II chronicles three particular strategies of addressing premature birth, from the technological intervention approach to the public health perspective, which centers on public education and raising awareness through the use of numbers. I conclude with the prevention approaches that have been utilized by radical birth workers.

Chapter 4, "Saving the Babies," examines several interventions used to address premature birth. In this chapter I bring together a range of documents and sources to create an archive of "baby-saving" strategies from the early twentieth century to the present. The strategies point to efforts to decrease prematurity and infant and maternal mortality through program implementation, policy, and technological development. Below the surface of saving intervention strategies, the archive reveals that a racial calculus—sometimes political, sometimes not—has thwarted the ability to successfully address birthing outcomes of Black women and infants. Essentially this chapter explores the tension between the state's long-standing interest in addressing infant, child, and maternal mortality and how that interest has lacked strength when viewed through a critical race lens. While in earlier chapters the narratives of mothers' and doctors' voices took center stage, in this one we will hear from NICU nurses and administrators from the March of Dimes to reveal some of the apprehensions they have concerning the idea of saving.

Chapter 5, "Narrowing the Gap of Black Women's Burden," examines a public health approach to addressing the racial disparity of prematurity. Historically, the March of Dimes has developed public education campaigns to address child-related health issues, and race has always factored into those health concerns. While the organization has been successful in raising awareness of public health issues, including premature birth, this chapter examines how the use of data to illustrate the scope of premature birth, as an intervention, also raises questions about the use of data to address racial disparity.

The final chapter is "Radical Black Birth Workers," whose emphasis is on the preventive approaches that Black (and other) women embrace, specifically doulas, midwives, birth workers, and advocates. They engage in birth work not only as care and service providers but also as part of a political project to stem Black women's high rates of adverse birth outcomes and to transform the medical-industrial complex. In this chapter, interviews with birth and reproductive justice advocates point to the role that community-based midwives and doulas play as they seek to establish humane birthing practices geared to all women in general, but Black women in particular.

The conclusion reflects on the themes raised in the chapters. This book elucidates how racism is experienced by Black women at a time when Black maternal and infant mortality and morbidity are a major concern in the United States. Because each chapter highlights various aspects of the persistently high rates of adverse birth outcomes and the ways that race and medical racism have disrupted Black women's and men's reproduction, the conclusion highlights some approaches that may deal with the problem. Importantly, it is through the care practices of radical Black birth workers and expanding care and birth options that we find a potent response to medical racism and effective work to attain outcomes that are more in alignment with the goals of reproductive justice.

PART I

1

Premature Predicaments

It was not natural. And she was the first. Come from a country of many tongues tortured by rupture, by theft, by travel like mismatched clothing packed down into the cargo hold of evil ships sailing, irreversible, into slavery.
—June Jordan, *Some of Us Did Not Die* (2002)

When my babe was born, they said it was premature. It weighed only four pounds; but God let it live. I heard the doctor say I could not survive till morning. I had often prayed for death; but now I did not want to die, unless my child could die too. Many weeks passed before I was able to leave my bed. I was a mere wreck of my former self. For a year, there was scarcely a day when I was free from chills and fever. My babe also was sickly. His little limbs were often racked with pain. Dr. Flint continued his visits, to look after my health; and he did not fail to remind me that my child was an addition to his stock of slaves. . . . As the months passed on, my boy improved in health. When he was a year old, they called him beautiful. The little vine was taking deep root in my existence, though its clinging fondness excited a mixture of love and pain. When I was most sorely oppressed I found solace in his smiles. I loved to watch his infant slumbers; but always there was a dark cloud over my enjoyment. I could never forget that he was a slave. Sometimes I wished that he might die in infancy. God tried me. My darling became very ill. The bright eyes grew dull, and the little feet and hands were so icy cold that I thought death had already touched them. I had prayed for his death, but never so earnestly as I now prayed for his life; and my prayer was heard. Alas, what mockery it is for a slave mother to pray back her dying child to life!
—Harriet Jacobs *Incidents in the Life of a Slave Girl* (1861)

This epigraph is from an autobiographical narrative written by Harriet Jacobs under the pseudonym of Linda Brent, which is how I will refer to her in this chapter. *Incidents* chronicles the excruciatingly painful life of a girl born around 1813 in North Carolina and forced into bondage in the Flint household in 1825 around age twelve. Brent's life was cloaked in abuse enacted by her owner, Dr. Flint, a physician, who emotionally abused and threatened her, as did his wife, Mrs. Flint, who despised her. Brent informs readers that she was also in a sexual relationship with an older man: a white lawyer, Mr. Sands—who ultimately became a congressman. While that relationship appears to be one into which she *entered* of her own accord, it is difficult to embrace the characterization that a fifteen-year-old enslaved girl "chose" to have sex with an older white man. If nothing else, it was a survival strategy—a move to ward off Dr. Flint's advances. Mr. Sands impregnated Brent when she was fifteen, and she subsequently gave birth to her son, Benny, described in the epigraph. At twenty, Brent was pregnant again and this time had a daughter, Ellen. Both children, fathered by Sands, were Flint's property. Believing that if she ran away Flint would sell her children to their father, Mr. Sands, Brent hid for seven years in the attic crawl space of her grandmother's shack.[1]

Brent's story haunts the more contemporary stories told in this book in its evocation of the temporal persistence of Black women's premature births. Several compelling themes emerge from this excerpt, which speak to my aims here. This book represents a vantage point of reproduction that has been overlooked in the anthropological literature, that of Black women. It serves to illustrate how archival sources, of which slave narratives are but one example, can be used to contextualize current issues. In this book, the archives consist of materials—narratives, medical and popular journals, and autobiographies, among other sources. The time period of these documents ranges from the 1700s to the fairly recent past. Notably, the archival sources and primary documents elucidate contemporary concerns. Some aspects of Brent's account of the premature birth of her son—the actual event and ensuing angst—echo those by the contemporary Black women whose stories we will hear. Black women's reproductive lives have historically been controlled by a predominantly white medical profession (J. L. Morgan 2004; Schwartz 2006). This fact directs us to consider that Linda Brent's owner was a physician. Even though medical knowledge—especially knowledge of reproductive health—was nascent at the time, that does not preclude raising questions about the medical care that Brent, as a Black woman, received. Indeed, the question is an entrée into considering the present-day prenatal and obstetric care Black women receive in light of their high rates of adverse reproductive outcomes. These are outcomes that exist despite advances in medical knowledge.

Brent's account enables consideration of three questions this chapter seeks to answer. First, the passage suggests that prematurity is defined based on weight. Brent's son, Benny, was not expected to live because he "weighed only four pounds" at birth. But what is prematurity, and has race played a role in its definition? Although one might suspect what may have led Brent to give birth prematurely, no cause is mentioned in the narrative. Thus, the second question concerns: What is the etiology of premature birth? And third, what do Black women's narratives about pregnancy and prematurity tell us about their medical care and race? These initial questions are important because reproductive disparities have beleaguered Black women for more than two centuries in the United States. During the antebellum period, infant mortality rates overall in America were excessive, but enslaved women lost nearly 50 percent of their children (Berry and Alford 2012). Linda Brent's narrative demonstrates this disparity. Her experience as described in *Incidents* affords us one way to think about the issue of pregnancy and premature birth—from Black women's standpoint. This is important, especially given the limited attention Black women's reproduction has received (except, see Mullings and Wali 2001; Bridges 2011; D. E. Roberts 1997).

When Linda Brent gave birth in the 1830s, prematurity and infant mortality were events in the lives of many enslaved women—indeed, of most women. Rates of premature births were inestimable because childbirth typically took place in the home, rendering it essentially a private, familial matter. However, the consequence of premature birth, infant mortality, *was* recorded. Beginning in the 1850s, birth and death rates, by race—including infant mortality—were calculable.[2] We know that, just twenty years after Linda Brent gave birth prematurely in 1830, the white infant mortality rate was 216.8 per 1,000 compared with a Black infant mortality rate of 340 per 1,000 (Haines 2008). Table 1.1 illustrates the Black-white differences for a range of reproductive issues: birth rates, fertility rates, life expectancy, and infant mortality rates over the last two centuries. Infant mortality rates are germane to this discussion because the dominant cause of infant mortality was and still is premature birth. The table also shows that birth and fertility rates are calculable and that by 1850 a more detailed picture of the racial disparity in birth outcomes had emerged. According to the table, in 1850, the Black infant mortality rate was one and a half times higher than the rate for white infants. In 2000, the disparity was two and a half times higher. It is astonishing to see that even under the strictures of enslavement, Black women had significantly better birth outcomes than they do today.

Early in US history, premature births were not framed as a health crisis because in cases when births were attended by physicians, they "saw no effective means of aiding these babies in their doomed struggle to survive" (Golden 2001, 180). Child death was unremarkable. Indeed, premature births, like infant mortality, did not become an urgent public concern until the early twentieth century (Zelizer 1994). Ultimately, both prematurity and infant mortality materialized as crises during the Progressive Era, leading to the establishment of the Children's Bureau in 1912.[3] At that time, the bureau sought to rectify the mercurial infant mortality rates in the United States, including by documenting rates of births and deaths. From that point on, life and death became institutionally "registerable" events, with many states collecting birth and mortality statistics, although the entire nation did not participate in vital registration until 1933 (Haines 2008).[4]

This chapter includes four sections. It begins with a discussion of how prematurity was defined. This was a process that began in earnest in the nineteenth century, and one that continues, relative to the way that prematurity needs to be medically managed alongside shifts in knowledge and technological advancement. Yet defining prematurity not only has served the purpose of medical management but also has been used as an adjunct of racial science—by which I mean aiding scientific inquiry for the purpose of proving the existence of racial categories in support of racial hierarchies. The second section brings select documents from the Children's Bureau archive into conversation with the history of racial science through the lens of prematurity. The third section explores the causes of prematurity. The final section offers four accounts of pregnancy, labor, and birthing by Black women over three centuries. The

TABLE 1.1 Fertility and Mortality in the United States, 1800–1999

Approxi-mate Date	Birth Rate[a]		Child-Woman Ratio[b]		Total Fertility Rate[c]		Life Expectancy[d]		Infant Mortality Rate[e]	
	White	Black[f]	White	Black	White	Black[f]	White	Black[f]	White	Black[f]
1800	55.0		1342		7.04					
1810	54.3		1358		6.92					
1820	52.8		1295	1191	6.73					
1830	51.4		1145	1220	6.55					
1840	48.3		1085	1154	6.14					
1850	43.3	58.6[g]	892	1087	5.42	7.90[g]	39.5	23.0	216.8	340.0
1860	41.4	55.0[h]	905	1072	5.21	7.58[h]	43.6		181.3	
1870	38.3	55.4[i]	814	997	4.55	7.69[i]	45.2		175.5	
1880	35.2	51.9[j]	780	1090	4.24	7.26[j]	40.5		214.8	
1890	31.5	48.1	685	930	3.87	6.56	46.8		150.7	
1900	30.1	44.4	666	845	3.56	5.61	51.8[k]	41.8[k]	110.8[k]	170.3
1910	29.2	38.5	631	736	3.42	4.61	54.6[l]	46.8[l]	96.5[l]	142.6
1920	26.9	35.0	604	608	3.17	3.64	57.4	47.0	82.1	131.7
1930	20.6	27.5	506	554	2.45	2.98	60.9	48.5	60.1	99.9
1940	18.6	26.7	419	513	2.22	2.87	64.9	53.9	43.2	73.8
1950	23.0	33.3	580	663	2.98	3.93	69.0	60.7	26.8	44.5
1960	22.7	32.1	717	895	3.53	4.52	70.7	63.9	22.9	43.2
1970	17.4	25.1	507	689	2.39	3.07	71.6	64.1	17.8	30.9
1980	15.1	21.3	300	367	1.77	2.18	74.5	68.5	10.9	22.2
1990	15.8	22.4	298	359	2.00	2.48	76.1	69.1	7.6	18.0
2000	13.9	17.0	343	401	2.05	2.13	77.4	71.7	5.7	14.1

a Births per 1,000 population per annum.
b Children aged 0–4 per 1,000 women aged 20–44. Taken from US Bureau of the Census (1975), Series 67-68, for 1800–1970. For the Black population 1820–40, W. S. Thompson and P. K. Whelpton, *Population Trends in the United States* (New York: McGraw-Hill, 1933), Table 74, adjusted upward 47 percent for relative undernumeration of Black children aged 0–4 for the censuses of 1820–40.
c Total number of births per woman if she experienced the current period age-specific fertility rates throughout her life.
d Expectation of life at birth for both sexes combined.
e Infant deaths per 1,000 live births per annum.
f Black and other population for birth rate (1920–70), total fertility rate (1940–90), life expectancy at birth (1950–60), and infant mortality rate (1920–70).
g Average for 1850–59.
h Average for 1860–69.
i Average for 1870–79.
j Average for 1880–84.
k Approximately 1895.
l Approximately 1904.
SOURCE: Haines 2008.

stories of Aunt Nancy, Anne Lewis, Ashley Bey, and Melissa Harrison illuminate how Black women have had, and continue, to bear the burden of premature birth. They do so to a greater degree than any other group of women in the United States.

Defining Prematurity

Prior to the late nineteenth century, physicians did not even classify infants who were born early; such infants were simply categorized as weak and feeble (Baker 1996, 4). Members of the medical profession used the terms "feeble" and "premature" interchangeably based on the assumption that premature babies would not survive. Defining prematurity played a critical role in ensuring classificatory uniformity. That is to say, defining the term facilitated both the documentation of the event and the medical management of premature infants' health needs. To do so, it was necessary to designate a consistent set of characteristics as to what constituted prematurity. Classificatory uniformity, then, made it possible to compare data on premature births and deaths.

Prior to the adoption of a formal definition of prematurity by US-based professional associations, prematurely born infants had been a subject of medical inquiry in Europe and the United States since the mid-1800s (Baker 1996), mostly in relation to poor women, who often gave birth in lying-in hospitals. Early on, the definition of prematurity was based on characteristics such as the weight of the infant, along with indicators such as skin texture, undeveloped nails, and fluctuating body temperature (Hughes, Black, and Katz 2017).

Among the events that precipitated the standardization of prematurity's definition, one stands out: the findings of Arvo Ylppö (1919), a Finnish pediatrician who laid the foundation for defining prematurity based on anatomical and pathological analysis. From 1909 to 1918, Ylppö conducted a study of 2,168 births at Charlottenberg's Empress Auguste Victoria Center for the Prevention of Infant Mortality in Germany, with the goal of identifying the clinical course and autopsy findings among neonates born prematurely. Of the 2,168 births he studied, 114 were preterm based on a weight of 2,500 grams, or approximately 5.5 pounds. Interestingly, Ylppö never provided a justification for the 2,500-gram weight limit, but it became the standard and has influenced public health practice into the present (Salihu n.d.). By 1935, the American Academy of Pediatrics had resolved that all live-born infants weighing 2,500 grams at birth should be treated as premature regardless of the length of gestation (American Academy of Pediatrics 1936). By this measure, Linda Brent's son Benny, at four pounds, certainly fit the criteria for prematurity and provides context for its definition during the antebellum period.

However, what is indiscernible is the length of time that Linda Brent was pregnant. This was likely because gestational time did not command a great deal of attention until 1922, when Dr. Julius Hess—considered to be the father of American neonatology—published the first book on prematurity and birth defects. In that text, he stated that when the designation of prematurity "is used, it refers to those infants born three weeks or more before the usual termination of pregnancy" (Hess 1922, 9). Hess classified two types of premature infants: those who were born possibly at term but were weaklings, and those who suffered severely during their intrauterine existence through factors that interfered with their nutrition and thus their development. Classifying prematurity in this manner paved the way for the US Bureau of Census and the American Public Health Association to recommend gestation as the definition of prematurity in 1935. Ultimately, prematurity was defined as a pregnancy of less than forty weeks, with birth taking place three or more weeks before the baby is due, around the start of the thirty-seventh week. The lower limits were set at twenty-eight weeks "because it is the consensus that a fetus of less than 28 weeks' gestation has not developed sufficiently for extrauterine survival" (Dunham 1948, 1). Gestational age gained greater currency in understanding prematurity in the 1950s, partly due to its relationship to infant mortality (Hughes, Black, and Katz 2017).

Weight, length, and gestation were all presumed to be factors in a premature infant's viability. For example, Fred L. Adair, a founder and former president of the American Congress of Obstetricians and Gynecologists, argued that newborns between 400 and 1,000 grams in weight, and twenty-eight to thirty-five centimeters in length, or of twenty-two to twenty-seven weeks' gestation, were products of conception that did not require being reported as premature. Instead, he said newborns born so early were termed abortions "because even if they showed signs of life at birth, they could not survive due to insufficient development" (Adair 1940, 904–5).[5] The expectations for survival were so low that weight and gestational age sometimes precluded an infant from even qualifying as premature. In some cases, they were classified as previable (Dunham 1948, 3). Previability, however, came with a caveat, since some infants survived who had been born at previable weights and gestational age. Those who did live, no matter how long, *could be designated as premature* because the definition was modified by a live-birth statement. "A live-born child is one which shows any evidence of life (breathing, heartbeat, or movement of voluntary muscle) after complete birth. Birth is considered complete when the child is altogether (head, trunk and limbs) outside the body of the mother, even if the cord is uncut and the placenta still attached" (Dunham 1948, 1–2). This history of defining prematurity illustrates the medical construction of prematurity and how its definition shifted over time relative to the development of medical specialties such as pediatrics, public health, and obstetrics and gynecology.

The 1948 pamphlet *Premature Infants: A Manual for Physicians*, by Ethel C. Dunham, chief of child development at the Children's Bureau, offers insight into the meaning of prematurity and its characteristics. *Premature Infants* is comprehensive in scope, covering definitions, causes, and treatments for premature infants. Dunham, a pediatrician who earned her medical degree from Johns Hopkins University, gained expertise in prematurity and established standards for the hospital care of newborn children (National Institutes of Health, n.d.). Dunham argued that gestation, as the defining feature of prematurity, posed some difficulties due to the uncertainty of the exact date when a pregnancy began "because duration of human gestation has been shown to vary considerably" (Dunham 1948, 1). Prematurity, in fact, has no one set of characteristics, and a more granular analysis of prematurity by gestational age is useful, at least in determining potential outcomes (Shaw et al. 2014).

In reading *Premature Infants*, one finds that it not only describes prematurity's definitional and etiological parameters but also shows that medical science viewed the scientific understanding of adverse birth outcomes, specifically premature birth, through the lens of social relations and in the context of race. A number of twentieth-century studies conceptualized prematurity with reference to ideas of racial difference that served as identifying features of prematurity itself. Some studies looked to weight and race, for example, as factors that defined prematurity (Brown 1922; Lyon 1941; Anderson 1947). Each study explored the proportional difference in "Negro" and white gestational periods to determine if weight differences could be used when considering the definition of prematurity.

Ideas about race and reproduction—or, more pointedly, race, pregnancy, and prematurity—have traversed time. The search for ties between race and prematurity bends an ideological arc toward contemporary medical practices and care. In other words, racial difference releases a paradox. On the one hand, racial difference confounds the idea of a standard in biomedical research—the white male—against which diagnostic and analytic determinations are measured. On the other hand, racial difference becomes the point of departure for holding up white supremacy, because race has been viewed as medically meaningful (S. Epstein 2007, 10).

Race-ing Prematurity

Science and technology studies scholars have explored the ways in which racial, gendered, and sexed bodies have been produced and manipulated in the interest of creating categories of difference. Typically, categories of difference are rooted in standards that have been produced from male bodies. Feminist science and technology studies scholars, such as historians Laura Briggs (2002) and Londa Schiebinger (2004) and anthropologist Emily Martin (1987), have investigated how gender standardization has been constructed through the medicalization of women's bodies. What I attend to here is how the standardization of race has been linked to prematurity through scientific racism's migration from the 1800s to the twentieth century. In this case, what is being manipulated into a racial category is the fetus and the prematurely born neonate.

We see evidence of this manipulation in relation to variables used to delineate prematurity, such as weight and gestation. *Premature Infants* references studies that were grounded in and echoed the US-based racial science of the 1800s, in which difference was captured through biotypologies. To be clear, the author, Dunham, did not embrace the racial science used to understand prematurity. Nonetheless, the manual's inclusion of studies as part of the literature review on premature birth gives some indication of the degree to which science was in search of evidence of racial difference. Racial hierarchy proponents have used science to distinguish "Negroes" from whites. It is interesting to consider that medical researchers viewed "Negro" bodies as appropriate sites of knowledge for understanding prematurity, given the flawed status that accompanied all racially produced groups other than "whites," who are typically people without race.

Racial science research has included the use of various procedures to prove that human racial hierarchies exist. Take for instance, the nineteenth-century physician Dr. Samuel Morton, who deployed "objective" craniometrical measures to establish the veracity of racial hierarchies (Gould 1978). Similarly, premature birth was an event in which "objective" measures were used to confirm racial difference. One study, for example, analyzed the role of occipitofrontal circumference—the largest horizontal circumference of the head—in an effort to distinguish between Negro and white premature infants (Dunham 1948, 6). Consequently, researchers made connections between prematurity, race, and sex by drawing on the formation of bone tissue and X-rays (7–8). The medical educator and pediatrician Dr. Amos U. Christie took X-rays of three areas where tissue was formed: the proximal tibia or the thigh shaft; the cuboid, which is the bone on the outer side of the foot; and, the capitate, which is a carpal bone found at the base of the palm of the hand (wrist). He was trying to determine whether bone tissue formation (or lack thereof) could be estimated by weight, and thus serve as a predictor of maturity or prematurity based on race or sex. Negro infants were used to validate medical incommensurability with ideals of a standard human—the white male. As it turns out, the scientific gymnastics required for this racial formulation were not good predicators of prematurity (Christie et al. 1941; Dunham 1948, 8).

Importantly, the scientific classification of race was not uniform; rather, it was the social conceptualizations of race that informed the categorization of racial subjects (Smart et al. 2008). Although science and technology scholar Andrew Smart and his colleagues (2008) discuss the use of racial classification in biomedical research, adopting such classifications, regardless of the sphere—be it biomedical, social, or legal— aligns with the state's socially and politically constructed meanings of race with science.

Malleability in terms of who was included in a particular racial category is evident, for example, in a report for the Children's Bureau by Elizabeth C. Tandy, who was the director of the bureau's statistical division. In her introduction to *Infant and Maternal Mortality among Negroes*, Tandy acknowledges that the mortality of Negro infants and mothers has been "extremely high, but the actual situation has been obscure, because statistics for Negroes . . . customarily are combined with those for other nonwhite races such as Indian, Chinese, and Japanese" (1937, 1). Tandy's reference points to the fact that race was unstable for nonwhites and "customarily" included a number of groups under the category of Negro.

A less conspicuous manner in which race was connected to prematurity comes from a review conducted by the physical anthropologist Howard V. Meredith (1946), who analyzed fifty studies completed between 1850 and 1945 that examined the head size of North American infants and children. Meredith's analysis revealed a composite mean head circumference at birth of 34.5 centimeters for nearly 2,500 white full-term males and of 33.9 centimeters for an equal number of white female infants. In the article, notations suggest that all of the infants were white. Thus, the standardization of the mean circumference of a mature birth was rendered normative based on whiteness.

Early racial science attempted to solidify the idea that Negro infants mature in utero more quickly than white infants, and these efforts to prove racial difference obscured other reasons that lead to premature birth. Where racial differentiation *can be* factored in as part of a disparity analysis is in terms of social, economic, and political disparities that place people at various types of disadvantage.

Contemporary ideas about pregnancy and the causes of prematurity can be traced to earlier racial ideologies documented in manuals such as those described here. A case in point is the work of Theresa Overfield, a nurse-anthropologist whose well-known, but simultaneously critiqued, 1995 text argues that race *is* a way to distinguish genetic breeding populations, despite research by biological anthropologists to the contrary (Blakey 1999; Goodman 2000). In her chapter on gestation and birth weight, Overfield notes that Black infants have shorter gestation length and thus are premature, which she suggests may be adaptive. The adaptation, she says, is an accommodation for Black women's smaller pelvises. In other words, race is linked to prematurity (or shorter gestational length) because Black women have smaller pelvises than white women: presumably they are thus unable to carry their babies to term. Overfield (1995, 26) makes this claim while at the same time indicating that there are few studies that substantiate it.

Based on Overfield's analysis, it is possible to arrive at a "logical" conclusion that premature birth is woven with the thread of racial difference and human variation. Race has been used in the service of understanding prematurity and marking difference. What is interesting about Overfield's perspective is that at a different point in time, Black women's pelvises were seen as a reproductive advantage. For example, Miriam Clause Meijer, a history of science scholar, writes that Petrus Camper (1722–89) was believed to be the first person to conduct comparative measurements of African, Asian, and European women's "pelves." According to Meijer, Camper placed various female pelvises, from different nations, in his private museum collection and "claimed that Asian and African women enjoyed easier deliveries than European women—thanks to their advantageous pelvis or foetus morphology" (2014, 11). As we will see, ideas such as ease of childbirth have crept into contemporary medical care.

I would be remiss if I did not point out that some researchers are interested in race, but not for nefarious purposes such as the ascription of racial hierarchies. Instead, they seek to account for racial and ethnic differences, for example, in intrauterine growth, to develop more accurate diagnoses of fetal abnormalities (Madan et al. 2002). Further, these scholars express concern that white infant's gestational time has become the standard for all infants when there may, in fact, be some ethnic and racial distinctions that are important in facilitating the medical management of premature birth, not to prove the existence of racial difference.

Causes and Associated Factors of Premature Birth

While race has played some conceptual role in the "scientific" understanding of prematurity and has framed at least part of our understanding of premature birth, racial biological markers for premature birth are unclear (A. K. Knight and Smith 2016). The potential causes for premature birth are many, situated along a continuum of medical and behavioral reasons.

They include "plural-born infants, mothers in the lower economic groups, and those with inadequate prenatal care" (Dunham 1948, 15). Other causes include premature separation of the placenta, premature rupture of the membrane, toxemia, cardiac disease, diabetes, thyroid disease, acute infectious disease, genital tract abnormalities, trauma, and the mother's economic and nutritional status (16–33).[6]

Race, according to the Centers for Disease Control and Prevention (CDC), is considered to be a personal marker. Until 2017, the CDC's website included an infographic depicting a white woman, identifying the risk factors associated with preterm or premature birth (Figure 1.1). Multiple factors that contribute to premature birth are categorized as belonging to three domains: Social, Personal, and Economic; Medical and Pregnancy Conditions; and Behavioral. The first category, Social, Personal, and Economic, identifies three risk factors: (1) low or high maternal age, (2) Black race, and (3) low maternal income or socioeconomic status.[7]

The medical indicators associated with risk for preterm birth include infection, prior preterm birth, carrying multiples, and high blood pressure during pregnancy. Behavioral characteristics include tobacco and alcohol use, substance abuse, late prenatal care, and stress. This latter category is often the spotlight of health education campaigns that reflect concerns about maternal carelessness.

Public education campaigns such as this one can be harmful to the intended audience. Recent research assessing perceptions of alienation in health care contexts found that the experience of being evaluated is connected to negative opinions of health care. The extent to which people fear being judged on such factors as race/ethnicity and age holds implications for the success or failure of public health campaigns. For instance, exposure to a negative message, such as "Black race" being a risk, is an example of a health care stereotype threat (HCST), which is "the threat of confirming negative group-based stereotypes" (Abdou and Fingerhut 2014, 316). HCSTs, often used in health education promotion campaigns, reinforce ideas about certain groups of people. For Black women, HCSTs may be a barrier to health care utilization and result in negative assessments of providers.

Beyond the characteristics on the CDC lists, other factors can lead to premature birth, although there is some debate about which of the factors occur more frequently (MacDorman and Mathews 2011). Although

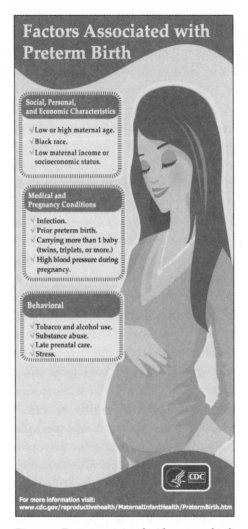

Figure 1.1 Factors associated with preterm birth

there are multiple causes for premature birth, the primary reason is due to medically indicated birth induction or C-section. Birth induction or C-section delivery accounts for 30 to 35 percent of preterm births and has often been planned.[8] The second is spontaneous preterm labor, which is said to account for 25 to 30 percent of preterm births. The last reason, which accounts for 40 to 45 percent of preterm births, is premature rupture of the membranes (PROM), which occurs before the onset of labor.

At term, the amniotic sac breaks, which results in ruptured membranes. This is a normal process commonly referred to as having one's water break. But preterm PROM (pPROM) likely occurs due to activation of these processes before it is time and appears to be linked to underlying pathological processes, most likely due to inflammation and/or infection of the membranes. PROM has also been associated with low socioeconomic status, low body mass index, tobacco use, and a history of preterm labor.

In other instances, the placenta does not grow or detaches, or a woman has what is disparagingly referred to as "cervical incompetency." This term, which harkens back to Emily Martin's (1987) astute observation, in her cultural analysis of women and reproduction, of the denigrating language used to describe women's reproductive processes, refers to when the cervix dilates early, or a urinary tract infection or vaginal bleeding occurs at any time in pregnancy. Cervical cerclage, also known as a cervical stitch, is a treatment for cervical incompetency or insufficiency, which can cause either a late miscarriage or preterm birth. Preterm PROM, which can result from the bleeding associated with placenta previa, is said to be more common among Black women (MacDorman and Mathews 2011).

What might be characterized as a mixed-model explanation is illustrated by a 1987 study that identified four predictors of prematurity: being under twenty years of age, being single, receiving welfare, and not having graduated from high school. The research concluded that racial difference (a "personal characteristic," according to the CDC) in premature birth rates was attributable to a specific medical issue; hematocrit, or the ratio of volume of red blood cells to the total volume of blood (low red blood cell is anemia); and socioeconomic characteristics (Lieberman et al. 1987).

The explanations for premature birth include epigenetics—the result of interactions between the social and physical environments that produce genetic modification. Beyond tobacco smoke exposure, most preterm birth investigators overlook the environmental exposures that often correlate with poverty (Burris et al. 2016). For example, environmental exposure (such as lead in water) tends to track along both socioeconomic and racial/ethnic lines. However, the extent to which disparities in preterm birth result from interactions between the social and physical environments *that produce epigenetic modifications* remains unclear. Natali Valdez (2018), a feminist science and technology scholar, notes that for pregnant women there are multiple environmental factors that are unequally weighted as individual behaviors end up being the focus of policy.

Reframing the generally accepted view that Black women are subject to adverse birth outcomes due to economic inequity, the behavioral scientist Arline Geronimus (1992) suggests that early health deterioration among Black women, which she termed the "weathering hypothesis," has negative cumulative effects. She is referring to the accumulation of discrimination that "settles" in the body as a result of chronic exposure to social, economic, and political exclusion. Therefore, even before pregnancy, Black women have stress levels that age the reproductive system and increase the likelihood of poor birth outcomes.

In troubling the assumption that low income is a primary determinant in premature birth, I draw from studies conducted with Black mothers, all of whom either have some college, have completed college, or hold advanced degrees. Higher levels of education are typically a good predictor of positive birth outcomes. Yet research has shown that Black women with the highest levels of education are still twice as likely as whites with the lowest levels of education to give birth prematurely (Mullings and Wali 2001; F. M. Jackson 2007).

In their groundbreaking book, *Stress and Resilience: The Social Context of Reproduction in Central Harlem (2001)*, Leith Mullings and Alaka Wali found that African American women of all socioeconomic levels experienced chronic stress, which played a mediating role in their birth outcomes. Just six years later, anthropologist Fleda Jackson (2007, 1) authored a report for the Joint Center for Political and Economic Studies in which she made a similar argument, namely, that more attention must be given to the psychosocial risk factors that may trigger physiological responses leading to premature births and low birth weights. Jackson's analysis stresses that poverty alone does not account for reproductive disparities. In fact, she points to a study conducted in the early 1990s that found that well-educated African American women's likelihood of having a preterm birth was more similar to the reproductive outcomes of non-college-educated, unemployed, uninsured white women than to those of college-educated, employed, and insured white women (Schoendorf et al. 1992).

PREMATURE PREDICAMENTS | 45

Premature Births in the Nineteenth, Twentieth, and Twenty-First Centuries

The etiologies and associated risks of prematurity described here are not comprehensive. Nor do they show how women themselves describe and understand giving birth prematurely. By presenting Black women's birth narratives going back to the mid-1800s, the next section aims to illustrate just how long Black women have given birth prematurely and the circumstances under which they did so, thus offering some context for the contemporary complexities of birthing from their perspective.

Aunt Nancy (Sometime between 1830 and 1850)

Linda Brent's story of the premature birth of her son is not the only narrative of premature birth revealed in *Incidents in the Life a Slave Girl*. Another chapter in the book, titled "Aunt Nancy," tells of a second instance in which a premature birth and infant mortality occurred. Aunt Nancy was also enslaved by Dr. Flint and, with the Flints' consent, was "married" at age twenty. When Nancy's husband, a seafarer, was home, she was permitted to stay with him in a small outer house, and over the course of her life she was pregnant six times. All six of her children were born prematurely and subsequently died. Aunt Nancy's duties involved tending to Mrs. Flint, and she was constantly at Mrs. Flint's beck and call. At one point, both she and Mrs. Flint were pregnant at the same time. Because Aunt Nancy had to continue serving Mrs. Flint, her own health was compromised due to the workload she was forced to undertake, including having to sleep on the floor near the entrance to Mrs. Flint's bedroom in case she needed anything. Consequently, on that occasion, Aunt Nancy gave birth prematurely, and just two weeks after the birth of her premature child, she resumed her place at the entry of Mrs. Flint's bedroom to attend to the Flints' infant. We can assume that the work-in-captivity that Aunt Nancy performed and the stress under which she lived were among the reasons for the premature birth and death of all her children. Aunt Nancy's story raises several points. First, Dr. Flint's children were able to flourish, but her children did not. She was available to care for his offspring while being unable to tend to her own health needs or those of her children. Second, her role as a mother was marginalized, a situation that has plagued Black women into the twenty-first century. In the following stories, we will see how the after-life of slavery persists, influencing birth outcomes well *after* the time of slavery, up to the present day.

Anne (Gave Birth in 1988)

When Anne Lewis gave birth prematurely in 1988, she already had one son. It was her second child, a daughter named Zora, born in Colo-rado, who was born prematurely. When I interviewed Anne, she was enjoying life as a sixty-two-year-old retiree. We arranged to speak by phone one afternoon. Anne called as she ran errands and had me on speaker phone while she drove. Before we even began, Anne stopped at a Dunkin' Donuts. "Excuse me, honey. I need coffee for this," she said to me, then ordered a sixteen-ounce decaf vanilla latte. In the background, I heard her blowing on the coffee to cool it. It took a while for her to start telling me her story—maybe she was delaying, gathering up the wherewithal to relate the details of what sounded like a very scary and mind-numbing pregnancy:

> My daughter was born in a very small private hospital. I can't remember how many beds there were. You know, I was in the military during this time. I had only been in the military three months when I got pregnant. I was in a brand-new job. I was the only female and the only Black [per-son]. So, it was a little stressful.

When she became pregnant, Anne was the executive officer coor-dinating and planning for a high-level change of command, involving dignitaries, senators, and congressmen. She was in charge of the entire event, which was to take place on June 1. When Anne first discovered she was pregnant, she had planned to deliver her baby at a hospital near her home. Anne reports that she made and kept all of her prenatal care appointments, and there was no indication that anything was wrong. However, that hospital closed. The physician who had overseen Anne's care up to that point, a white physician, was transferred, and she was as-signed a new doctor—also white—of whom she spoke very highly. She said he was very attentive to her, but her new ob-gyn was affiliated with a hospital twenty-five miles away from Anne's home. She continued to tell me about her pregnancy:

I had been married for five or six years. It was not an ideal marriage, but we were working on it. If I had not been pregnant I might have gotten a divorce, but we separated instead because the pregnancy made things a little better. When I was pregnant, I was in excellent shape because I had just gone through all the training with the military. So, I was doing OK as far as my weight [was concerned]. All those things were perfect, and I had no signs that anything was wrong. Whatever day was Memorial Day that year, I woke up to get dressed to go to work, and I started, what I would call hemorrhaging. I did not know what else to call it. I got up, and it was like a water faucet. Blood was everywhere, and of course I had no warning that anything was wrong. Friends were visiting before transferring to England. The woman [of the couple] was pregnant as well. I screamed for her, and by the time she got to me the floor was completely covered with blood. Every time I moved I would gush. My first thought was, "I am losing my baby." This was May and the baby was due on August 28.

Concerned about her well-being, Anne's guests contacted her new doctor, who instructed them to bring Anne to the ER right away. They also called Anne's husband, with whom she was no longer living, to come pick her up and take her to the hospital. She bled so much that, according to Anne, her husband and friends put down a large black garbage bag in the back of the car, like a tarp. Anne lay down in the back of the hatchback with her feet up on the headrest of the passenger seat, hoping the bleeding would subside. Anne recalled that when she arrived at the hospital and exited the car, there was literally a huge puddle. It took two people to move the bag out of the car, which was weighted down by the blood she had had lost. Anne said, "I was horrified. I didn't know which one of us was dying, me or my daughter, but I knew one of us was." No one at the hospital was able to figure out why she was bleeding. "Of course, the first thing they did was go back to my records. But there was nothing indicating that I had any problems. I was admitted and gave them permission to use—I can't remember what it was called—a new drug that was supposed to stop the bleeding."

Unable to determine the cause of her bleeding, according to Anne, the hospital called her original doctor. She was informed by the ER doctor that her original doctor said he had noted in Anne's records that she had placenta previa. When I asked Anne to explain what that meant, she said that her "placenta never moved on top: it was laying across my cervix." According to Anne, no one ever located the physician's notation indicating that he had diagnosed her with this condition.

After a few days, the medication Anne had been given to stop the bleeding seemed to work, and she was able to return home with strict instructions to be still. Two weeks later, though, Anne was back at the hospital because she had started bleeding again while making a pie. This time, she required a C-section, and her daughter was born at twenty-eight weeks' gestation. What Ann likes to remember is that her new doctor was very attentive during the entire ordeal and attempted to make the C-section surgery tolerable by turning down the lights and playing music.

Anne found both the doctors and nurses at the small private hospital where she gave birth to be wonderful. She was pleased to report that Zora has done well. "Developmentally, she was behind in sitting up and crawling until she was a little over a year. Now to fast forward she went through high school taking Advanced Placement classes. And wound up with a music scholarship. It's a miracle!" But at the same time, Anne's pregnancy was marked by a major misstep. The omission of placenta previa from Anne's records could have been fatal because she had not been properly monitored for complications that could arise from the life-threatening bleeding. Another major concern is that placenta previa, if not monitored and resolved, can result in the need for a C-section before the baby reaches term, as in Anne's case. A preterm infant can end up with many physiological and developmental issues, such as pneumonia, meningitis, vision problems, delays in physical development, or autism.

To be sure, continuously high levels of stress can increase the chance of giving birth prematurely. Black women's care is cloaked by race and tense interactions with medical providers (Hill 2016), but one of the themes of Anne's birth experience—and those of others in this book—is that tense interactions or overtly racialized experiences are not necessarily a consistent element. That is, despite positive experiences with health professionals, where care does not experientially take on a racialized or discriminatory tone, the subtle accretion of mistakes, errors, or bias can still result in racially unequal birth outcomes.

Based on Anne's account, stress was obviously a major factor; in addition, the apparent mistake on the part of her initial doctor, while not necessarily intentional, was life-threatening to both Anne and Zora. One of the important aspects of the afterlife of slavery is that racist intention is not necessary in the creation of racist outcomes. As recent studies have shown, a surprising proportion of US medical students hold erroneous racialized beliefs about Black peoples' experience of pain; these beliefs may well contribute to the documented inequities in providing Black patients with appropriate pain relief (Somashekhar 2016). As a result of the lingering legacy of the afterlife of slavery, errors such as neglecting to note a particular condition—in this case placenta previa—may be more impactful for Black women because they are layered on a foundation where care and diagnosis are, potentially, already compromised.

Ashley (Gave Birth in 2013)

We met Ashley earlier and heard about her first premature birth. Because one premature birth is predictive of another, it is not really surprising that Ashley's second child, Justin, who was born five years after Jamie, was also premature. As with her first pregnancy, the second one was riddled with accidents and neglect. Ashley received prenatal care, beginning at eight weeks, until Justin was born. Unlike during her first pregnancy, Ashley had private health insurance, which led her to believe that she would receive better health care than she did during her pregnancy with Jamie. She was particularly hopeful that this pregnancy would turn out differently than her first because her medical team consisted of two female physicians, who Ashley thought would be more concerned about her health status, which included seeing spots and throwing up every day. Neither of those two symptoms had occurred during the first pregnancy. Ashley reported that her doctors' response to these symptoms was, "Every pregnancy is different."

Ashley was aware that she had high blood pressure, not because anyone informed her but because she saw the numbers on the monitor and understood what they meant. She said that when she asked about her elevated blood pressure, her concerns were met with misdirected blame. Ashley recalled that her doctor said her "blood pressure was high because you came to the appointment on the train." Then, they would take her pressure again. This happened repeatedly. Ashley also said that the doctors were aware that she worked, but they presumed she stood all day and sometimes attributed her high blood pressure to her job. However, Ashley worked at a call center where she sat, so this presupposition was incorrect. Sometimes the doctors blamed her blood pressure on her eating habits. But Ashley insisted that she ate well. The problem, as Ashley saw it, was that her medical treatment was inappropriate:

> I never got diagnosed with preeclampsia until I went for an emergency visit. I gave them my previous history. I should have been seeing a high-risk pregnancy doctor. I told them [the doctors] my symptoms and about the previous C-section and premature birth. At one point, I had blood in my urine and they sent me home.

Preeclampsia, which is also known as toxemia of pregnancy, is characterized by swelling, proteinuria (excess protein in the urine), and hypertension. The condition often occurs late in pregnancy and, if left untreated, leads to eclampsia, which is when the blood pressure is so high that it results in seizures. Sometimes, preeclampsia, or at least its symptoms, is caused by heart disease or diabetes. Lack of prenatal care and poor nutrition are also high on the list of contributing factors for preeclampsia. Yet Ashley says she was diligent about keeping her prenatal appointments. She also pointed out that she ate well, was employed, and had private insurance—unlike during her first pregnancy, when she had public insurance. Yet, she reported that each time she went for a checkup they sent her back home. "No one diagnosed me," Ashley repeated. When she arrived at the hospital with swollen legs, the nurse took her blood pressure; it was 270/60 (a typical blood pressure is between 110/70 and 120/80). At that point the doctor said, "We are taking the baby as soon as the OR [operating room] becomes available." Justin was born at thirty-three weeks and was immediately admitted to the NICU.

In Ashley's case, two significant factors potentially contributed to her second premature birth: a prior premature birth and preeclampsia. At the same time, we must not overlook that there was a lapse in Ashley's care and, based on her own testimony, her concerns were repeatedly brushed aside by her physicians. Despite sharing her worries that something was wrong with her pregnancy, according to Ashley, the doctors blamed her for the high blood pressure—for example, it was high because she had taken the train or because she had a job that required her to stand. From Ashley's point of view, no one listened to her. Instead of having her concerns taken seriously, she was dismissed.

Regardless of where she received her medical care, whether it was a public or private hospital, whether she received public assistance or had private insurance, Ashley believed that racism played a part in how she was treated during her pregnancies. She was nineteen and twenty-three, respectively, when she had her children, Jamie and Justin. She was young enough to be on the receiving end of widely held assumptions about young Black women's fecundity, immaturity, irresponsibility, and lack of knowledge (Luker 1996).

The medical-industrial complex is defined as "the large network of private corporations engaged in the business of supplying health-care services to patients for a profit" (Relman 1980, 963).[9] More than forty years ago, journalists Barbara and John Ehrenreich (1970) described the medical-industrial complex, which includes the entirety of the health care system, every single aspect, that is geared toward profit—not patient care. In their book *American Health Empire: Power, Profits, and Politics*, they wrote that Black and Puerto Rican patients complained of being treated badly. They also noted, "Since blacks are assumed to be more ignorant than whites, they get less by way of explanation of what is happening to them" (Ehrenreich and Ehrenreich 1970, 14). Ashley's assessment of the medical care she received aligns with the Ehrenreichs' analysis. From her point of view, racism played a role in her care based on the way doctors treated her—as if she lacked the ability to understand what they were explaining. Although the underlying causes behind the interaction between Ashley and her medical providers cannot be confirmed, the fact that she thought racism played a role draws our attention to the overall stressors faced by Black women in a society where bias—while not always observable—is indeed an ever-present possibility in the context of a medical structure that has historically failed to fully embrace caring for Black women.

Melissa (Gave Birth in 2016)

Assisted reproductive technology is another factor that can lead to premature birth. This could have accounted for why Kyle, Melissa Harrison's son, was born prematurely. Melissa is a forty-six-year-old Black lesbian who became pregnant in 2016, after nearly eight years of trying to conceive through artificial insemination. Melissa, who has a college degree, was a successful small-business owner who closed down her business to pursue conception.

Melissa's initial attempts at conception involved going from the United States to the Caribbean, where she tried artificial insemination on four occasions. On the fourth try she became pregnant but miscarried at eighteen weeks, most likely because she had fibroids. Melissa decided to have the fibroids surgically removed, a procedure known as a myomectomy,[10] and more than one pound of tissue was removed. Following the surgery, Melissa did some research and chose another route to achieve conception: in vitro fertilization (IVF), which cost her somewhere between $16,000 and $20,000. Melissa made all of these attempts without the benefit of insurance, paying for them out of pocket.

Although Melissa could have purchased an IVF package, which costs about $30,000, she did not. She told me, "With these packages you can get multiple tries. And if they don't work they return 20 percent." Melissa's desire to become pregnant led her to broaden her transnational reproductive circuit, and she chose to go to India for IVF. The desire to conceive draws many individuals and couples into circuits of transnational reproduction—that is, the border-crossing threads of commerce that facilitate reproduction, such as surrogacy and use of ARTs—but Black women's participation in this circuit is not well studied, except for scholarship illuminating how Black women are excluded (Campbell 2015). Melissa's choice to go to India was not unusual because, at the time, the country had a well-developed ART infrastructure. It was a desirable destination for medical tourism and reproductive commerce due to low costs, well-trained English-speaking doctors, and well-equipped private clinics (Deomampo 2016).

As we spoke on the phone, Kyle made noises in the background, which caused Melissa to alternate between talking to me and attending to Kyle. Melissa told me:

I moved to IVF and did the first one in India, in Mumbai. I had been in touch with a guy who was a sperm donor who had successfully helped a woman in England conceive. The doctor's fee was $5,000 plus airfare, accommodations, and drugs. I had this romantic idea, I thought it was an adventure. I always wanted to visit India; I was interested in the culture. Being from New York, I thought I would be prepared for being in a big city. But when I got there [India], it was crowded. It was intense; I had to have an additional procedure to remove scar tissue from my uterus as a result of the fibroid removal. And then there were the hormonal drugs. It was a lot emotionally.

Eventually, what occurred was more complicated than Melissa had anticipated. "I felt like my doctor in India was a little bit of a scam[mer]. I was alone. And I felt like the doctors were fishing to see if I could pay more." She recalled they asked questions like, "What do you do for work?" Or they would comment that she had a lot of money. "It was all very financially driven," Melissa told me, referring to how the doctor searched for health issues that would require additional services and/or tests, ultimately costing her more money. She did not become pregnant on that try but made two more attempts.

The third attempt was a success, which came after Melissa met Chris, who is three years older, and they were married. Melissa's ability to conceive seemed easier, she believed, possibly because she was less anxious, had access to Chris's excellent insurance plan, and did not have to go through the process of conceiving alone. She recalled:

Chris and I had gotten together. She is an ER doctor but did not know that much about all of this. She was interested, though, and she performed artificial insemination on me three or four times, but it did not work. I was interested in having IVF again, but Chris did not want me to get pregnant outside of the country. She wanted to talk to doctors and have me give birth here in the US. I got access to my eggs, I think I had three left. The doctor in India charged me $5,000 again, to send them back to the US. Another try did not work, but then, the last attempt was at a clinic on Long Island and it took. I was highly monitored because of my age and that was I high-risk, but everything seemed fine.

Melissa achieved conception through ART, but three months before the due date, she started cramping. On a return trip from Boston, Melissa decided to stop by a house she had purchased as rental property before she met Chris. She wanted to prepare the place for some new renters and did some light cleaning. In the middle of doing laundry, the cramps started. Melissa told me that she "called Chris, who wanted me to go the hospital, which I did. I was dehydrated and having intermittent contractions, so they kept me overnight and released me the next day. But they warned that I should go on bed rest for three days."

Melissa left the hospital and returned to the house. The day after her release, she noticed spotting and had more contractions. Again, she called Chris and her doctor, both of whom said Melissa should go to Alston State Hospital, which had a level III NICU. She described what happened after she waited there for about an hour:

> My water trickled, it didn't really break, just trickled. They gave me magnesium and steroids to stop the contractions. I was on bed rest for four days. Did you know they can only give you magnesium for four days?[11] I was lying in my bed and people came to visit me. They also wanted to do a cervical cerclage but decided not to, because I was dilating and my temperature was rising. They thought I may have had an infection. And then thirty minutes later, I had a C-section. Kyle was born at twenty-five weeks and four days. He weighed one pound and twelve and a half ounces, which is actually big for twenty-five weeks. He was in the NICU for three months. [When he was born,] Kyle was breathing on his own; he had no brain bleeds, nothing associated with a baby coming that early, and he had a healthy appetite. The only thing he needed was that after eleven days, he was intubated for three days and then on a low dose of oxygen.

Melissa acknowledged that the consequences of being born prematurely do not necessarily show up until later in a child's life. In many ways, Melissa was comforted by nurses and staff who were very encouraging about Kyle's progress. Given the difficulty of the circumstance, she felt supported. However, that did not prevent Melissa from feeling anxious about Kyle's well-being.

When we spoke, Kyle was meeting all of his milestones at his adjusted age of eight months. At that time, Kyle's developmental issues were minimal, although he had received physical therapy, in part because he was not walking at age one. Kyle was eligible for physical therapy, due to his birth weight, for which Melissa received ninety-two dollars a month toward the cost of his health care.

When asked if anyone ever let her know why she may have given birth prematurely, Melissa replied, "No." I asked if she thought it was due to the IVF, but Melissa said that her ob-gyn did not know why she had gone into labor prematurely. However, ARTs such as IVF are known to increase the likelihood of preterm birth (Koudstaal et al. 2000), as well as increasing the incidence of having multiples (twins and triplets).[12] Other than these obvious reasons, the other possible reason for Melissa's early birth was her "advanced" age.

In some ways, Melissa's story does not support the point that the other birth stories here, like Ashley's, make about medical interactions and care that may have compromised women's pregnancies, labor, and birth. Melissa's final comment on that topic was that she was "sure that the fact that Chris was a doctor made people more responsive to us." However, that does not preclude the inclusion of her narrative because, in truth, not all Black women have had questionable or negative interactions with care providers. Indeed, Melissa was among the minority of people interviewed who leveraged better care or had more positive experiences due to having a doctor as a spouse or a family member in the medical field. Including her story, in fact, is a reminder of the productive tensions in research when some of our informants' stories do not neatly align with the dominant analysis we are privileging.

Still, Melissa's premature labor was recorded in hospital data, and her son's birth counts as a premature birth. She is represented in the statistics of Black women who have given birth prematurely, making her narrative a valuable part of a discussion on race and premature birth.

* * *

Discussions of Black women's reproduction tend to highlight the negative webs in which they are caught. The problems women experience are often structurally provoked, and yet these structurally rooted problems are typically interpreted as individual women's bad behavior (K. R. Knight 2015). Generally, those webs are represented in the context of poverty or lack of access to resources. The stories are often of depraved circumstances, such as a chapter by sociologists Jeanne Guillemin and Lynda Holmstrom on Darlene Bourne—the surviving twin of a fifteen-year-old Black mother—in their ethnography *Mixed Blessings: Intensive Care for Newborns* (1986), titled "Darlene Bourne: The Patient as Social Problem."

The chapter's title labels its subject, Darlene, as a social problem and throughout the chapter Darlene and her entire family are depicted as social problems. Their depiction mimics the supposedly pathological qualities of Black families that have long been a staple in sociological discourse. Guillemin and Holmstrom narrate Darlene's life, and that of her family, in a fashion that hews closely to discourses of Black family dysfunction (Frazier 1939). These narratives are often ethnopornographic, focusing on sensationalized details, reducing human subjects to objects, and denying people agency or autonomy. For example, we are not privy to the words of Darlene's family: we do not get to "know" or "hear" them. Instead, Darlene's identity as a social problem, as described by Guillemin and Holmstrom, is a reflection of the staff and researchers' racialized gaze. This gaze was sharpened by the staff's inability to determine who Darlene's father was and the fact that Darlene's mother was young and single—all of these are factors typically attributed to Black family pathology. The chapter in *Mixed Blessings* represents a mordant example of Black women's pregnancy, birthing, and, potentially, mothering in a manner that reinforces long-standing narratives of Black familial incompetence, narratives that have their roots in the slavery era.

In the aftermath of enslavement, Black women's reproductive lives have habitually been "at risk." Despite the structural factors that challenge life chances, Black women frequently symbolize such reproductive atrocities as prematurity, infant mortality, and maternal mortality, as if they purposefully or willfully produce these outcomes in a surfeit of depravity. While it is true that Black women do have more frequent adverse birthing outcomes, the narrowly focused class dimension—typically a proxy for discussing behavior—inhibits the support of broad-based preventive measures in medical care. Indeed, US policies intended to address poverty and low income are often inadequate because poor and low-income people are reviled and blamed for their condition. Solutions that stress individual behavior change, for example, neglect the role of structure and infrastructure in providing access to the food, environment, education, and safety that are required for thriving communities, much less positive birth outcomes. To put it another way, in underserved communities, no amount of behavior change by residents can transform food deserts into sites of food abundance, provide experienced teachers and relevant curricula to schoolchildren, or create access to quality medical care.

The stories of Linda Brent, Aunt Nancy, Anne Lewis, Ashley Bey, and Melissa Harrison place Black women's pregnancy and premature labor both at the center of analysis and on a continuum of time from the nineteenth to the twenty-first centuries. They represent some of the causes that are also on a continuum of consequence—from the "unknown" cause in Linda's case, to Aunt Nancy's station as an enslaved woman whose racial status combined with crushing work demands resulted in a tragic string of six premature births from which not a single child survived. Anne's premature labor may have been the result of a combination of stress and medical oversight. Ashley's predicament suggests forms of medical or diagnostic neglect. Finally, Melissa's labor was bound up in surgeries and reproductive technology.

If the broad statistics demonstrate starkly that there is, indeed, a nationwide crisis of prematurity among Black women, in individual cases it is difficult to isolate the exact causes of premature birth. The tendency to individualize Black women's birth outcomes as a tactic for denying the well-documented truth that something is wrong is, once again, a tactic of the aftermath of slavery in which slaves' resistance to their condition was medicalized as individual psychopathology. In the aftermath of slavery, it is more comforting to stick with the story that each woman has her own history, biological or genetic expressions, and environmental exposures that *may have* contributed to premature birth than it is to point to the structural condition of medical racism and the toll it takes on Black women, children, and families. The numbers tell us that today Black women's birth outcomes are more tenuous than they were during slavery, but ethnographic inquiry is capable of bringing context to numbers, which is one of the goals of this book.

By offering women's stories, this chapter brings into relief a picture that is more expansive and expressive than numbers. Linda, Aunt Nancy, Anne, Ashley, and Melissa broaden our understanding of *who* is likely to give birth prematurely. In examining these stories, it also becomes possible to discuss premature births as a more generalized issue among Black women, not solely as a problem that impacts poor or low-income Black women. In the next chapter, we shift our attention toward the encounters that professional Black women (and, in one case, a father) had during the birth of their child and their experiences with having their newborns admitted to the NICU.

2

Into the NICU

If you come with me, I think someday, I can show you children you will never have to bury.
—Octavia Butler, *Wild Seed* (2001)

Neonatal intensive care units are insular spaces. They, like other areas
within hospitals, exist with a measure of sovereignty due to the specialized knowledge possessed by those who work there (Mwaria 2001). The
space of the NICU was where the newborns of the parents I interviewed
lived—some for as long as sixteen weeks. Yet, the NICU is not only a
space where newborns wait to be stable enough to go home with their
parents. It is also where parents' sense of self is challenged and emerges
relative to the staff working in the NICU. Some parents described dis-
plays of racism ranging from the minimal to the blatant during the time
they waited out their newborn's developmental maturation, explaining
that they felt that a racialized calculus was used by the NICU staff to
assess their worth and capabilities as parents.

Certainly, interactions with staff in the space influenced parents' assessment of the NICU. Therefore, in this chapter, I put race at the center of understanding prematurity and show that race and reproduction
are coconstituted. Thus, this chapter asks, What happens in the NICU?
How do parents feel within and about the space? And do race and racism "happen" in it? This last question seeks to discern whether parents
experience racism, how racism takes shape in the context of the NICU,
and the way medical professionals understand race.

First, this chapter offers an ethnographic description of the NICU.
Second it attends to the way NICUs were experienced by three parents
with differential access to resources. Parents' status is often linked to
their income, type of employment, form of insurance, and educational
levels. These points of reference often congeal, at least in the public's
mind, and become class. Class is frequently the dominant factor in un-

derstanding life chances and far too often overshadows the importance of race. But there are different ways to think about race in the United States; here, I explore how race may or may not be compatible with class distinctions.

In the final section of this chapter, conversations with neonatologists reveal the degree to which race, and by extension racism, was secondary to their class-based understanding of prematurity. In other words, neonatologists talked around race, a phenomenon that is an important element as we think through how care is delivered. If doctors do not want to talk about race, then they are not likely to talk about, let alone try to address, racism. Circumventing such discussions helps the medical-industrial complex to avoid having to undertake an analysis of how it is complicit in medical racism. To position class *over* race by referencing low income or low educational attainment as the dominant analysis for understanding prematurity is misguided and confounds the stories some women and men told.

The Space Between Womb and Home

Each time I entered an NICU, I gasped. Sometimes I held my breath, anxious to see who was lying in the nearest incubator. My senses were heightened, my hearing attuned to the frequency of a baby's breath such that the sound of an infant's inhalation and exhalation was disconcerting. At the hospital in Louisiana, I met with three NICU nurses. Sonia Jackson and Jacqueline Dixon are both Black, and Tiffany James is white. We all sat at what they jokingly called "central command," from which the care of newborns on the unit was orchestrated and administered. For most of the time we were together, my eyes remained focused on the wall-mounted monitors, which provided stats, such as heart rates, for each infant. When a buzzer went off, my body became rigid. "Whose monitor is that?" I asked, directing my question to Sonia. Then, they laughed when I asked, "Has one of the infants stopped breathing?" Sonia responded, "Don't worry, we are on it." The flashing yellow, green, and red lights indicated varying degrees of urgency regarding an infant's vitals. Tiffany told me that yellow and green lights were nothing to get worked up about. She said, "The baby was probably stretching or something." When red lights blinked, someone needed to go into the room. But to me, a novice visitor, all flashing lights were equally alarming. Perhaps the most appropriate comparison between an NICU and a starship has to do with perception. In fiction, starships have very long time scales, and the "action," if you will, takes place within the starship. NICUs look a lot like stationary starships; the nurses' description of "central command" drew on language that compares NICUs to spaceship control decks, and the units have pods where the incubators are located. Similar to NICUs, the outside world is cut off from the space, so outsiders have little idea what it even looks like.

NICUs are categorized from level I to IV, with different technology at each level. Level I NICUs have the least amount of equipment, since infants in those units tend to have fewer medical needs. Level IV NICUs have the most comprehensive technological equipment, capable of providing highly intensive interventions. Over three years, I visited four NICUs on several occasions: three of these were level IV units, one each in Louisiana, New York, and Connecticut; the fourth was a level III NICU in Minnesota. All the infants born to the parents I interviewed were admitted to level III or level IV NICUs. One cannot simply walk into any NICU at will. Sometimes, a passkey or front desk registration is necessary for entry. Some NICUs require an escort for anyone who is not a parent or an approved visitor. And, you must wash your hands—for as long as it takes to sing "Happy Birthday" twice—to ensure cleanliness.

During visits to the NICUs, I noticed that most of the doctors possessed cool veneers and were linguistically economical—no extra words, just pared-down verbal precision. Their voices were often just above a whisper. Most people, except visiting parents, moved with restrained but dexterous intentionality as they administered technology to save or address the needs of neonates—some whose whole hand was only slightly larger than an adult fingernail or whose bodies rested ambiguously on the border of being fetal.

NICUs are not necessarily related to maternity wards in hospitals. Some hospitals have both; other hospitals, for example, those that specialize in infant and children's health, do not have maternity wards. The NICU I visited in Louisiana did not have a maternity ward. Instead, newborns were transported there. The two in the Northeast had both a maternity ward and an NICU, as did the one in Minnesota.

A Level III NICU

After three hours of assisting in the birth of a baby at a hospital in Minnesota, Liza Gianelli, a white nurse who rotates between labor and delivery and the NICU, and I walked over to the NICU where the nurses, all of whom were white, were more animated than in the other hospitals I visited, possibly because the care for these newborns was less intense, since it was a level III hospital.

At the entrance of this unit, as was the case with every unit I visited, there was a sink for hand washing. Directly ahead of this area was the step-down unit, where infants close to being discharged rested in what seemed to be a cross between a crib and an incubator. I counted ten of these hybrid baby beds, situated in a semicircle. Two nurses sat chatting at a half-moon-shaped desk, enabling them to see all of the open cribs. Liza introduced me to both of them, and after we exchanged greetings, she took me into the NICU. This space was oval, also with the incubators along the wall. It had twelve incubators, two of which were in isolation rooms, which have very little light. The baby in one of the isolation rooms on that night had been born with neonatal abstinence syndrome (NAS), in which an infant is born addicted to drugs. The baby rested comfortably in a mamaRoo—a low swing with sea-like motion. The movement seems to calm babies with NAS, which may occur when a pregnant woman takes drugs such as heroin, codeine, oxycodone, or methadone. These substances pass through the placenta, and the baby, along with the mother, becomes drug-dependent. If the mother continues to use the drugs within the week or so before the birth, the baby may experience withdrawal symptoms as the drug clears from his or her system.

The second little one I saw that evening was a boy whose parents had taped their picture on the wall over his incubator. Both mother and father were dressed in traditional African clothing and were smiling into the camera. I then saw a little white baby in a cylindrical incubator with a dome-like top and a blanket covering the entire incubator. Along with the eye patches he wore, the blanket reduced the amount of light in contact with his eyes. As Liza, Katie, the neonatal nurse practitioner, and I moved around the oval NICU, we walked toward one neonate who had been born just the night before. This little girl, who was white, was so tiny. It was shocking that the only reason I could see this little girl was because she was at the end of a series of plastic tubes connected to machines that kept her alive. Walking behind Liza and Katie, I left the NICU and reached the hallway. Only then did I realize I had been holding my breath.

It is difficult for one to imagine the trauma of prematurity or the magnitude of NICU technology. Tubes, machines, isolettes—or incubators—and oxygen machines abound. The proliferation of NICU technology has changed so much about reproduction, including women's relationships to their bodies and their babies, as well as the practices of labor and delivery. For instance, Lee McFarland, who is white and has worked as a labor and delivery nurse for thirty years, noted that neonatal care has been introduced into the general labor and delivery environment. I learned of these shifts in labor practice while sitting in Lee's living room late one cold February night. Lee's wry sense of humor and infectious laugh punctuated the seriousness of her concerns about the degree to which labor and delivery has changed over the last three decades—from when she worked in hospitals in Virginia, Ohio, and the District of Columbia. She told me:

> When I first started working in labor and delivery, the girls from the NICU did not come down for the delivery, they stayed up there and we worked with the neonatologist to stabilize the infant, and then they [the infants] would proceed to the unit, if necessary. Only the neonatologist would come to the deliveries. So back then, we [the labor and delivery nurses] had to be both labor nurses *and* emergent neonatal nurses. The first fifteen years I worked, that's how it was. And then eventually that changed.

Lee described what she viewed as the enhanced medical management of birthing, noting that at one point only two or three professionals were present when a woman went into labor. Now, there are several nurse practitioners, one or two neonatal nurses, and respiratory therapists. As many as fourteen people can attend a woman's labor and birth, especially if there is any chance whatsoever that there might be a problem. For each neonatal specialist involved in a labor and birth, there are fees attached to their presence. If a neonatologist is asked to be present for a suspected problem, that is considered a consult, for which there is also fee. Having NICU personnel present enhances an NICU's bottom line.

There is also a racial component to the NICU that may also be linked to the bottom line. Another nurse disclosed that the NICU at her hospital gets used for "holds." A hold occurs if a mother has an open case with a children's services agency. After the birth the mother's newborn is taken to the NICU as a precautionary measure to ensure she does not leave the hospital. While the infant may not require NICU care, the fact that he or she is part of the census, or the daily count of the number of people in the hospital, means that the unit can request payment. "The thing is," the nurse told me, "is that most of those mothers are Black. Race is all up in the NICU."

"I Had a Great Experience": Sheila's Story

Prematurely born babies and those born with congenital illnesses are dependent on the NICU personnel to see them through discharge. Specialists on this unit collaborate to usher babies from fragile to resilient, and from tiny to larger. By many accounts, premature infants in the NICU live in a sphere of intermediacy, between stages of development, between womb and home, living liminal lives in a liminal space. Sheila Sundiata's daughter, Ciara, lived in an incubator for two months until she weighed in at four pounds.

Sheila Sundiata, an African American woman now in her fifties who is an art consultant, was living in San Francisco in the 1990s. Just before she became pregnant, Sheila had embraced a very healthy lifestyle; she gave up smoking and drinking and incorporated eating more nutritious food. When Sheila discovered she was pregnant, she decided she wanted a midwife rather than a doctor to usher her through her pregnancy. Doctors were more system-oriented, Sheila thought, and she preferred to have the care and closeness of midwives attending to her. Her goal was to have a less medicalized childbirth. Other women I interviewed also chose traditional birthing practices. While most of them ended up having births that involved medical interventions, including Sheila, their desires for more natural births were rooted in a critique of and resistance to the medicalization of the labor process. Instead, what Sheila wanted was a *birth*, not a delivery.

During a prenatal checkup, when Sheila was almost seven months pregnant, she was surprised when her midwives said they needed to talk about her diet. Her weight had ballooned, and although overall she had a healthy pregnancy, she was leaking ten times the amount of protein from her kidneys that she should have, which is an indication of pre-eclampsia. When her midwives asked how she felt about being admitted to the hospital, Sheila responded that she still had to work. After resisting her midwives' push to be admitted, Sheila said she eventually agreed in part because she had chosen this particular midwife practice because they were connected to the chief of obstetrics. Sheila went home and told her family, her boyfriend, and her boss that she was going to be on bed rest at the hospital. The following day, after being admitted, as she put it, "Things went worse."

> When I was admitted, they turned my case over to the obstetrician. He said they wanted to monitor me and I would go into the ICU, where I would stay. They would have to insert a catheter, and I would be bed-bound—my blood pressure could cause a stroke. They were hoping I would get to seven and a half months. That did not occur. I was in the hospital for one day in the ICU and then my daughter went into distress; I went into distress—my blood pressure rose so they gave me magnesium sulfate to prevent seizures induced by the high blood pressure.

The doctors and nurses monitored everything, Sheila said. The obstetrician decided to perform an emergency C-section. Although she does not remember much about what happened before the surgery, Sheila recalled thinking that she might not survive. "Early on, I had a sense that something would happen during my pregnancy. That is why I read a lot. I had even talked to my mom and stressed that if I didn't make it, or if there was a choice, I wanted Ciara to make it."

When Sheila woke up, after the C-section, she was surprised to be alive. It was then that she learned that her daughter was in the NICU. Sheila was unable to see Ciara for a week. "My baby was one pound," she told me, "and I couldn't see my child." Photos of Ciara, which Ciara's father took and shared with Sheila, helped to compensate for the lack of in-person visits. Sheila recalled:

She looked perfect, but nothing in the pictures prepared me for when I saw her in person. In the pictures, she was perfectly formed, she was just tiny. She had blinders on her eyes because she was under the incubator light. Proportionately she looked perfect. Her father would come back and report how wonderful she was. But when I saw her for the first time, I was wheeled over to the NICU, and she was in the incubator. She was too small for diapers so she was just laying on top of diapers. I was shocked. She didn't look at all like the pictures I had seen: she looked like a bird that had fallen from its nest. I thought, "Don't get attached to this little girl."

Sheila's comment led me to wonder if her thoughts of not being attached were at all related to how she perceived the hospital's care of her daughter. I asked Sheila if she thought race or racism factored into her or Ciara's care. She responded, "I had the best staff. I had insurance. They [the hospital staff] doted on me, and they were responsive. They explained everything and consulted with me and let my partner at the time stay overnight. I was treated really well." Sheila told me that if she had been at a public hospital, she may not have been treated as well, and the fact that she and Ciara's father were not married also could have been a factor if Ciara had been born at a public hospital. Sheila's comment bore the mark of knowing that race, reproduction, morality, and societal angst because being Black and unmarried with a child is often deemed a social problem. Sheila realized that the way one is treated and the care one receives is mediated by race, class, and gender (and I would add sexuality). A single Black woman holds little moral authority in the public's eye, and Sheila understood that. But that was not Sheila's situation. "My experience was really beautiful. Even though it was a horrifying experience."[1] According to Sheila, the NICU staff treated both her and Ciara very well, and race was not an issue in her birthing experience or in her care after she gave birth.

However, even when race does not factor into a parent's assessment, it is still salient. Race factored into Sheila's birth in ways about which she may not have been aware. For instance, Sheila had a C-section, an all too common surgical procedure, and thus joined the ranks of Black women who are disproportionately more likely to have C-sections (Roth and Henley 2012). This is not to suggest that the C-section was unnecessary. However, a number of midwives, doulas, and mothers remarked that when some doctors see a Black woman, they tend to corral the evidence needed to insist she will need a C-section. The purpose of this "diagnostic performance," birth workers say, is to secure a higher reimbursement rate. Although the physician fees may be comparable for a C-section or a vaginal birth, the hospital fees may be considerably higher for the former—between $7,000 and $14,000 depending on where one lives (O'Brien and Rebala 2017). Of course, there is another reason, which is also financially driven, not from an interest in increasing income but based on the fear of being sued. The issue of liability is one taken up by sociologist Theresa Morris (2013), who argues that the exponential increase in C-sections is driven by decisions to avert being sued and hospital policies feed into that fear.

The overall possibility for the surgery is higher for Black women than for any other group, according to the CDC (Centers for Disease Control and Prevention 2015). C-sections are not benign surgeries; associated complications can include blood clotting and potential infection. So, the fact that Sheila had a seemingly nonracialized experience because she had private insurance and gave birth at a private hospital did not immunize her from the procedures to which Black women are subjected, placing them in greater danger for maternal mortality.

As she continued talking, Sheila revealed that every day when her mother visited the hospital, she arrived in her nurse's uniform, although she did not work there. It was interesting that Sheila did not view her mother's arrival in professional dress as a possible factor that influenced how she and her daughter were treated. Black people move through life knowing what being Black means in the United States. As one doula stated, "Racism is in circulation even when we don't talk about it." Sometimes there is a need to project credibility, as Sheila's mother did, which serves as a form of insurance to secure respect.

"Waiting": Sam and Lisa's Story

When I called Sam Rollins one night in May for our interview, we quickly settled into a two-hour conversation. I met Sam through his wife, Lisa, who, at the end of our interview, suggested that I also talk to Sam. Sam is African American, and Lisa is white; both were in their early fifties at the time of the interviews. Sam is a developmental biologist, and Lisa works as an administrator at a community-based organization. Sam spoke with a degree of intensity and precision when discussing what he felt about having his child, Alyssa, in the NICU. Alyssa was born in 1998 at twenty-four weeks' gestation, weighing just one and a half pounds.

Lisa's preterm labor was precipitated by a staph infection, according to Sam. Lisa had already been in the hospital on bed rest and while there became infected. According to Sam, Lisa had a very high fever, and one night she was going in and out of consciousness—in other words, she was having a seizure or was delirious. At some point, Lisa asked Sam to lift her leg, and within seconds, the baby just "popped right out." Panicked, Sam called for the staff, who came and "swept her up," and took her to the NICU, where she was placed in an incubator. Sam confessed that he was unaware of NICUs prior to Lisa's admission to the hospital for bed rest. Up to that point, he did not think of them as a place for specialized care.

During Alyssa's stay in the NICU, Sam and Lisa took turns visiting her, "four to six hours a day, virtually every day." Generally, Sam felt like the NICU was a place of waiting because no one ever told him and Lisa that the outcome of Alyssa's care was going to be good. Sam said, "They never built up our hope; they said it's a moment-to-moment experience. There'll be good days, and there'll be bad days. So, the NICU, was a place to wait for her to come home."

In an earlier conversation with Lisa, I asked how she and Sam were treated at the hospital. Speaking only for herself, she thought they were treated well, but that as a white woman she said she did not want to speak for Sam. That was when she encouraged me to interview him. Of course, during our conversation I asked Sam about the issue of race and racism at the hospital where Alyssa was born, and he responded by saying that because he was a scientist in a lab setting near the hospital where Lisa gave birth, he was certain his profession helped to make their experience with the NICU staff very positive. When I inquired if racism was part of their experiences, Sam said, "No, in fact, I think everyone was deferent because I am a scientist."

Negotiating the uncertainties of a neonate's survival is not the only issue in having a child in an NICU. But one might not get that sense from these two vignettes. Neither Sheila nor Sam reported having to confront medical racism. This was also the case with Melissa, whose birth story we encountered earlier. Melissa and Sheila had medical care providers in their families—Melissa's wife was an ER physician, and Sheila's mother was a nurse whose daily visit at the hospital in her nurse's uniform signaled legitimacy. Sam worked in a science setting. None of them felt the sting of racism. But even when people do not perceive medical racism, or it is not asserted, or people feel protected because of their class position, the legacy of medical racism is still a factor that influences health and treatment. Sam's comment about the deference of hospital staff hints at a recognition that his status as a lab scientist prompted those in the NICU to treat him with respect. Underlying this comment is also the recognition that if Sam had not held a prestigious position, his treatment might well have taken on racial overtones. Racism constantly circulates, and Black people know it. Racism dictates how Black people know the consequences of being Black in medical spaces— being dismissed, not being taken seriously, suffering mistreatment, and being misdiagnosed—and they self-consciously end up negotiating interactions to achieve better care. Unlike Sheila and Sam, Veronica did encounter racism after the premature birth of her son.

Race in the NICU

When Veronica Newsome walks, she appears to be gliding. Sometimes, when carrying her son, Igbe, she props him on her hip, and his legs dangle atop her flowing skirt. Gliding and carrying an infant is no easy feat, but Veronica somehow pulls it off. She is intentional in her speech and thinks carefully before making a comment. Veronica is a caseworker, but she could have easily been an anthropologist, because her observational and self-reflexive skills are quite sophisticated for a young Black woman in her twenties.

Veronica was very happy when she discovered she was pregnant. She made sure to obtain prenatal care and took very good care of herself nutritionally, drinking green juices. What did not feel "right" was that Igbe's father, Hakim, who is an actor, was on location filming in Los Angeles during most of the pregnancy. Maybe that was what contributed to the solemn tone of her voice as recalled her pregnancy.

Like many women who are pregnant for the first time, Veronica said she had no idea she was in danger of delivering prematurely. When her water broke early and she went to the hospital, they disclosed to her that she had pPROM. It was *after* she gave birth that Veronica took it upon herself to do research on her reproductive health because she wanted to determine the potential risks involved with getting pregnant again. She ascertained that a procedure completed years earlier probably had caused the premature birth. When Veronica was eighteen, she had a LEEP cone biopsy after a Pap smear showed the presence of precancerous cells. LEEP cone biopsies involve cutting out a cone-shaped section of the cervix, and the size of the piece that is removed can increase the likelihood of giving birth prematurely (Nam et al. 2010; Castanon et al. 2014).[2] Although there is some conflicting research about the degree of the risk associated with LEEP cone biopsies, the fact that no one conveyed to Veronica the links between the surgery and the possibility of preterm birth is what she found so upsetting. She was also disturbed that she had repeatedly told her obstetrician at the clinic about her earlier surgery, but no one seemed to take it into account. During an interview with Dr. Leslie Farrington, a retired obstetrician who is Black, and with whom I shared Veronica's story, she told me that Veronica *should have been considered high-risk* because of the earlier cervical procedure. If Farrington had been her care provider, she said, she would have requested a vaginal sonogram to measure Veronica's cervical length. She would have then counseled Veronica about the possibility of her giving birth prematurely. But, according to Veronica, her doctor gave no indication that Veronica was likely to have a premature birth. She also said, "I had no idea that I should have been an advocate for my care during my pregnancy."

Veronica was thirty weeks pregnant when she was admitted to the hospital. A week prior to her admission, she had contractions, but they were sporadic. She was not especially concerned because false labor had been discussed at the birth education class Veronica attended. Because it was too soon to be in labor, she thought she was having Braxton-Hicks contractions, which are intermittent uterine contractions that mimic labor. Veronica said, "One Saturday morning I woke up and the sheets were wet, I stood and water dripped down, I was freaking out. I called Hakim and asked him if I should go to the hospital. He said I should listen to myself. I had planned to have a home birth, so I was completely unprepared for this."

Veronica arrived at the hospital and was put on bed rest, with the hope that she would not deliver for at least two weeks. She was given medication to speed up fetal development. Hakim flew in from Los Angeles and was there when Veronica went into labor. Igbe was born vaginally, breathing on his own, and Veronica held him for a few minutes before they took him to the NICU. Veronica said she felt like everyone took good care of her and Igbe. "I asked lots of questions, I had a doula, I had people advocating for me, including my mother and my doula. I had Hakim's mother doing research for me on birthing and prematurity. I was very educated." However, Veronica was discomfited by two things. First, was the fact that her son was in an incubator, which brought up feelings of shame. Second, was the way that Hakim was treated after he arrived from Los Angeles.

The NICU at the hospital where Veronica gave birth had recently undergone renovation and was an aesthetically pleasing place. A main island, where medical personnel did their paperwork, allowed them to see all the incubators. Veronica's voice dropped a little when I asked about what it was like having her son in the NICU. Igbe's care was generally good, but having her child in an incubator, she said, "was intimidating especially since this was my first baby." Veronica's mixed feelings about the NICU were particularly focused on the incubator:

It is hard to put into words. It was a vulnerable experience. I felt like my baby should be in my body and yet the baby was in the incubator. So, it was overwhelming to be hit with the visual of babies, multiple babies, as well as my baby in this thing [the incubator] that is doing its job. But it was doing *my* job. I felt a little ashamed, like I was supposed to be doing what the incubator was doing.

In a beautiful and soul-wrenching account of her attempts to conceive, her pregnancy, and the premature birth of her son, queer butch-identified author Cherríe Moraga eloquently describes the loss she felt over her son Rafael's premature birth: "What is hardest to write about is the loss I feel not having brought Rafael to full term. At times, I think it is loss, then wonder if it's really guilt I feel that my son had to go through so much suffering outside the womb because I couldn't protect him inside" (1997, 98). Veronica's lament had a similar quality as Moraga's. Both of them felt responsible for being unable to bring their pregnancies to term. It was as if *they* were dysfunctional—shifting from being mothers in the biological sense to becoming displaced by NICU technology.

As complicated as Veronica's reproductive health history was—the possibility of cancer as a teenager, the premature labor, and having her son admitted to the NICU—the unexpected aspect of her care was how racism was expressed with regard to Hakim's treatment. Veronica said she felt that Hakim was denied his right to be a father, making her role as a mother and partner more complicated than she had anticipated. Managing life as a new mother, with a child in the NICU and a partner who was viewed with suspicion as a parent, was tension-filled. But how does one complain about or raise such issues when one is in such vulnerable circumstances?

The Subtleties of Racism

Veronica had not expected to be talking about racism when she thought of her pregnancy. None of the women interviewed did. But when asked, the story Veronica told about Hakim's visits to the hospital unraveled:

> I don't think Hakim's experience [of the NICU] was good. A lot of the time, when he walked in, they would look at him like he didn't belong there. They would not acknowledge his existence. I had to negotiate on his behalf. I felt like a lot of time, there is a lot of hate for Black men. Men are just not welcome in the NICU, because they don't expect Black men to be doing the right thing. Often, I felt like I had to legitimize Hakim being there and I think it had to do with skin color. I am light-skinned and he is dark. People were nicer to me, and I had to be the go-between, saying, "This is a safe guy, treat him nicely." I think they treated me nicer because I am light-skinned.

When Igbe was born, Veronica said, the nurses, most of whom were Black, commented, "Look how long and pretty and beautiful he is." And then they looked at Veronica and away from Hakim, as if he was not even present: There was no acknowledgment of him as Igbe's father. And, while the nurses were very welcoming to other fathers who were white, Veronica said, they were not warm toward Hakim.

Veronica believed that what Hakim wore also contributed to the nurses' impression of him. His clothing choices are part of his personality, but they also reflect the work he does: Hakim is an actor who has starred in off-Broadway plays and television, sometimes typecast as a drug dealer, sometimes not. The degree to which the nurses were rude, as Veronica put it, likely had to do with what he was wearing and how they perceived him. Veronica said, "If he was dressed 'urban,' people looked at him negatively. When people saw him, they thought he was scary."

One incident that Veronica found especially upsetting was when it was time for skin-to-skin contact with Igbe. She and Hakim had decided that he would participate in that process. Skin-to-skin contact typically occurs just after a baby is born. Generally, newborns are placed in skin-to-skin contact with their mothers to make the transition from fetal to newborn life with greater respiratory, temperature, and glucose stability. It is a sacred time that should be honored (Phillips 2013, 67). But when that time came for Igbe, according to Veronica, the nurses hesitated to include Hakim. She said they stared Hakim down, like he was not good enough to be the parent and to hold his own baby. In turn, Veronica said that she insisted that Hakim had the right to be part of the skin-to-skin process; this was what they, as a couple, had decided. Exasperation filled her account as she told me that she had to remind the nurses that Hakim was the father and had the right to be there. Thus, the woman who had just given birth to a child who was in the NICU was forced to play the role of mediator on her partner's behalf with a staff member who, according to Veronica, viewed him with suspicion.

Although Igbe was well taken care of, Veronica says she felt safer in labor and delivery than in the NICU. Her son was well tended to, but Hakim—and by extension Veronica—was treated with hostility. To underscore their displeasure, Veronica called me from a cast party she and Hakim were attending. She wanted me to hear what Hakim had to say about what it was like for him at the NICU. Over loud voices and laughter Hakim projected his voice so I could hear, "They didn't treat me like they did other fathers, and it was like I wasn't even there. I saw them treat the white dads with respect. But not me."

Veronica surmised that the staff in the NICU "don't really care about you, the parent." She continued by saying:

> You can come in every day, but they act like they are just there to take care of the baby. And I was feeling like fuck you and thank you, at the same time. I felt like each time I went to the NICU, I had to prepare myself to go in, because they did not welcome me with open arms. Just having your baby in the NICU is traumatizing.

Of course, there was no way Veronica could be certain what the NICU staff were thinking about Hakim. But she *felt* it based on their actions. The same may be said of Ashley, whom we met earlier, who had come to the same conclusion. Her interpretation was that the doctors and nurses mostly ignored her because she was young and Black. Ashley and Veronica were unprepared for the versions of medical racism that plagued, respectively, their pregnancy and postpartum period. Both Veronica's and Ashley's encounters with medical personnel illustrate the insidious ways in which race and racism play a part in Black women's reproduction. Because, however, they were a little hesitant about describing the incidents as racism, I want to attend to this issue of uncertainty.

Uncertainty, in this case, must be understood not only as the absence of proof or not knowing something due to ignorance. It also reflects the vague wondering whether racism is an explanation for the care or attention women receive or fail to receive. It is a way of explaining feelings in the face of a complex arrangement of power—the medical system—that promotes its own indemnification by holding up *its knowledge* of medicine as the arbiter of appropriate care *over* the intuitive knowledge that women possess about their own bodies and experiences. Uncertainty derives from racism permeating many aspects of Black people's lives, including high rates of incarceration, experiences of police brutality, premature death, and, especially in this case, experiences of medical bias. Medical bias has a long legacy that still influences overarching approaches to treatment and patient relations today, as evidenced by the significant number of reports and studies showing racial bias, so it is suspect even if a particular encounter is not definitively categorized as racist (Trawalter, Hoffman, and Waytz 2012; Hoberman 2012).

Unworthy Parents

Veronica's comments brought to mind an earlier conversation I had with an African American physician, Dr. Shane Anderson, a neonatology fellow at a well-respected hospital in Louisiana. Anderson, who prefers the pronoun "they," was the first and only doctor with whom I spoke who admitted that racial stereotyping and differential treatment of Black patients took place in the NICU. The subject came up when I asked Dr. Anderson whether there were differences in how neonates were treated in the NICU based on race. They shared the following story of a Black mother who was receiving social services, had given birth to twins, and was characterized as unfit to parent by medical staff:

> There was a Black mom who had twins, let's call her Juliette. Juliette was around sixteen or seventeen. She had the babies prematurely, but I don't remember at how many weeks. They had been in the NICU two months. Then, one of the twins went home, but the other stayed. There was a permanent shunt in the boy's head. By shunt I mean there was a little reservoir in the baby's head that had to be drained every day. The mom would come once every week or week and a half. The nurses got pissed off, and said, "If I were his mom, I'd be out here every day. We should get children's services involved because this is neglect." When Juliette would come in, they [the nurses] were cold to her. If she asked a question, they would say things like, "If you were here you'd know what was happening to your baby." They [the nurses] came to us [the fellows and neonatologists] saying, "You need to get family and children services involved." But she was just sixteen years old. I just don't think that she understood the gravity of the situation. And also, I think there were barriers to her being there more often. She lived an hour away, and that was the thing, it was a whole-day thing [trip]. . . . It is really complicated. But they read it as neglect—that she did not care about her babies.

On the surface, one might think Dr. Anderson's discussion reveals more about class than race, based on the presumption that what was questionable about this young woman's ability to mother centered more on the fact that she was young and possibly without income. The evidence that she was without income might have been inferred from the fact that she did not live close to the hospital. Although this may be true, Juliette was Black, and race and class are entangled, and this entanglement emerges from the US history of racism, enslavement, and segregation. Class does not isolate Black people from racism, and being a Black woman with access to resources is not necessarily a protective measure against medical racism. When race is placed at the center of reproduction, reproductive outcomes, and mothering, we find that the history of medical abuses and the mistreatment of Black women (and men) begun during slavery has continued in its afterlife (D. E. Roberts 1997; Ross et al. 2017). The examples of how race and class intersect that illustrate medical racism's afterlife include the abuse enslaved women experienced by being forced to reproduce and the medical community's near decimation of granny midwives, who provided care for pregnant women in the 1920s and 1930s. Segregated hospitals were also a form of medical racism, as was the sterilization of poor Black women and girls in the 1970s or the sterilization of incarcerated Black women in twenty-first-century California (McGreevy and Willon 2013). In 2016, a New York City–based report showed that Black women with some college had higher rates of severe maternal morbidity—that is, the unexpected outcomes of labor and delivery—than women of other races or ethnicities without a high school degree (New York City Department of Health and Mental Hygiene 2016). Sadly, we have the 2017 misdiagnosis of Shalon Irving, a CDC epidemiologist who died after giving birth despite having made multiple medical visits to determine what was wrong (N. Martin 2017). What these examples show, according to cultural theorist Stuart Hall (1980), is that class is lived through race, and racism operates in concert with and despite class.

One cannot tease out the fact that Juliette was Black and argue that the nurses were concerned about whether or not she could care for her children because she may have been poor or low-income. The reality is that Black women have historically been denied the "right" to mother, and their efforts to do so have been criticized (Moynihan 1965; D.-A. Davis 2016). Recall that Ashley received public insurance and had her child at a public hospital. Ashley showed up every day knowing she was good mother. But still her perception was that racism was the reason she felt disrespected and that her child might be taken away.

Dr. Anderson's recollection of Juliette serves as a reminder that mothering has been viewed on a continuum, which ranges from the ideal to the unruly. The ideal mother is a type that is fetishized and exists in perfect unity with her child (Kukla 2005). Alternatively, there is the notion of "monstrous mothers," whose class and race often indict them as being dangerous for all manner of reasons ranging from unassisted childbirths (Tsing 1990) to being vectors of disease (Reagan 2010). Dr. Anderson's observation illustrates that motherhood is constructed by medical professionals who may perceive maternal failure if mothers do not visit their NICU-admitted child every day. What operated in the cases of Veronica, Ashley, and Juliette was the power medical professionals had in *refereeing* Black women's and men's worth and status as mothers and fathers. Black women, in particular, have not been respected as mothers.

Indeed, as historian LaKisha Simmons points out, "Blackness is defined through cultural incompetency and Black motherhood was a particular problematic because racist ideologies of Black maternal failure blamed infant mortality on improper parenting" (personal communication, March 30, 2017). Such calculations of maternal failure represent a logic of racial hierarchies similar to the way racial scientists described in the first chapter constructed race. Logics of racial hierarchies are the rationalities that are superimposed on and justify racial ordering. In this case, racial ordering centers on Black parents who are viewed as unable to parent well, in contrast to white parents who do—an appraisal emboldened by perceived incompetence (Ferguson 2004). In other words, NICU staff used the power of their profession and their status to code Black behavior both differently and negatively (Browne 2015).

Delving a little more deeply into Veronica's and Ashley's stories and Juliette's story as told by Dr. Anderson brings to light an earlier observation of how the tentacles of insurance status, class, and race can collude to inform how Black women may be treated. Dr. Anderson described a situation that took place with Juliette, the young Black woman, described earlier, who was receiving social services. Juliette, along with Veronica and Hakim, and Ashley, were all young, but they were in very different life stages. Juliette was sixteen or seventeen, according to Dr. Anderson. Veronica (and Hakim) and Ashley were in their twenties when their children were born. In terms of education, Juliette was not in college. Veronica had completed college, as had Hakim, and Ashley was attending college part-time and worked while raising her children. All of them had public insurance. It could be that how they were viewed and treated was through the prism of their insurance coverage.

The point here is that socioeconomic status, class, and even type of insurance coverage can be orchestrated and lived through race. The description of each situation is held together by the narrator's sense that judgments were made based on race, not only their class status as evidenced by insurance type. As noted previously, poverty and low income as indicators of class are raced as Black. Veronica, Ashley, and Dr. Anderson, who retold Juliette's story, reported sensing that NICU staff gauged the ability to parent based on race, which cannot easily be disentangled from perceived class status through the lens of insurance. In fact, it can be argued that these women's insurance status intensified their racialization rather than in any way operating separately from race in terms of the way they were treated.

Ideals of "true motherhood" or "true fatherhood" in some instances involved the presentation of specific qualities and behaviors that NICU staff deemed important. On the one hand, motherhood—indeed parenthood in general—could coalesce positively around the care of a premature newborn, with an "ideal" parent being involved and spending a lot of time with his or her fragile infant. Sam, with his prestige as a scientist and his five to six hours per day in the NICU, felt well treated at the hospital. In contrast, the younger Hakim, dark-skinned and wearing clothes that intensified his Black identity, was challenged and ignored and felt constantly disrespected. On the other hand, through the apparatus of stereotyping, Black parents' worthiness may be diminished for anything that contradicts an ideal, for example, as was reported by Dr. Anderson of Juliette and in Veronica and Hakim's case. From Ashley's standpoint, she was dismissed and not taken seriously *because* she was young and Black.

In some ways, aspects of each of their accounts reflect the fictive history of Black parental failure, which is part of the US narrative that undoubtedly did not *begin* with sociologist Daniel Patrick Moynihan's report *The Negro Family* (1965). However, his characterization of Black women, men, and children in that report has done much to contribute to negative views US society holds about the Black family. Moynihan's work helped to shape the idea that Black families were pathological, which he attributed to female-headed households. His argument was that Black women were obstacles to male ascendency as heads of households. In the report, Moynihan aligned societal racial disparities with the nontraditional family structure.

Interpretations of Black women (and men) vacillate between a narrow range of preoccupations: they pose "danger," are inept, and are immoral. Even Sheila, who had a positive experience in the NICU, was aware of the potential for being viewed negatively. Thus, the tradition of locating Black women (and men) as the problem, regardless of class, remains intact. Being stereotyped as a "bad" parent or one who poses a danger is not the only manner in which racism has been meted out against Black women. As we will see next, various forms of racism are coded through Black women's reproduction within the medical system still refracting the danger they presumably pose.

* * *

Liza Gianelli, the white nurse introduced earlier who works in labor and delivery, made a point of telling me that all the babies in the NICU are taken care of in the same way. But she also indicated that leading up to the birth there are different ways that care is managed. Racialization, the process of attributing specific behavioral attributes based on perceived racial designations, was coded in stereotypical comments that Liza found disturbing. She said she has heard nurses say such things as "She's got eight kids, why are we even saving this one?" What Liza said she overheard was confirmed by another nurse, Lee, who worked at a different hospital. Both white, Liza and Lee disclosed incidents of stereotyping women that led to categorizations of women and their families as good or bad. It is not unusual for categorization to be a routine feature of bureaucracies, including medical settings (Lipsky 1980). Liza continued, "I think this is how we end up with disparities in health care. Everyone *wants* to treat all patients the same. But, no you don't, I see you."

Liza's description tells a story illustrative of stereotyping, or what British sociologist Isobel Bowler (1993) calls "typification." Bowler's insightful research involved three months of observations at a hospital in a South Asian working-class community located in the south of England.

Bowler points out that the way midwives stereotyped patients led to negative clinical assessments. Patients come to be viewed as undesirable, and their inability to present themselves in a manner estimated to be appropriate by the staff makes them subject to being viewed with condescension. Bowler's reports included descriptions of mothers' lacking maternal instinct, making a fuss over nothing, making demands, and being noncompliant. Veronica's description of how she had to navigate race in terms of Hakim's presence in the NICU and Dr. Anderson's description of Juliette being judged as not fit for parenting represent just two of the ways that race happened in the NICU. Hakim and Juliette were classified in ways similar to what Bowler describes.

In addition to parents' trauma and vulnerability due to having an infant in the NICU, they also faced being evaluated. Recent research suggests racial differences in parental satisfaction with NICU nursing care. One study exploring the kind of support that nurses, in particular, provide to parents found that Black parents were less satisfied than white parents with how they were treated by nurses. Parents wanted more compassion and respectful communication (A. E. Martin et al. 2016). Though it is neonates who are admitted to the NICU, the NICU is also where some parents are forced to negotiate not only the fragility of their child's health status but also racism.

Because race and racism are so salient in discussions of birth experiences and outcomes, I raised the topic with neonatologists. Problematically, the subject of race was barely acknowledged by most of the white doctors I interviewed. What are the investments cultivated by medical staff that prevent them from talking about race? According to comparative race scholar Paula Ioanide (2015), it is a labor that involves concealment but comes with some kind of reward. Part of the reward may be the avoidance of guilt because there is so much invested in *not* being seen as racist that one way to address that concern is to not center race.

Refusing Race and Racism in the NICU

At every hospital I visited, the NICU doctors were predominantly white, as were most of the nurses, therapists, and social workers. The nursing assistants and housekeeping staff, however, were predominantly Black or Latinx. Of the eight doctors interviewed, three were Black and five were white. The national physician workforce is predominantly white male (Nivet and Castillo-Page 2014). Racial and ethnic ratios among physicians offer some insight into the racial structure in which medical racism exists, although balancing the ratio does not guarantee that the system will necessarily change practices and beliefs.

During each conversation, I inquired about race and prematurity and found that the issue of race was intentionally ignored by all but one of the white neonatologists. Only Dr. Alfred Angliotti, the chief of neonatal medicine at a Connecticut hospital, admitted that there are racial differences in premature birth, noting that 50 percent of the infants born prematurely at his hospital "were born to African American and Latino mothers." None of the other white neonatologists disclosed the racial census of their NICUs. In fact, there was a refusal to even talk about race. It was not that the doctors thought race did not exist as a dimension of social and political life, but they seemed wholly willing to forgo having discussions that considered race in discussions of prematurity.

My first encounter with a neonatologists' refusal to talk about race occurred while I was visiting an NICU in the middle of Louisiana.

* * *

Dr. Jason Harris's office seemed small for a person who headed up an NICU, but then he was not in it very often, he said. When I entered his office, I was greeted by a tall, cordial, and reserved white man in a white coat. Although he shook my hand firmly, I detected some reticence about our meeting. Dr. Harris was extremely busy and in fact was scheduled to meet with some fellows shortly after our interview. Nonetheless, we spent a good deal of time—maybe an hour and a half—talking about how his NICU was structured, its history, and its growth. Before we got to that point, however, Dr. Harris shared with me that he loved what he did—saving babies—and that he was personally pro-life. I recall that admission came on the heels of a question about the increasing viability of lower-weight newborns and his thoughts about saving extremely preterm infants.

Near the end of our conversation, I broached the subject of race and inquired about the demographics of Dr. Harris's patient population in the NICU. I asked what percentage of patients were Black, white, and Hispanic and how many were on Medicaid.[3] He responded as follows:

In Louisiana and this hospital; it is probably 65 to 70 percent Medicaid funding for newborns, which includes sick and nonsick babies. It might be a wee bit higher here because the segment on Medicaid is probably at risk for worse outcomes because of health care disparities by choice, by education, by substance abuse, et cetera. So, that's the numbers. The age range of kids we see here are kids born that day to all the way up to a year before they are able to go home. Right now, the oldest kids are probably four or five months old.

Medicaid is not race. But it is, apparently, a proxy for both race and economic status. And while it is true that in Louisiana there are more Black than white people enrolled in Medicaid, nationally, white enrollment is about twice that of Black enrollment, 41 percent and 22 percent, respectively (Kaiser Family Foundation 2017). Dr. Harris's response led me to ask about the mothers, specifically, what were the demographics of the mothers whose newborns were in the NICU, and what was the relationship between race and premature birth? In answer to those questions, Dr. Harris stated that his hospital had cared for the child of a thirteen-year old mother. He said, "We get thirteen- and fourteen-year-old moms. I wasn't intimately involved in caring for the thirteen-year old mom, but I knew [her age] from reading the chart. So, we do see that. Pregnancy in young teens is more likely to be compromised. There is higher chance of predelivery and preeclampsia and things like that." "Was she Black?" I asked. "Yes," he said. Harris's near refusal to explicitly discuss race was not antagonistic. But it was unexpected.

Louisiana has one of the worst birth outcomes in the country. Among the six parishes listed for Louisiana in the March of Dimes Racial Disparity Index, the premature birth rates range from 9.9 percent to 18.6 percent—much higher than the goal rate of 8 percent that the March of Dimes wants to achieve. When race is accounted for, the disparities are stark: for Black women the rate is 15.6 percent, compared with 10.7 percent for whites. Despite this knowledge, which is readily accessible on the March of Dimes website, Dr. Harris never once mentioned race. But, when pressed, he used Medicaid and the example of a teenage pregnancy as its proxy. I soon discovered this was not uncommon.

Dr. Lawrence Edelson is chief of a neonatal intensive care unit in New York. To get to his office, one must pass through a set of glass doors. An oval reception area is at the center of the suite, with hallways on either side. Offices are carved out of the exterior walls, such that each room has a view. The panoptics would not be lost on anyone who has the slightest familiarity with Jeremy Bentham, the eighteenth-century philosopher and social theorist who designed institutional spaces that optimized the ability to observe inmates (Semple 1993). At the end of a suite is Dr. Edelson's office. As he emerged from his office to greet me, I was struck by how well-dressed he was—he looked as if he had just wrapped up a *GQ* magazine photo shoot. Dr. Edelson was calm, even-toned, and not given to flourishes.

After an obligatory handshake, Dr. Edelson directed me into his office, warmly blanketed by the afternoon sun streaming through the windows. Taking a seat at the small, round conference table, I scanned the room: the walls were adorned with photos of people who had contributed to the NICU he operates. During that first meeting, we settled in to an interesting conversation about his decision to attend medical school. As he reminisced about his early training and his desire to help people, I found him to be a sympathetic person. The longer he spoke, the more it became apparent that he had some knowledge and concerns about class politics. The same was true of his staff, two of whom I also interviewed.

When we got to the task at hand, which was to talk about premature birth, I asked about the rates of premature birth, the kind of care infants received, and how he characterized the NICU. He told me, "We make babies here. We take something not babyish and make it into a baby." This comment was both disturbing and curious. Maybe other neonatologists feel similarly because with the technological dimensions of saving life—when infants are attached to machines that help them breathe, clean their blood, control their body temperature, and provide nutrients—it could seem that is what is happening. Dr. Edelson's comment provoked me to reconnect with some of the mothers I had interviewed earlier, to ask what they thought of this idea of NICUs "making babies." Each one was deeply offended and thought the comment was pompous. "How dare he," said one mother. Another mother wholly rejected this concept that babies are made in the NICU.

Returning to the conversation with Dr. Edelson, as with all the physicians and nurses I interviewed, I asked about the relationship between race and prematurity. I said, "Here's what I've been grappling with—the literature talks about Black women being more likely to have pPROM and . . ." Before I finished my question, Dr. Edelson interrupted, saying, "There are probably small differences interracially, that I don't know [about]. I would say we probably don't understand that. But those are probably small differences, between the races."

Three months later, we met for a second time. Once again, I brought up the issue of race and prematurity. I said, "My first question has to do with the data on premature births. It is generally known that race is a factor in prematurity. Do you have some sense of what the reasons are?" Dr. Edelson responded, "How about [we talk about] poverty versus race?" Respectfully challenging him, I said, "But it says . . . it doesn't *say that* . . ." He then proceeded to use terms like "inner city" and "poverty" to describe his patients. "The much bigger [issue]," he said, "and this is just me, is poverty. Poverty and education are so far ahead of anything else in determining outcome. You know, inner-city African American, high school education at the most, all those track with prematurity and bad outcomes." In his discussion, Dr. Edelson focused on poverty, education, the inner city, and African Americans. He was, in a sense, talking around race but refused to think analytically about race beyond stereotypes. Why did he not mention that Black women who have attained degrees had a worse rate of prematurity than white women with the lowest level of education? Why could he not talk about race?

In these two exchanges, Dr. Edelson not only deflected the topic away from race, he intentionally operationalized its exclusion from the subject of prematurity. Scholars often depict the inattention to issues of race as invisible (see, for example, Stovall and Hill 2015). However, based on conversations with Drs. Harris and Edelson, race was not invisible. But neither one of them was *willing* to talk about race. They were, however, willing to link premature birth and adverse birth outcomes to teenagers and poor African American women. Race was not invisible; it was known, making the conversations feel like a sort of functional dystopia that, I would argue, aligns with the neoliberalization of race. That is to say, we live in an economic and political moment in which a preference for postracialism reigns. Race is flattened out by an imagined degree of agency that rests on self-help and moral responsibility (Giroux 2003). As educational scholar/activist Connie Wun so importantly argues, "Under the afterlife of slavery, anti-blackness and its specificities are consciously or unconsciously eclipsed or negated. This obscurity occurs despite the United States' legacy of violence against Black communities" (2015, 6). The tendency to not discuss, acknowledge, or deflect away from race is evidence of a refusal of sorts, where race is viewed as a distraction. And if it is not possible to talk about race, it is less possible to address racism. Hoberman reminds us that physician avoidance and evasion of discussing race is likely "out of fidelity to the dream of medical care that transcends color" (2012, 7).

Two other neonatologists, both white women, similarly refused to talk about race. One of them, Dr. Leah Kalin, is in her early fifties and, like Dr. Edelson, embraces the challenge of neonatology and providing care for fragile infants. I asked her the question, "So, in terms of outcomes, how does prematurity play out, racially?" Dr. Kalin responded, "It's more in terms of socioeconomic class in the population that we see, and what I mean by that is . . . we have patients who are Caucasian, Hispanic, African American, and Asian. Our patients are more affluent and less affluent." She went on to say that affluent patients, who have what she called "an intact family-ish structure," manage to get their kids to all of the follow-up appointments. After being released from the NICU, they do everything they can to maximize their premature child's potential. Other families—whatever their ethnic background—who are in a "socioeconomic state of emergency," whether it is because "there is only one [wage] earner, or because of drugs, or because of whatever, they are the least likely to get their kids to the follow-up appointments."

Dr. Kalin's attempt to depict racial heterogeneity privileged what she believed to be neighborhood class analysis. This was accomplished by conflating behavioral differences with class, so that race became a weaker measure of prematurity. Said differently, Dr. Kalin suggested that all racial groups—Black, white, Latino, and Asian—occupied two social positions, either affluent or less affluent, equally. By this logic, if the two social positions were equally populated with the four racial groups, then maybe her point would have been valid. However, her analysis was flawed for two reasons. First, she stereotyped both categories of affluent and less-affluent. Affluent people do not necessarily have "intact family-ish structures," and less affluent families are not necessarily defined by drugs, having one wage earner, or "whatever."

The second aspect of her flawed logic has to do with the community's demographics. The community served by the hospital where Dr. Kalin works does in fact have a racially and ethnically mixed population, but it is an uneven mix. Blacks represent 65 percent of the population, 17 percent are Hispanic, and 12 percent are white. Dr. Kalin's deployment of the neighborhood's racial heterogeneity muddies the fact that sometimes what is happening is related to *race*. The "affluent patients" of whom she spoke were identifiable by neighborhood. Using zip code and census data, I found that white and Asian residents lived in a completely different neighborhood than the predominantly Black and Hispanic communities. Patterns of residential segregation are quite profound: there are very few Black and Hispanic people living in the neighborhood where the white and Asian residents live, and vice versa. Therefore, Dr. Kalin's attempt to conflate the hospital's diverse clientele with the diversity of its catchment area to deflect the reality of racial differences in prematurity is to deny race by using class, which depended on racial tropes.[4]

In four out of five instances, white doctors avoided speaking directly about race (Bonilla-Silva 2002), a rhetorical strategy in which they articulated the medical world as if race is not a factor in understanding prematurity. However, the manner in which the doctors addressed the issue of prematurity was embedded in behavioral, personal, and social characteristics. For example, when asked about race and premature birth, Dr. Harris said that it happens "by choice, by education, by substance abuse, et cetera." For Harris, those were the determining factors for who ends up in the NICU. According to Dr. Edelson, disparities in premature births were attributable to poverty and education. But then he went on to link those issues to race by referring to inner-city or urban Blacks and adverse birth outcomes. Dr. Kalin's answer to the question of how race and prematurity were connected relied on notions of socioeconomic class and family structure in ways that echoed ideas in Moynihan's report *The Negro Family*.

Because race is so fundamental to how class is understood in the United States, in their attempts to differentiate class each neonatologist used long-standing racial tropes that marked a racial "other" to universalize class. The doctors' use of tropes shows the near impossibility of differentiating race from class. The motivation to address only class is a move that, in fact, makes race inconsequential. Ioanide argues that there is an emotional economy to being invested in "preexisting sensibilities about race, gender, sexuality, class, and national identity" (2015, 7). These beliefs are distinct from logics of reason and fact. In the case of these doctors, it could have meant that they did not have to consider that racism could have played a role in the birth outcomes of Black women, and that they—or the system with which they were affiliated—could be contributing to it. Alternatively, it is possible that they spared themselves from having to think about how racial justice might need to be addressed in medical practice.

NICUs, the actual spaces where a premature baby ends up, are tangled up in many webs of meaning, including how parents feel, the way parent-making occurs, and how race happens. To an outsider, they are a technological wonder where the medical management of the infants is spectacular. During NICU visits, I watched nurses and doctors as they attended to babies, which they did with aplomb, an observation supported by Anne, Ashley, Melissa, Sheila, Sam, and Veronica. Each one indicated that the children's care in their NICU was very good, although this was not the case for all parents.

Based on the narratives of two mothers, one father, doctors, and nurses, we see that the NICU held slightly different meanings for each person. For instance, one mother, when she saw her newborn in the incubator, prepared herself to let her child go. In another case, a father described the emotional weight of having his daughter born so early, as well as the wait for a medical turning point that would allow her to leave the NICU and go home. In addition to being in a state of suspension, or liminality, some parents also dealt with what they perceived as medical professionals' racism while their infants were in the NICU. With infants in the NICU, family members are at a vulnerable point, and it is likely that they may perceive adverse treatment more intensely. But these circumstances do not reduce their perceptions to being reactive. To the contrary, their defense mechanisms as parents or family members can guard against the feeling and/or mistreatment due to racism.

What was interesting was that parents' response to questions asking if race factored into their newborn's care were generally consistent. As it turned out, the newborn's care was not problematic for most parents, and they did not describe instances of racial disparity with regard to their child's treatment. A few parents did not encounter racism directed toward them while their infant was hospitalized. Instead, it was parents who experienced race and racism.

Strikingly, most doctors refused to discuss race and in so doing foreclosed the other discussion I wanted to have about racism, prematurity, medical practice, and treatment. Although they knew Black women were more likely to give birth prematurely and thus that their children were more likely to populate the NICU, Drs. Harris, Edelson, and Kalin discussed the problem of prematurity without discussing race. To talk around race and prematurity may be a strategic move to render prematurity raceless. Racial refusal, as conceptualized here, operates as a muted or silent form of racism (D.-A. Davis 2007) in which race is purposefully ignored. Instead, class became race's surrogate in discussions of the disparities of premature birth. It takes considerable audacity to refuse to engage about race and racism in medical environments. Perhaps not doing so justifies a particular ordering of society in which white supremacy sustains the care for particular groups of people through arrangements that are embedded in institutional settings.

As literary scholar and author Toni Morrison (1992) points out, in matters of race, silence and evasions have historically ruled. How can racial disparities and medical racism be addressed if professionals collude with postracial ideologies in the medical-industrial complex in not acknowledging race? Not acknowledging race perpetuates inequality and upholds the possibility of shifting systemic and structural problems to individual issues. In this way class, when viewed as behavior, and personal characteristics such as age, drug use, or lack of education, become more "reliable" explanations as the answer to the question, what causes prematurity? This in turn confers upon the problem the ability to self-manage: wait until you are older to have a baby, don't use drugs, attain higher education, and embrace personal responsibility. To ignore race is to ignore history and the effects of history on people's lives. The next chapter will examine specific racial dimensions of parental experiences of pregnancy, labor, and birth of a premature infant within a historical context.

3

Pregnancy and Prematurity in the Afterlife of Slavery

White people believed that whatever the manners, under every dark skin was a jungle. Swift unnavigable waters, swinging screaming baboons, sleeping snakes, red gums ready for their sweet white blood.
—Toni Morrison, *Beloved* (1987)

There is no reason that women giving birth should not receive the best of care. Yet, based on some of the stories we have encountered thus far, medical care was at times lacking, and at other times medical care placed women at risk for pregnancy-related problems. As I have been arguing in this book, the suboptimal care that some Black women receive may result in part from the legacy of racist treatment during the antebellum period and in the afterlife of slavery. This chapter offers examples of past practices and beliefs that constitute medical racism, culled from medical and public health journals and popular culture. Such sources contribute to understanding the accrual of assaults that may "weather," or wear Black women down, physically and psychologically, compromising their pregnancies and childbirths. Generally, the quality of health care that Blacks receive is poorer than that received by whites, according to the *National Healthcare Disparities Report* (Agency for Healthcare Research and Quality 2012). One reason for poorer health care among Blacks is attributed to doctors' stereotyping based on a patient's race, with those biases influencing clinical and care decisions (Ansell and McDonald 2015). Research shows that implicit bias or unconscious stereotypes derive from doctors' personal experiences and can contribute to health care disparities (Chapman, Kaatz, and Carnes 2013).

This chapter offers a close reading of the narrative of one woman, Yvette Santana. I place Yvette's story in conversation with those of other women, like Veronica and Ashley, to elucidate the cultural narrative of premature birth, even though no matter the number of narratives, the story will not be generalizable to all Black women. The analysis of Yvette's experience is framed around histories and ideas about Black women, their bodies, and reproduction. Racism is interpretable from Yvette's dramatic, indeed traumatic, experiences, that can be traced to enslavement and how its afterlife is expressed as racism and endures in the United States. Yvette's story provides critical insight into medical professionals' practices and elicits the question: How are Black women's prenatal, labor, birth, and treatment in medical environments today extensions of earlier racial thinking?

"If I Had Been White with Blond Hair"

Late one Sunday night, as Yvette Santana drove two hours to go home from a meeting, we spoke. She had me on speaker phone, and during that time, she chronicled her pregnancy and the birth of her twins. In her late forties when we spoke, Yvette is an administrator in higher education who waited to have children until she was forty years old. Yvette and her husband at the time, Carlos, were in a commuter relationship—he lived in Washington, DC, and she in Charlotte, North Carolina, and they shuttled between the two cities.

When Yvette and Carlos decided to have children, her physician told Yvette that her fibroids would complicate conception. To facilitate becoming pregnant, Yvette, like Melissa, whom we met earlier, endured two myomectomies. After the surgeries, which according to Yvette left her uterus compromised, she underwent in vitro fertilization (IVF). Although Yvette's age and use of ART should have signaled potential issues, she believed her ob-gyn—who specialized in high-risk pregnancies—viewed her pregnancy with too little concern. Yvette attributes his indifference to a comment she says he made that Yvette did not have the markers of "being Black," due to the absence of high blood pressure or diabetes, both of which are also indicators of high-risk pregnancy.

The physician's inattention in managing Yvette's pregnancy in a way she thought was appropriate exemplifies a form of medical racism. In other words, because she did not display illnesses associated with being Black, he neglected to attend to the danger her pregnancy *did* pose. In fact, according to Yvette, her doctor accused her of hypochondria and asked if she was trying to make herself high-risk. Her response to his question was, "I am almost forty and pregnant with twins. Yeah, I think that makes me high-risk. I have a very high possibility of delivering early."

Due to what she perceived as the physician's lack of concern, Yvette searched for and found another doctor in Washington, DC—a Black woman—from whom she received affirmation about the potential seriousness of her pregnancy. Speaking by phone, this doctor agreed that Yvette's pregnancy could pose problems and offered to provide care during her pregnancy, if Yvette wanted, but explained that she would need Yvette's records. Yvette then planned a trip to spend some time with her husband and meet with the potential new doctor.

Just before the trip to DC, Yvette visited her ob-gyn in Charlotte, for two reasons: she felt under the weather and wondered if she was well enough to fly. Yvette's ob-gyn said she was fine and told her, "Go for it, there's no problem." But when she got on the plane, Yvette said she did not feel right. "I called the doctor in DC, who said, 'Get off the plane and go back to your doctor.' But we were on the tarmac . . . so I stayed on and flew to DC." Upon landing, Yvette said she felt "like crap." She went to a hospital emergency room close to the airport. But the doctor with whom she had previously spoken was not affiliated with that hospital, so the two of them never met.

While in the ER, Yvette completed paperwork, but no one really attended to her, she said. Although she indicated that she felt ill and might be in labor, instead of addressing that possibility, the ER personnel ignored her. "I was not manifesting enough symptoms of distress for them to be concerned," she told me. Yet, Yvette said that she was continually asked if she was on drugs. The only medical attention Yvette reported that she received involved being tested twice to determine if she was on methamphetamines.

Several hours after arriving at the hospital, her twins were born—at twenty-six weeks' gestation. Yvette gave birth prematurely to a girl who weighed one pound and eight ounces and a boy who weighed two pounds and one ounce. Both were admitted to the NICU. During the infants' stay in the NICU, nurses insisted that Yvette's twins would survive, although they were small. "They kept telling me, 'Oh, you know Black babies make it all the time. There's nothing to worry about; they are so fit!'" Yvette never shared with me the race or ethnicity of the ER or NICU personnel, although it is not clear that it mattered. Racial ideologies wend their way into broader systems, becoming normalized in everyday practices regardless of the race, ethnicity, or gender of the practitioners.

Over the ensuing twenty-eight days, Yvette spent most of the time at the hospital with her children. One day, she decided to go home, take a shower, and return later to spend the evening with the babies. Within an hour of leaving the hospital, Yvette received a phone call asking her to return. When she arrived, Yvette found out that her son had died, having succumbed to methicillin-resistant Staphylococcus aureus (MRSA), a hospital-based staph or bacterial infection.[1] The nurses, she said, were shocked at his death, probably given their predictions that Black babies are "so strong and fit." Yvette concluded that the nurses' belief in strong Black babies had worked against her son. She confessed her true feelings: that if they had seen her children as fragile and not strong, maybe they would have taken better care of her son and she would have taken home both twins instead of one. At the end of that portion of our conversation, Yvette said, "If I had been white with blond hair, I bet my son would be alive."

Yvette then shared what happened when she returned to the hospital, after having received the call that her son had died. When she arrived at her son's room, Yvette found a security guard waiting for her. She said, "Not the social worker—they had security, like I was gonna come in there and shoot the place up! There was no psychologist. I thought that was very inappropriate." It is difficult to imagine a white woman having this experience.[2]

I asked Yvette if she thought a lawsuit could have been initiated, but she said she just did not feel like pursuing that route. I wondered if she thought that she would have been perceived as being demanding or overreacting, as Black women sometimes are. What Yvette did say was that she believed that her care and that of her newborns was "triaged," by which she meant her condition and that of her twins were viewed with less urgency, which in turn determined their treatment. Yvette attributed the fact that while in the ER her case was not viewed with concern to racism. It is easy to see why she would arrive at that opinion—she felt that the obstetrician, the ER personnel, and the NICU personnel dismissed, misread, or downplayed what Yvette believed to be the acuteness of her circumstance and that of her twins—only one of whom survived.

Racism in the Afterlife

Key events during Yvette's pregnancy and postbirthing experience—
from the doctor in North Carolina who did not consider her pregnancy
to be high-risk, to the ER hospital personnel who tested her for methamphetamines, to the NICU staff who assured her that Black babies
survive, to calling security—illustrate how racism and race-making
practices persist over time. Yvette's experience aligns with several events
in which Black women have been misdiagnosed (Suite et al. 2007),
positioned as superhuman (Mullings 2005b), and victimized by the
"troubling tradition," as journalist Harriet Washington (2006) calls it, of
medical experimentation and exploitation.

Washington's book *Medical Apartheid: The Dark History of Medical
Experimentation on Black Americans from Colonial Times to the Present* offers the first full history of Black people's mistreatment as experimental subjects in the United States. For example, most people may
be aware of the notorious Tuskegee experiment in which Black men
with syphilis were left untreated for forty years. What may be less well
known is the medical experiment that took place in the 1990s in Baltimore, Maryland, in which predominantly Black girls at a middle school
were implanted with Norplant, which suppresses ovulation. Of course,
community members were angered that Norplant was being distributed
without parental knowledge and that there may be side effects. Again,
had those girls been white with blond hair, it is hard to imagine their
being implanted with a contraceptive device while still in middle school
and without the permission of their parents.

Against this backdrop, Yvette's story is not exceptional. Repeatedly,
Black women face various forms of racism during their pregnancies. A
National Public Radio report that called attention to a similar situation
focused on three Black women who shared horrific accounts of their
pregnancies and births (Mogul 2017). One story was that of Charity
Hines, who went to Kings County Hospital in Brooklyn, New York, for
a forty-week checkup but was not yet in labor.

During what Charity thought was a routine prenatal visit, the doctor
performed a vaginal examination. Only when Charity yelled out in pain
and demanded to know what was going on did the doctor tell her that
she was probing to stimulate labor. According to Charity, the doctor

then apologized and admitted she should have told Charity what was going to happen, but noted that sometimes this causes patients to become worried. Subsequently, Charity began a twenty-seven-hour labor, had a C-section, and ended up with a mild infection; her son was admitted to the NICU. Essentially, Charity's protestations were dismissed, and labor was induced without her consent. What happened to Charity exemplifies how Black women's treatment during prenatal care in this contemporary moment has been traumatic (Abbyad and Robertson 2011). Experiences such as Charity's reflect yet another aspect of medical racism centering on the obstetric experience, in which condescension, lack of consent, and adverse birth outcomes amounted to a form of gender-specific violence, sitting on a continuum that includes what happened to Yvette.

The incidents marking Charity's labor and Yvette's pregnancy, labor, and postpartum period illustrate how racism is perpetrated on Black bodies. Medical exploitation and mistreatment have hinged on racialist presumptions. Yvette's story, in particular, opens a window onto four realms of medical racism: diagnostic lapses, obstetric hardiness, hardy babies, and menacing mothers who are seen as demanding and problematic.

Diagnostic Lapses

According to Yvette, her ob-gyn neglected to identify her pregnancy as high-risk, what I term a "diagnostic lapse." My use of this term is inspired by medical anthropologist Duana Fullwiley's enculturated gene concept. In her ethnography *The Enculturated Gene: Sickle Cell Health Politics and Biological Difference in West Africa* (2011), Fullwiley focuses on how people with sickle-cell anemia in Senegal in the early twenty-first century embody sickle-cell variation and different lived expressions of the disease. However, the disease ontology, she argues, cannot be separated from history. Fullwiley offers an account of sickle-cell that is influenced by Senegal's economic situation in the 1970s and 1980s, when the country was resource poor and people were forced to develop survival strategies to deal with many issues, among them, sickle cell. This accommodation resulted in low-level disease management, and everyday practices came to be viewed as a form of competence. In other words, disease embodiment and management on the part of Senegalese themselves *minimized the perception of the gravity of a severe medical situation by others.*

Fullwiley's analysis corresponds to Yvette's experience because the gravity of Yvette's medical condition, which did not manifest alongside a co-occurring population-specific and population-expected illness, was minimized. That is to say, her pregnancy did not correspond to a medical context that the physician associated with high-risk pregnancy. But this was a perverse situation: in the absence of a "race"-specific disease—hypertension or diabetes—Yvette's physician took her health status to be atypical of what was expected of a pregnant Black woman. Consequently, it was possible for him to ignore the other aspects of her pregnancy that were unequivocally cause for concern: she was forty years old, had undergone two myomectomies, used IVF, and was pregnant with multiples. In this way, Yvette was the casualty of a diagnostic lapse that was a consequence of racism.

Examples of diagnostic lapses, as they pertain to Black women's health, are found in the annals of medical racism. For instance, historian Marie Jenkins Schwartz's (2006) discussion of the manner in which physicians came to wield control over enslaved women's reproduction provides a clue to how race assumptions (and status) have obscured physician's abilities to make appropriate diagnoses. The case Schwartz summarizes to make her point comes from a medical journal published in 1854. A reading of the original article, which documented the case of a "negro girl, who was aged nine, and the property of J. Haywood Jones, Esq., of Mooresville, Alabama" (Gantt 1854, 336), was very disturbing, indeed.

In the article, Dr. Gantt reports that in June 1852, a Dr. Hussey was called to address the medical needs of a nine-year-old girl. She had a swollen abdomen, and Dr. Hussey had no doubt the girl was pregnant, noting that "the abdomen was distended and rounded, as in pregnancy. . . . I attempted to pass my finger into the vagina, but could not find success, from the smallness of the canal. . . . It became the undivided opinion of all who saw her that she was pregnant" (Gantt 1854, 336). Of course, this is unnerving on many levels: first, that the physician would normalize that a nine-year-old girl could be pregnant; second, that the physician assumed the girl was pregnant; and, third, that the physician attempted to conduct a vaginal examination. It is striking that it never occurred to the doctor or the girl's owner that she could be anything but pregnant. This, I argue, exemplifies the operationalization of diagnostic lapses. The girl's race and status as an enslaved person predisposed those around her to assume a *diagnosis* that aligned with the perception of her race and her position in the slave economy, as a reproducer. As such, no other diagnostic option was "available." Obviously, the girl's situation differed from Yvette's because she was enslaved and had no say over her health. But in a contemporary context, the "unavailability" of another diagnosis was true for Yvette as well. The young girl could only be viewed as pregnant because of who she was—Black and enslaved, a person likely representing future revenue through her reproductive potential. Yvette could only be viewed as "healthy" and in no danger of an adverse birth outcome due to what she *did not* have and who she was—a professional Black woman with no diagnosis of diabetes or high blood pressure. Diagnostic lapse operates in both directions, the absence of a diagnosis due to indicators that are, or are not, present.

The young girl died just three months after Dr. Hussey's examination. The author of the article, Dr. Gantt, conducted an autopsy of the girl and found she was *not* pregnant. Rather, she had a tumor on her liver that was "fifteen inches in circumference and weighed over two pounds" (Gantt 1854, 337). Similarly, Yvette had *not* used methamphetamines. However, she was pregnant with twins, over forty years of age, and had a compromised uterus. In both instances, diagnostic lapses operated. Yvette and the young girl both had health issues that were viewed too narrowly, based on race, which led to misdiagnosis.

A second example of diagnostic lapse comes from the archive and is based on an article published in a 1951 issue of the *Journal of the American Medical Association*. Historian John Hoberman recounts how earlier biological rationales merged with "inferior status" and impacted Black women's medical treatment. Physicians believed that Black women "enjoy a racial immunity to endometriosis" and, consequently, received less monitoring and treatment than their white counterparts (Hoberman 2012, 140). Medical racism, in this case, was asserted based on the assumption of a condition associated with race. Instead of Black women who presented with symptoms of endometriosis being diagnosed *with* endometriosis, they were diagnosed with pelvic inflammatory disease (PID) because they were assumed to be sexually promiscuous. The consequence of such a misdiagnosis is sterilization.

Lee, the labor and delivery nurse introduced earlier, attested that stereotypes about Black women leaked their way into the provision of care at a clinic in Virginia where she worked. Based on her estimation, most clinic clients were employed; 80 percent were government workers, and most were college educated. Lee recalled that one day, a Black woman in her thirties or forties came in complaining about vaginal discharge. She wanted to make an appointment to see a physician, but the nurse—a white woman—did not want to give her an appointment even though the doctor had time available. Lee said, "The nurse on call did not want to give the woman an appointment because she did not feel the client was having an emergency." And then, according to Lee, the nurse said to her, "'Oh, I am sure she just has another STD, every Black woman in Northern Virginia has PID. They all have PID; they just sleep with everybody.' I stood there with my mouth open. I went to my boss and filed a formal complaint. The woman was transferred." From this story, we can see the how racial stereotypes bleed into practice, jeopardizing Black women's health.

Diagnostic lapses result when medical professionals lack the ability to think about disease, illness, and discomfort—or to make diagnoses— outside of racial, gender, or sexuality categories and associated stereotypes. In Yvette's case, it was the absence of something presumed, the absence of a Black woman's race-specific or race-attributable disease— hypertension or diabetes—that led the doctor to neglect the potential danger she faced during her pregnancy, which resulted in diminished monitoring of her situation.

One final observation with regard to Yvette, as compared to Ashley or Veronica—who both received public health insurance due to low income—is that no matter how far one moves up the social or economic ladder, resource accessibility does not necessarily serve as a protective measure against medical racism. Yvette's status, despite her profession and her health insurance, still resulted in her feeling disregarded and that her care led to her having to face pregnancy-related perils similar to Ashley and Veronica. Black women's medical care and the racism they face, which possess traces of the antebellum period and colonialist medical treatment, end up being translated onto the Black body in general and the Black reproducing body in particular.

Obstetric Hardiness

The ER staff's refusal to attend to Yvette's claims of being in labor and the issue of whether or not she was in pain resonate with beliefs that Black people experience pain to a lesser degree than whites. One rationale that has persisted over time is obstetric hardiness, which, in theory, applies to both white and Black women. Obstetric hardiness centers on the ease with which women bear children—reflecting a toughness that is constructed as primitive in nature. Russian women, for example, are thought to be obstetrically hardy, but they are considered to be an anomaly among white women. The thesis has been most successfully choreographed onto Black women's bodies, based on the argument that they are more capable of dealing with the painful ordeals of pregnancy (Hoberman 2012, 141).

History provides insight into the presumption accompanying the obstetric hardiness thesis: a belief that particular groups of people have high pain tolerance. In the early to mid-nineteenth century, one area of scientific inquiry involved the use of enslaved women in experiments. According to historian Deirdre Cooper Owens (2017), Black women were the test cases for the development of gynecology. For example, J. Marion Sims, the "father of gynecology," conducted surgical experiments on three enslaved women—Anarcha, Lucy, and Betsey—to correct vesicovaginal fistula, a condition in which a hole between the vagina and the bladder results in involuntary urine leakage. Sims wrote, "The vagina may become inflamed, ulcerated, encrusted with urinary calculi, and even contracted; while the vulva, nates, and thighs are more or less excoriated, being often covered with pustules" (1853, 3). This condition is sometimes the result of unrepaired tears from childbirth or another type of uterine trauma: the uterine wall becomes thin due to multiple pregnancies, or as the result of rape (Nordland 2006).[3]

Scholars have argued that enslaved women, particularly after legislation ending their importation, were forced to increase the value of slaveholders' property through reproduction (Washington 2006; Dudley 2012) and thus were likely to develop vesicovaginal fistula. According to her owner, Anarcha had such a condition and underwent about thirty operations, involving multiple incisions. The absence of anesthesia clearly made this a painful procedure. One indication that Sims's operations were likely quite painful is based on his description of how he handled a small fistula. According to Sims's book *On the Treatment of Vesico-Vaginal Fistula*:

> Here the fistula is very small, say not larger than a common-sized probe, or even as small as a number seven or eight sewing needle, the best plan to scarify is, to hook up the part with the tenaculum, pull it forward, and by a thrust of the knife transfix the entire thickness of the vagino-vesical septum; then by a circular sweep of the instrument, the whole fistulous track may be removed at once; which substitutes for the small and callous opening, a smoothly cut orifice of rather a conical shape, large enough to admit the end of the forefinger. (1853, 4)

Needles, thrusts, knives, and removal—there was no way these experiments were not extremely painful.

Rationalizations of Sims's experiments have taken at least two forms: the laudatory contributions of his work and the racial endowment justification. In defense of Dr. Sims, bioethicist and professor of anthropology L. Lewis Wall (2006) argues that the charges against Sims for conducting experiments without anesthesia are without merit. Wall states that the fistulas themselves caused more suffering than the surgeries to correct them. Further, Wall says that the charges against Sims for not providing anesthesia to his patients are unfounded because anesthesia was not introduced into surgical practice until the mid-nineteenth century. Such justification clouds the issue of pain, care, and ethical practice. Intentionally causing pain is not the only measure of unethical practice—although, to be sure, I heard many stories of women who experienced a tear during childbirth but received no anesthesia before the tear was repaired, even when women said it was painful. Other unethical practices include not securing consent for procedures and the use of vulnerable populations. Sims was known to have conducted his experiments on enslaved women and poor Irish women, who in that period were not considered white.

The second rationale, the racial endowment justification, acknowledges the pain that women felt but dismisses it due to racial hardiness. Dr. Seale Harris, one of Sims's many biographers and the founder of a clinic in Birmingham, Alabama, in 1922, wrote, "Sims's experiments brought them physical pain, it is true, but they bore it with amazing patience and fortitude—a grim stoicism which may have been part of their racial endowment or which possibly has been bred into them through several generations of enforced submission" (1950, 99). Under the broad concept of racial endowment comes such notions as hardiness, which intersects with Yvette's experience.

Yvette's labor was illustrative of a perverse manifestation of the hardiness thesis. Whatever the ER personnel's analysis of Yvette's behavior, it *did not* lead to the assumption that she was in labor or pain. Maybe a different racializing calculus was in operation, one linking race to drug use. Yvette says she did not scream or moan, which *was* in keeping with the idea that Black women are able to withstand labor pain. But the possibility exists that the hardiness thesis took a detour and was transfigured into a different probability. Indeed, it is likely that Yvette's reading of her own calmness, as she insisted *something* was wrong, was interpreted as a manifestation of having used methamphetamines, which can have the effect of stimulation or sedation.

During and after enslavement, ideologies of endurance and durability, as well as expendability, framed Black bodies. Research shows that medical professionals hold beliefs about racial difference that result in disparities, for example, in administering pain medication (K. M. Hoffman et al. 2016; Singhal, Tien, and Hsia 2016). Hardiness, then, becomes the justification for forcing women to withstand pain while at the same time placing them in the position of being violated (Schiebinger 2004).

What, one might ask, can be the reason for practitioners to dismiss the signs, disclosures of fear, sense of endangerment, and knowledge of a woman who is concerned about her health? Racial science, medical racism, ideologies of pathology, and hardiness have been marshaled in ways that mark Black women as both flawed and superhuman. On the one hand, hardiness positions Black bodies as flawed because the "strength" possessed does not register as human, and Black nonconformity is almost always in need of intervention—usually in the form of policing. Simultaneously, the idea that Blacks are impervious to pain enables diagnostic lapses. Based on her account, we might say that Yvette was treated as not quite human, and she "wore" the afterlife of slavery, in the form of medical disregard.

Hardy Babies

Black babies are so fit.

Some version of the strength and fitness accorded to Black babies was a refrain Yvette and other mothers heard, which relates to women's obstetric experience. Fit Black babies can hold an important place in the hardiness thesis. Racial science has undeniably contributed to the tropes used in the service of representing Blacks as superhuman.

A useful text from the nineteenth century, although not focused on children, explored the limited mental capacities of Negroes but regaled their physical strength. The English translation of French naturalist Julien-Joseph Virey's book *Natural History of the Negro Race* is a foundation on which claims of Blacks as hardy have been built. Virey, whose work was lauded by twentieth-century racial scientist Paul Broca, described Negroes as being more prone to feelings than thoughts and claimed that they possess small brains. He continued, noting that Negroes are "superior to all other men in agility, dexterity, imitation, as respects to body. . . . Their feats of agility are surprising. They climb, vault on a rope with wonderful facility, equaled only by monkeys, their countrymen, and perhaps, their eldest brothers in the rank of nature" (1837, 26). Negresses, he wrote, when dancing are indefatigable. These characteristics are suggestive of the same attributes associated with hardiness: endurance, strength, and toughness. Over a century and a half later, the controversial psychologist J. Philippe Rushton, who promoted similar racial science claims, argued that Blacks have an advantage in sports based not only on their physiology but also because of their small brain size. Rushton (2000, 147) has also asserted that Black babies are more physiologically mature than white babies.

In the medical field, two papers, one written in 1967 and the other in 2004, connected gestational maturity to race. The forty-year time span between the two articles reflects a "fruitful" continuity of locating functional differences in premature infants by race. One study of premature infants in the United States supports the idea that prematurely born "Negro" babies survive better than white prematurely born babies (Henderson and Kay 1967). In 2004, a study based in the United Kingdom found that, when compared with white European women, Black and Asian women's fetuses required shorter gestational lengths (Patel et al. 2004). Perspectives such as these serve to instantiate the fragility of whiteness, equate blackness and "Asianness" with difference (Balchin and Steer 2007, 751), and exaggerate those differences such that nonwhite infants are viewed as superhuman or in need of less care.

Endorsing the hardy Black baby thesis has consequences, one of which is that throughout their life span, Black children tend not to be viewed as children. Instead, they are represented as big and scary. The repercussions of this mischaracterization include Black boys and girls being deemed as malicious and "a menacing threat to white lives," as argued by historian Stacey Patton (2014). This has led to premature deaths—like those of Tamir Rice and Michael Brown, both of whom were shot by police and described in terms of possessing a physical presence that intimidated police. For instance, Cuyahoga County prosecutor Timothy McGinty suggested that twelve-year-old Rice was threatening. According to the prosecutor, Rice looked bigger than most children his age (Marans 2015).

Commenting on the fatal shooting of Michael Brown in Ferguson, Missouri, journalist Ben Stein disputed the description of Brown as unarmed. He said that calling Brown unarmed, "when he was 6'4", 300 pounds, full of muscles, apparently, according to what I read in the *New York Times*, on marijuana. To call him unarmed is like calling Sonny Liston unarmed or Cassius Clay unarmed. He wasn't unarmed. He was armed with his incredibly strong, scary self" (Rothkopf 2014). Ideas about Black boys' difference and denying the possibility of their innocence extends to Black girls as well. A gender analysis of maturity described in a study of girlhood found that childhood innocence is also elusive for Black girls. Starting at age five, Black girls are viewed as less innocent, more adultlike, and less in need of protection than their white peers (R. Epstein, Blake, and González 2017). Depictions of Black children as strong and scary can lead and has led to outcomes such as premature deaths and overincarceration.

Popular culture also promotes the idea of strong babies. For example, imagery found in the 2011 Strong Baby advertising campaign, a health education campaign developed by the city of Milwaukee to address the city's high infant mortality rate, does double duty by situating adverse birth outcomes as the responsibility of the mother as well as constructing some babies as superhuman (Figure 3.1).[4] In Wisconsin, Black infants were three times more likely to die than white infants, and the campaign involved providing prompts to ensure stronger babies. In this campaign, the infants are posed in a manner suggestive of enormous strength. These ads thus both reinstantiate the idea of the strong baby and are a problematic representation of maternalism. Through the imagery and text the mothers of Black babies are held differentially accountable for the outcome of their births than are white women (Walters and Harrison 2014). The message these ads send is that the neoliberal subject, the Black mother, should take full responsibility for the health of her baby and should self-manage her pregnancy to bring it to term.

The captions in the ads "shore up old ideologies" of racial mothers, even though the mothers are visually absent (Waters and Harrison 2014, 40). The ads ratchet up anxiety about preterm birth and loss along racial lines: Black mothers place their children in harm's way differentially than white mothers. Putting their infants in jeopardy is one implication of these ads, which convey the impression that Black mothers do not seek out prenatal care—for which they are to blame. The ads suggest that Black women can control whether or not their babies are born at term. They also blame unhealthy Black babies on mothers who smoke— which studies have shown to be exaggerated in some cases and untrue in others.[5] In fact, smoking as a toxic factor leading to premature birth or infant mortality is often associated with Black women, but this link is questionable. Some research has shown that among pregnant women who smoke, Black women actually smoke less than white women (Palmersheim 2012).

Alternatively, the representation of the white infants' strength is associated with directives for them to be immunized and breastfed, potentially far less complicated solutions than carrying one's infant to term. Through the text and images, the causes of infant mortality and morbidity are presumed to be different for Black infants than for white infants. Locating the mother as the site from which infant mortality and premature infants emanate reduces complex social and structural etiologies down to the body of the mother. Using an article from the journal, *Vir-*

Figures 3.1a–3.1e
Strong Baby
campaign

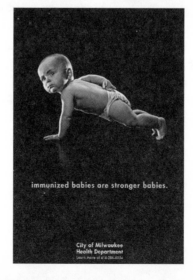

ginia Medical Monthly, anthropologist Gertrude Fraser aptly illustrates the reductionist racial logic of blaming the mother for her own and her children's health problems—even in death. In the article, a selected case of maternal death centered on a twenty-three-year-old "colored" woman who was in labor for fifteen hours and bleeding. A hospital review panel noted the inappropriate care on the physician's part. At the same time, the review classified the mother's death as preventable "due to the absence of prenatal care, the failure to seek medical attention. . . . The failures were due to neglect or ignorance on the part of the patient and her family" (Maternal Health Committee 1942, 35; cited in Fraser 1998, 133). Deflecting the problem away from racism was pro forma and an easy way to deny the structural causes of birth outcomes. But the reality of racial discrimination informed how people viewed the issue.

Black people have indeed blamed the loss of their children on racism.[6] For instance, Mary Church Terrell, a prominent civil rights and suffrage activist and the first Black woman appointed to the American Association of University Women (AAUW), lived through the premature births of her children, all of whom died. In her autobiography, *A Colored Woman in a White World*, she tells the story of one of these births, and the inferior incubator that her baby was placed in (in a segregated hospital) and laments that it was racism, writ large, that put her infants in jeopardy. She writes:

> When my third baby died two days after birth, I literally sank down into the depths. Of despair. For months, I could not divert my thoughts from the tragedy, however hard I tried. It was impossible for me to read understandingly or to fix my mind on anything I saw in print. When I reached the bottom of a page in a book, I knew no more about its contents than did someone who had never seen it. Right after its birth the baby had been placed in an improvised incubator, and I was tormented by the thought that if the genuine article had been used, its little life might have been spared. I could not help feeling that some of the methods employed in caring for my baby had caused its untimely end. (2005, 142)

Together, the Strong Baby ads and the discussion in the *Virginia Medical Monthly* highlight that Black mothers are required to govern their own health issues and those of their babies in utero, which is strikingly in line with neoliberal ideologies. The Strong Baby ads, though, can be contextualized by neoliberal logics that invoke self-disciplinary actions that resolve not only social problems but also medical problems. Political theorist Barbara Cruikshank (1999, 3) makes the point that such governance practices, in the Foucauldian sense, guide the actions of others: they are any program, discourse, or strategy that attempts to alter or shape the actions of others or oneself. Essentially, the images of the Black infants and the accompanying text insinuate that prematurity and infant mortality are "social condition[s] forged in Black women's wombs" (J. L. Morgan 2004, 56), for which the women are at fault.

Menacing Mothers

As mentioned earlier, when Yvette arrived at her son's room, she found a security guard waiting for her. It should be startling that hospital personnel would call security as the response to Yvette's mourning. Instead, based on interviews I conducted, it was not unusual.

Subjecting Black women to behavioral inspection and seeing them as threats was not unusual, according to Sara Roberts, a thirty-year-old African American mother of four children whose professional success included being a master's-prepared NICU nurse and a doula. Although Sara said she loved her job, the hospital where she worked was not above her critique, particularly as it related to the racial dynamics of the hospital vis-à-vis the population it serves. Sara reported, "The patients are mostly Latino, African, African American, and Asian, but *all* the nurses are white [except Sara]. There is not one doctor of color on the NICU staff. So, there are cultural barriers that need to be considered."

One of those barriers concerned how white nurses responded to Black mothers and treated them as suspects. For example, on one occasion Sara recalled she was on NICU duty with another nurse, who was white. Among the infants in the NICU was a little boy whose mother was Black. Sara described an incident in which she believed racism factored into the white nurse's decision to call security. According to Sara, the nurse who was on duty with her called the mother of a newborn who was in the NICU. The nurse wanted to check in about when the mother would be returning to the hospital. When the mother returned the nurse's call, Sara says, she overheard the mother on the phone say, "Who's calling me from the hospital, twice? I am on the way." Sara shared her evaluation of the mother's response; the mother was likely anxiety-ridden, no doubt *because* she had received two calls from the hospital. Sara explained that she thought the nurse who initiated the call had perceived the mother's tone differently, believing that the mother was intimidating and feared that the mother was going to hurt her. Sara's outrage was clear as she told me that the nurse called security to ask them to be on the lookout for the mother when she arrived. "I mean, come on!" Sara lamented. Other nurse informants revealed that it was not uncommon for white nurses to perceive Black women as menacing and to treat them as if they pose a risk.

Risk. Black women are *at risk*, and they are *a risk*. When something (or someone) is considered to be a risk, a state of unease takes over. This is the central argument that Didier Bigo (2006), a French critical security studies scholar, makes about the concept of risk and security. Risk can contribute to states of anxiety, to which the response is various forms of governmentality. While Bigo is referring to global threat, it is not difficult to see how similar logics can be applied to groups of people. Once danger is established, as sociologist Simone Browne (2015) states, security measures can be deployed with ease. Simply *being* Black indexes distrust and precipitates profiling and assignment into risk categories based on nonthreatening behaviors. Labeling is a dangerous endeavor, as Browne points out, in which "anxieties and the anticipation of risk stemming from those deemed 'dangerous minorities' then shape security measures" (2015, 38). How is it, one might wonder, that women who have given birth fit into categories of risk? Or is it that racialized bodies are in constant need of surveillance regardless of circumstances? Again, it is hard to know, but this is the kind of uncertainty that plagues many Black people in the United States.[7]

Enslaved people were under almost constant watch; slave patrols and overseers are the best-known examples of such surveillance, but physicians were frequently called to ensure that women did not attempt to abort their pregnancies or end an infant's life after giving birth. Behaviors were watched, especially when related to reproduction, which contributed to the plantation economy. They were not, however, always controllable, as enslaved people consistently resisted scrutiny and regimes that regulated their lives (James 1989).

Under the watchful eyes of NICU personnel, surveillance of mothers held implications beyond their being viewed as threats. Surveillance also lent itself to determining parents' worthiness to be parents. As we have seen, race became a critical edge from which some nurses judged mothers—constructing them as worthy or unworthy. Conferring value in the making of parents is derivative of an analysis by feminist science and technology studies scholar Charis Thompson (2005) of how parents are made. Although Thompson focuses on the biomedical and legal interventions that congeal to create kinship through ART, parents are also *made* in the technology-laden domain of the NICU—in this case at the intersection of medical professionals' determination and race. Medical professionals described some of the circumstances in which they believed race played a part in judging whether parents met a particular standard of being good enough. Within the context of the power that medical staff can wield over Black parents due to their children being in the NICU, determinations of (un)worthiness intersect with racism, forming a web that supports or disrupts parenting.

Again, it was Sara who confirmed that African American families with children in the NICU were watched and judged, based on race, when she shared the following incident:

> I recently had a patient who I was helping. She was frustrated because she wanted to stay in the parent room because she was homeless. The caveat was she had another young child who also needed to stay [at the hospital]. Her baby had been here four and a half months. No one else picked up on the cues [that she was homeless]. Sometimes this mother said, "I need to leave for a couple of hours." What she was going to do was go see about an apartment. I told her, "You know they are watching you, so you need to be careful. You will be judged based on what they see you do." There were so many things that consumed her, but that didn't mean she didn't love her baby. Families struggle and they are trying to figure out how to get to the hospital on the bus in the snow, with other children. That is not necessarily the struggle of white nurses.

Sara's observation speaks to the reality that parenting ability was appraised. She was not at ease when doctors and nurses parlayed *their* ideas about mothering or parenting into a tool to assess others.

Assessments of whether African American mothers could mother took the form of concern about whether they possessed the skills necessary to attend to their children's medical needs. For example, Sara said some nurses viewed African American women as "bad" mothers if they thought the mothers would be unable to operate an oxygen machine for their infants. But when oxygen tanks are delivered to the home, training in using the equipment is also provided. Constructed under the watchful eyes of some doctors and nurses, the Black mother of a premature infant could be held accountable and judged as good or bad, based on a scale of the professional's own making. Sara said she felt that "doctors and nurses do not actually believe some African American women can *be* mothers."

Race and the Labor of Care

Sherry Gordon is a friend of Anne Lewis, whose traumatic pregnancy was described earlier. Anne introduced us, knowing that Sherry's son, Michael, had been in an NICU. Michael was neither premature nor underweight, having weighed about nine pounds and three ounces at birth. Sherry chuckles when she says, "He was a C-section baby; born big and beautiful." Michael was in the NICU as a result of a congenital disease: his stomach became enlarged, and the doctors diagnosed a bowel obstruction. They eventually had to perform surgery—an ileostomy.[8] Michael was in the NICU for forty-seven days, and every day Sherry visited because she lived less than a mile away from the hospital and because, as she pointed out, "I breastfed all my children. It was very important to me. So, I went to the hospital several times a day to feed my baby."

Sherry found most of the hospital staff to be very supportive. In particular, she said the certified nursing assistants (CNAs), most of whom were Black, were very kind. According to Sherry, the split in job responsibilities by race and duties resulted in white nurses putting out the medications and the mostly Black CNAs doing what Sherry called "dirty work." But Sherry said that it was the CNAs who kept her informed and let her know what was going on when she was not around. Sherry recalled:

I specifically left instructions to not give my child formula. I said to them, "I will be here. This is my schedule, I will be here to nurse him or give milk. But I don't want him to have formula." And twice I caught them giving him formula. I don't know if they didn't read the chart. I can't say the circumstances, but I was not a happy camper.

Sherry firmly stated that she was not one to let an incident go by unacknowledged. So, she confronted the West Indian neonatal physician about not following her directive. The physician dismissed Sherry's complaint, considering it acceptable to give Michael formula. In fact, the doctor thought formula might be better for Michael's intestinal recovery. Sherry disagreed and said she had to explain to the doctor that breast is best:

> I gave him this whole litany—a big discussion on that topic. I don't care what you say, you obviously don't know . . . there is no way you will ever make me believe that there is anything better for my child than my milk. And do not allow the nurses to do it. Or there will be hell to pay . . .

In recalling what happened, Sherry registered the event with disgust and interpreted the nurses' and doctor's responses to her demands about how her baby should be cared for as disrespectful. As Sherry described it, "A few of them [the nurses] thought I was too much, that I was meddling too much—that I was coming too often. But I was coming to see my child!" Seemingly, no matter what some Black women do, it is not enough to garner admiration for their maternalism.

Similarly, Veronica, whose story was shared earlier, also demanded that the NICU staff give her son, Igbe, only breast milk. On one occasion, the nurses told her that the nursery had an adequate supply of her breast milk, so she decided to go out to dinner and return later to spend the evening with Igbe. Yet when she was dining about forty-five minutes away from the hospital, one of the nurses called her to say they had run out of breast milk. She returned to the hospital and found a nurse feeding Igbe formula. Like Sherry, Veronica said she felt that the nurses found her request to be "too much." Maybe it was a silent judgment because, according to Sherry and Veronica, no one said anything to either of them. But they *felt* it.

Another mother was actually discouraged from breastfeeding her child on demand. Crystal, about whom we will learn more later, had developed a clear plan for breastfeeding her child who was in the NICU. But the NICU staff rarely let her do so. In fact, she said, they would tell her that she needed to return to feed him and sometimes made her wait three hours. Crystal felt that the medical staff used their power to monitor her ability to see and feed her son. She believed they were being retaliatory because of the demands she made about how she wanted her son to be cared for.

If Sherry's, Veronica's, and Crystal's sense that they were perceived as demanding sounds familiar, it is because Black women are often represented as such. Stereotypes circulate that explicitly portray Black women as unreasonable and demanding. These representations were so chilling that, back in 1920, W. E. B. Du Bois pointed out that as a group, Black women suffered from damnation and devaluation, which has had a particularly cruel and long-lasting effect on them (Gammage 2015). All three women felt that medical professionals viewed their labors of care as problematic. Being viewed as a problem and watched with caution operated in the case of the young mother whom Sara described—with no attention to the structural barrier, homelessness, that she faced, which influenced the mother's ability to be present. Sherry, on the other hand, was made to feel like she was a problem because she was a highly involved mother. The duality is almost like a condition of attack with specific entailments in nearly every case. In other words, the young woman Sara discussed and Sherry, Veronica, and Crystal were not opposites but were on a similar scale in terms of the way Black women are subjected to being controlled, having their behavior pathologized, and being in need of intervention.

Connecting what we might call these "breastfeeding episodes" to what Sara Roberts shared, we can surmise that some of the intermediaries of care in the NICU refuse to view Black women positively or support their decisions regardless of a woman's behavior or desires. While some mothers are framed as irresponsible or not caring enough, others suffer because they want too much; no matter what they do, Black mothers are interpreted negatively (Menzel 2014, 11), and the labor of their caring is consistently minimized or disregarded.

Leith Mullings cogently points out that stratified reproduction is reinforced by gender constructions in which "women as mothers becomes master symbols of family, race, and civility" (1995, 129). This symbolic reckoning, however, is available only to white women because Black women are seen as promiscuous, bad, and ineffective mothers (Mullings, 1995; Collins 1991). Racial hierarchies of motherhood are built on legacies that privilege white over Black mothers. Black women have been denied the right to assume revered positions as mothers (Spillers 1987), although they resist that ideological prison by framing the importance of sacrifice, teaching children self-reliance, and being protective as crucial components of their child-rearing practices (Glenn, Chang, and Forcey 1994; Elliott, Powell, and Brenton 2015). The ideological prison into which Black women are often thrown is an expression of stratified reproduction.

Stratified reproduction, or the systems of inequality that structure women's reproduction differentially based on class, race, and ethnicity, is a useful way to consider who is able to legitimately assume a revered position of motherhood (Colen 1995). Black women's ability to mother is undermined at almost every stage, from the time at which she is pregnant, the fact of her pregnancy, how she wants to give birth, and how she raises her children. Here again, we can see how mothers may be judged and their worthiness to parent questioned. Take, for example, Yvette: even as she grieved the loss of her son, she was apparently not deemed good enough to have a therapist console her; instead she was confronted by a security guard. The mother described by Sara was viewed as a threat. Being a threat positioned Yvette and the mother Sara discussed as potentially unworthy parents. Sherry was viewed as too assertive—maybe even truculent—for showing up every day and being clear about the care she wanted her child to receive, which left her feeling disrespected.

By and large the complex interactions between medical professionals and Black pregnant women, or Black women who have just given birth, as described here, demonstrate how power is asserted over Black women, regardless of class. Race confounded whatever cultural capital—in the form of educational attainment and income—these particular mothers may have possessed. Yvette's and Sherry's stories reveal the ways in which these women were susceptible to configurations that disadvantaged their right to be listened to and to be presumed competent; their value and the value of their concerns and opinions were mediated in the context of race.

Racism coalesces through different processes and practices in the sphere of prenatal care, birth, and the admission of a child to the NICU. These practices are not necessarily articulated in terms of direct statements. They may be explicit or subtle. An explicit version of racism is illustrated in the production of biological suitability, which anthropologist Daisy Deomampo documents. In her work on race and surrogacy in India, Deomampo shows how Indian medical professionals use *essential characteristics* to determine race in the egg selection process for commissioning parents using surrogates (2016, 147–62). An example of the subtleties of racism is described by Khiara Bridges, whose research among uninsured pregnant women in New York revealed that they are racialized through what she calls "deracialized racialist discourse." This discourse creates new pathologically laden groups of poor minority women without ever explicitly mentioning race (Bridges 2011, 160).

A close reading of Yvette's narrative and the inclusion of other accounts help to illuminate the kinds of situations that led women to characterize their experiences as medical racism. We see that historically constituted racist ideas and practices have migrated to Black women's contemporary experiences of prenatal care, labor, birth, and postpartum. I have termed this "diagnostic lapse," which is a slip or a failure to address a woman's health issue for any number of reasons, such as was the case with Anne Jackson, whose first physician did not note in her records that she had placenta previa. Diagnostic lapse is also exemplified in Ashley's and Yvette's cases, where both of them had a sense that something was wrong, but their concerns were not taken seriously by their respective physicians. Diagnostic lapses mimic the historically constituted ways that the black and brown bodies of women have been treated, mistreated, or dismissed, because professionals modulate the alarm that a woman feels about her own health condition.

In closing I want to return to the earlier mention of Yvette Santana in relation to Harriet Washington's book *Medical Apartheid*. Although Yvette was not the subject of medical experimentation, her pregnancy, labor, and premature birth, when analyzed in the context of the afterlife of slavery, may have been easily nestled in the pages of Washington's book between the description of Fannie Lou Hamer's sterilization and the eugenic program initiated by Margaret Sanger. Yvette's story, like that of Hamer and the subjects of Sanger's program, rests at the intersection of neglect, violation, and exploitation, which are common manifestations of Black women's reproductive experiences in the United States. We can wonder how the situation may have ended up if Yvette had a birth worker to help navigate the medical system that failed her.

Witnessing a Birth

An Interlude

The first part of this book has emphasized birth stories told by Black women and two Black men. These have frequently been angst-filled narratives, often soldered with histories and interpretations of racial stereotyping and the experience of racism. Up to this point the chapters have interrogated premature birthing experiences from the vantage point of Black mothers and fathers, who have been subjected to articulations of racial bias. Most mothers, but by no means all of them, described interactions with medical professionals that may be characterized as being caught up in webs of racism based on how they were treated.

The second part of the book shifts the lens in a slightly different direction while still keeping Black women and race in the line of sight. This tilt is toward technology, data, and birth advocacy to examine different modes of intervention and prevention. Part II explores approaches that have been undertaken to address premature birth, including saving technologies, the statistical bureaucratic approach taken up by the March of Dimes, and the critical prevention approach that has led to an increase in the number of doulas and midwives who engage in birth work as part of the larger political project of reproductive justice. Though the accounts offered here may raise concerns about generalization or critiques of omission, the intent is to offer insight regarding how the "problem of prematurity" has been and is currently being addressed.

Before moving on to part II, however, I share here the story of a birth that I witnessed and of which I was a part. The details of prematurity are difficult to live through, listen to, write about, and read. For that reason, I offer this interlude to help remind us what a birth could be like. I do not know what the pregnancy was like for Idalia, the mother, as I only arrived at the hospital about three hours before her daughter was born.

What I do know is that Idalia's birth story—or one like it—is one that most of the women interviewed wished they had experienced.

* * *

Liza Gianelli is the labor and delivery nurse who allowed me, with permission from her nurse supervisor, to shadow her during her shift at a hospital in central Minnesota. We arrived at the hospital on a Tuesday in November, just before 3:00 p.m. I stood at the reception area as Liza discovered that although she thought she was working until 11:00 that night, she might not have to work at all. I detected disappointment because I think that in addition to loving her job, Liza was excited to have me see the action on a maternity ward, which had both the labor and delivery unit and a level III NICU. We waited to hear if Liza was on that day, and at last she received word that, indeed, she was. Liza had a four-hour shift that night with me shadowing her and wearing scrubs, like Liza and the other nurses.

At the beginning of each shift, all the nurses attended a meeting. The head nurse reviewed the status of each woman who was in labor, and each nurse selected a mother to work with. Liza chose to work with Idalia, who had been in labor for about eight hours before we arrived at 3:00 p.m. It was likely Idalia was going to be the only one delivering that night, which turned out to be the case. After the shift meeting, Liza and I immediately went to Idalia's room, which was the size of a studio apartment in New York City, about 600 square feet. Standing at the foot of Idalia's bed was Jill, a midwife; she would be delivering Idalia and Juan's baby in the birthing room (Figure I.1).

Idalia lay on the bed, moaning softly. She looked weary. Another bed was parallel to hers, where Juan could rest or sleep. There was also a sink and an infant bed with a radiant warmer. There were no drugs administered, such as Pitocin, which brings on labor. Everyone just waited until Idalia's body was ready to deliver. And together, we used all kinds of strategies to facilitate that birth, but nothing high-tech or involving medication. When a doctor came in to check on Idalia's progress to see if Idalia wanted to speed up the birth, Jill just encouraged everyone to be patient. There was no need to rush.

Idalia's birthing room was spacious. But what caught my attention was the bathroom with a very large tub. Within ten minutes of our arrival,

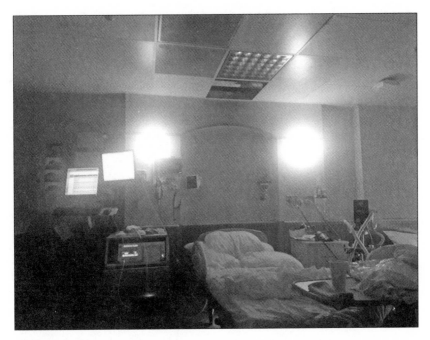

Figure I.1 Birthing room

Liza and Jill determined that Idalia would benefit from sitting in a tub of water. During labor, warm baths are used to reduce stress hormones, which can elevate pain levels; this is helpful because pain can slow down labor. But water immersion shifts that dynamic and can also ease involuntary muscle tension and lower blood pressure.[1] As Liza filled the tub with water, I asked Jill to explain to Idalia, in Spanish, her native language, what I was doing there. I wanted to secure her permission to remain in the room while she was in labor. Idalia and Juan looked in my direction, conferred in Spanish, and agreed that I could stay. Then they returned to the business of laboring.

Liza thought ambient lighting would be good for the bathroom, so we went in search of battery-operated candles. Once they were found, Liza prepared the bathroom, and Idalia walked slowly from her bed to the bath and submerged herself in the water with Juan's help. She stayed in the bathtub for a while, and then a flurry of activity took place to help her along. In the absence of a rebozo—a long piece of cloth worn as clothing or to carry items but also used as an aide in labor—Liza tied a knot at the end of a sheet and threw it over the bathroom door, closing the door tightly. This allowed Idalia to pull her weight against a sheet so that she could crouch and bear down. After that I helped set up a contraption that attached to her bed so that she could put her legs up in a stirrup-like position so that she could push down. Three hours later a beautiful baby girl, named Dalgis, arrived. It was both incredible and an honor to witness Juan cutting the umbilical cord.

PART II

4

Saving the Babies

Strategies to save premature infants and to prevent infant mortality have been deployed in earnest since the early 1900s, although the interventions have met with varying degrees of success. Saving premature babies, like all reproductive politics, involves racial politics, as Dorothy E. Roberts (2014) argues, and this chapter shows that over time, the interventions used to save infants have generally been uneven in terms of racial outcomes. In this chapter I explore the racial politics of saving by examining a limited number of interventions used to address newborn mortality and premature birth in the United States.

The strategies under investigation include the campaigns and programs developed by the Children's Bureau, which was founded in 1912, and the Sheppard-Towner Act of 1921 which provided federal funding for maternal and infant care. Then I consider two presidential directives that contributed to saving efforts: President John F. Kennedy's creation of the National Institute for Child Development in 1962 and President Ronald Reagan's Baby Doe mandates in the 1980s. Finally, I examine two advancements to address the manifestations of prematurity—surfactants used to maintain lung function and NICUs. NICUs dominate the field of possibilities as *the* technological intervention to save infants. However, the narratives of nurses and March of Dimes personnel, which raise questions about NICU technology, trouble their glorification.

Technologies of Saving

Saving has many valences, as medical anthropologist Risa Cromer (2016) notes, and in anthropology is most often referred to in terms of reproduction (see, for example, Fitzgerald, Legge, and Park 2015) and market culture and capital accumulation (see, for example, Riles 2013). Sociology and anthropology scholars have theorized saving in a number of contexts located within the domain of the political, ethical, and moral. Relative to reproduction, the subjects of saving range from newborns to abandoned infants to embryos (Buchbinder and Timmermans 2013; Oaks 2015; Cromer 2016). Medical anthropologist and sociologist Mara Buchbinder and Stefan Timmermans, respectively, theorize saving by exploring how parental testimony wielded political influence that led to the passage of the Newborn Screening Saves Lives Act in 2008. The act established national screening guidelines for the assessment of newborns for twenty-nine possible genetic, metabolic, and congenital conditions. Affective economies proved useful toward the goal of passing the act and included drawing on feelings such as fear and compassion and the use of narratives to elicit emotional investment in the political project to save newborns.

Sociologist Laury Oaks (2015) offers a thoughtful analysis of the development of "safe-haven" laws, a movement that has raised awareness of the problem of child abandonment. Safe-haven laws allow for mothers who are unwilling or unable to care for their infants to drop off their children at designated locations. Included in this movement are "unborn babies," who antiabortion activists also seek to save. In Oaks's analysis, saving assumes the form of preventing "infant abandonment and honoring the souls of abandoned babies" (2015, 49). Baby-saving efforts are orchestrated by activists, and the notion of saving takes on ethical dimensions that are legitimized through the law.

Christian ideals of rescuing the soul factor into the moral dimensions of saving (Cromer 2016). Using frozen embryos as her unit of analysis, Cromer places the concept of saving at the nexus of medicine and morality. Cromer explores the moral orientations that make saving frozen embryos urgent, and her work examines the ethical terrains of fetuses, potentiality, and value. One primary observation is that saving is practiced and operationalized differently depending on the circumstance.

Cromer's perspective is useful in considering that saving has various dimensions, which I position here as technologies. I import feminist theorist Teresa de Lauretis's (1987) use of the term "technology," which she situates as both a process and a product of social and political relations. Similarly, theorist Nikolas Rose argues that technologies are an "assemblage of social and human relations within which equipment and techniques are only one element" (2007, 16). Thus, I use "technology" in a capacious sense to represent a broad range of saving interventions. The saving technologies used to address premature birth and infant and maternal mortality include not only breathing machines and intravenous tubes but also programs, practices, and policies, examples of which are described in the following.

Saving Babies

During the antebellum period, enslaved women "lost about 54 percent or more of their pregnancies to stillbirths, infant mortality, and early childhood mortality" (Steckel 1986b, 452). For every 1,000 white infants born, 179 babies died, compared with 350 for every 1,000 Black babies born (Steckel 1986a). By 1915, although the rates had declined to 100/1,000 and 181/1,000 for whites and Blacks, respectively (Ladd-Taylor 1993, 122), Black infants were still twice as likely as white infants to die.

It is important to know that infants and children in the United States were not always viewed as worthy of saving. However, in the context of rapid industrialization, urbanization, and global economic prosperity and dominance, the US predicament of infant and maternal mortality came under intense scrutiny (Zelizer 1994). Alarmingly high rates belied the nation's sense of international superiority, since infant mortality served as a benchmark of the nation's health (Levander 2006).

By the 1890s, US reformers urged the state to play a role in assisting mothers to raise healthy infants, homing in on maternal, infant, and child death. Infant mortality rates were so high from the end of the nineteenth century through the beginning of the twentieth century that President Franklin D. Roosevelt remarked upon the crisis during his 1909 talk at the National Conference on the Care of Dependent Children. Conferees included Lillian Wald, founder of Visiting Nurse Services, who first suggested that there be a Children's Bureau; Jane Addams, social worker and settlement house activist; Julia Lathrop, who became the first chief of the Children's Bureau; and Booker T. Washington, an educator and leader in the African American community. They all heard President Roosevelt open his address with the following words:

> There can be no more important subject from the standpoint of the Nation than that with which you are to deal, because when you take care of the children, you are taking care of the Nation of tomorrow, and it is in-

cumbent upon every one of us to do all in his or her power to provide for the interests of those children whom cruel misfortune has handicapped at the outset of their lives. (Children's Bureau 1967, 4)

The president's comments, and the meeting in general, galvanized attendees to propose the development of a Children's Bureau, with affluent women from the settlement movement at the forefront of saving children and their mothers.

Importantly, while children's needs varied within the context of race, little or no discussion took place at the meeting concerning Black mothers and children. In fact, according to historians, Booker T. Washington toned down the needs of Black children, despite the fact that very few services were available for them and their families at that time (Lindenmeyer 1997). By 1912, President William H. Taft signed the act that created the Children's Bureau, which operated as an autonomous unit until 1969. Upon its founding, the bureau constituted the first public recognition by the federal government that it had a vested interest in ensuring and a responsibility to promote the well-being of the nation's children. However, well-being was contingent on race, and most efforts were in the service of the mothers of white infants.

The original mission of the Children's Bureau was to "investigate and report . . . upon all matters pertaining to the welfare of children and child life among all classes of our people," with special concern for "infant mortality, the birth rate, orphanages, juvenile courts, desertion, dangerous occupations, accidents and diseases of children, employment, [and] legislation affecting children in the several States and Territories" (Harwood, Yu, and Kavanagh n.d., 2). The Children's Bureau upheld the ideal of saving babies and became an important political player in some areas of the country (Wailoo 2001). However, agency personnel also had to be careful of what they found and reported on, in terms of children's health, because the findings could tarnish a community's reputation. Thus, bureau staff often had to adopt what historian Keith Wailoo calls "a habit of diplomatic caution" when writing reports (2001, 72).

One of the first tasks Julia Lathrop, the new chief of the Children's Bureau, faced was to concretize what, up until that point, had been just estimates of the infant mortality rate. Based on census data, she estimated that of the 2.5 million babies born in the United States, 200,000 died before their first birthday. This, Lathrop argued, was "human waste," and she believed that probably half of the deaths were preventable (Lindenmeyer 1997, 35). She recognized that understanding the scope of the problem required accurate data. Under Lathrop's leadership, birth registration drives focused on data collection in cities with populations of more than 50,000. But registrations were part of the scientific discourse, "imbued with curative efficacy" (G. Fraser 1998, 56), and ultimately contributed to the elimination of midwives—due to their refusal or inability to complete them properly—leaving poor and Black women with little access to care during childbirth. Just one year after the bureau was established in 1912, it produced the first study on infant mortality based on data from Johnston, Pennsylvania, which had completed its birth registration.

Beginning in 1913, a number of strategies were implemented in response to the Children's Bureau "baby-saving campaigns." In a preliminary report on such campaigns, Lathrop summarized various programs that had been implemented to reduce infant mortality. For example, New York City had created the New York Milk Committee and reported attempts to reach expectant mothers as early as possible to connect pregnant mothers to nurses who visited them every ten to twelve days. As explained by Lathrop, "The object of this campaign is to show that, under existing conditions, the mortality during the first month of life can be greatly reduced; also, that the number of stillbirths and premature births can be greatly reduced" (1913, 39). Materials such as pamphlets outlined directions for child care and child welfare and were used "as part of the training for vocational teachers of home economics" (6). Accompanying all of these programmatic technologies were hygienic standards and instructions for maternal and child care.

Armed with knowledge about saving babies, the bureau's slogan, "Save 100,000 Babies," was a one-year campaign that ran from 1918 to 1919 (Figure. 4.1). This wartime program mobilized 11 million volunteers around the nation to help reduce infant mortality.

The effort to save infants persuaded the majority of state governments to form child welfare programs or agencies. Even though infant welfare campaigners were ostensibly interested in saving all American babies, their efforts did not necessarily translate into saving Black infants. In fact, Black infants were almost entirely excluded from the early infant welfare campaigns, particularly in the South (Meckel 2015). However,

The health of the child is the power of the nation

APRIL 1918   Children's Year   APRIL 1919

UNITED STATES CHILDREN'S BUREAU AND WOMAN'S COMMITTEE OF THE COUNCIL OF NATIONAL DEFENSE

Figure 4.1 Children's Bureau poster commemorating Children's Year

the same was also true in the North. While maternal and infant campaigns were directed at most communities, it was "not until 1916 that the New York Association for the Improvement of the Condition of the Poor pioneered the first attempt to deal with Black urban mortality by conducting an infant welfare demonstration in a Black neighborhood" (Meckel 2015, 142). One reason for the delay was that some Progressive Era reformers thought it unnecessary to "waste public funding to protect the lives of racially inferior poor women and their offspring" (Hart 2015, 71). Many Progressive Era infant and maternal health care advocates and activists viewed immigrant and Black women's birthing practices as inferior. Advocates' and activists' concerns centered on the ability to become Americanized and assimilate. Americanization and assimilation "depended on the racial identity of the group under consideration" (Hart 2013, 170). In other words, Progressive infant health advocates viewed the health, or lack thereof, of infants on intrinsic characteristics, not structural deficits. By this logic, Black infants died not because of poverty or racism but because they were born into racially inferior homes with neglectful parents who were culturally retrograde (F. L. Hoffman 1896). These discourses interfered with the state's willingness to address Black prematurity and maternal and infant mortality.

Saving Mothers and Infants: The Sheppard-Towner Act

From 1909 until 1936, infant and maternal mortality were treated as public, social, and political issues reflecting on the nation. During the early twentieth century, the confluence of Progressivism, feminism, and medical specialization raised interest in infant and maternal mortality, propelling these issues to the forefront of popular and political debate (Gertz 2013). Between 1915 and 1920, "Negro" infant mortality was 65 percent higher than white infant mortality (Meckel 2015). Yet, "Negro" infant mortality rates were neglected even though the rate in 1915 was 181 per 1,000 compared with a rate of 100 per 1,000 for whites (Ladd-Taylor 1993, 122). Directing attention to reducing Black infant and maternal mortality, particularly in the South, was not a central issue of concern until after the enactment of the Sheppard-Towner Act in 1921 (Meckel 2015, 142).

The Promotion of the Welfare and Hygiene of Maternity and Infancy Act, also known as the Sheppard-Towner Maternity and Infancy Protection Act, was signed into law by President William G. Harding in November 1921. It was enacted to combat the high rates of maternal and infant mortality through the provision of federal funding to state programs for mothers and babies. It was the first women's bill to pass into law after women won the right to vote, and it remained in effect until 1929. Initially, medical societies and organizations opposed Sheppard-Towner on several grounds: some believed the bill brought the nation one step closer to socialist medicine, others argued that the bill infringed on state rights, and still others viewed it as a feminist plot. It did pass, however, primarily because politicians, who were fearful that women would vote as a bloc, wanted to appease women in the hope of securing their votes.

Decreasing premature birth and infant and maternal mortality rates involved using federal funds to disseminate information and instruction on nutrition, hygiene, and prenatal, neonatal, and postpartum care. Funds supported conferences and provided maternity nurses for pregnant women and new mothers. Saving babies and mothers was now legislated, yet maternal and child health services in state health departments were uneven. Some states did not participate in the effort, and other states participated in some years but not others. Funds distributed by the Sheppard-Towner Act assisted states in establishing, for example, midwife training programs. However, some were less effective than others, in part due to their administrative operation. Using a decentralized administrative model, Sheppard-Towner allowed communities to develop programs that met their needs. Some have argued that this structure made it easier to discriminate against Blacks since there was little administrative oversight to ensure even distribution of services (Moehling and Thomasson 2012). Thus, racial stratification impeded the success of the Sheppard-Towner Act. While public health nurses were hired by departments of health, Black nurses faced barriers in their fight to meet Black people's health needs.[1] Black women were recruited to assist in health promotion for their communities. However, many of them reported discrimination, and there is evidence that efforts on behalf of all children were uneven. For example, a 1921 report on maternity and child care in rural Mississippi by Helen M. Dart, who worked with the Hygiene Division of the Children's Bureau, found that "the quality of nursing care was poorer for Negro mothers than for white" (30). Further, the only African American physician to assist in the effort to decrease infant mortality was Dr. Ionia Whipper, who worked for the bureau from 1924 to 1929. Her job was to assist nurses who trained midwives in southern states where white physicians often did not go (S. L. Smith 1995, 138). Dr. Whipper toured the South as an assistant medical officer for the Children's Bureau, instructing midwives in childbirth practices. According to her diaries, Whipper encountered prejudice from whites and suspicion from Blacks (S. L. Smith 1995; Lewis n.d.).

To be sure, infant mortality declined during the time Sheppard-Towner funded states' efforts, with national infant mortality rates dropping from 76 to 69 per 1,000 between 1921 and 1928 (Ladd-Taylor 1993, 128). However, among Black babies, rates improved only minimally. In 1921, when Sheppard-Towner was initiated, the infant mortality rate among Black infants was estimated to be 108 per 1,000; by 1928, the rate was 106 per 1,000 infants.

The limited success in decreasing mortality rates among Black infants was attributed, among other factors, to administrators' inability to reduce tensions that arose between traditional healing practitioners, such as midwives, and the modern medical approach offered by Sheppard-Towner, particularly among Native American, Mexican, and Black clients. Many birth attendants had learned more "modern" methods of health care, but some still drew on old-fashioned, culturally specific practices. In one instance, a Virginia midwife who, although trained, "refused to give up the practice of placing a pocket knife under the mattress to cut the after pain" (127). The idea was that if a knife was under the mattress, the pain associated with having given birth would be "cut," in other words, the pain would subside. This, of course, was viewed as a "primitive" practice by more modern-minded nurses.

Some scholars have pointed out that most of the nurses were white, and even though the Children's Bureau did employ Black and Mexican nurses, their participation, and in some cases their impact, appears to have been negligible. One telling case came out of Georgia, which had high death rates among Black infants. The Georgia State Board of Health hired an inexperienced nurse to work with Black midwives because it considered the salary demanded by an experienced white nurse "too much for any negro" (Ladd-Taylor 1993, 127). Overall, according to Gertrude Fraser, for Black women, and poor white women as well, the "ideals of a federally funded health care program were never realized" (1998, 52). Alongside the uneven outcomes of the Children's Bureau and the Sheppard-Towner Act in addressing the racial dimensions of premature birth and maternal and infant health, there was a lack of political will to fully fund federal prevention programs. According to historian Richard Meckel (2015), by the 1950s the privatization of medical care over government support for maternal and infant health was solidified. Low-income and poor people and racial minorities had limited access to private care. In the absence of Medicaid coverage, which only became available in 1965 and made it easier for low-income and poor populations to access private medical care, the United States once again saw a widening racial gap in birth outcomes: a gap similar to the one at the turn of the century and that made the United States pale in comparison to other countries that had lower infant mortality rates.

The Presidential Politics of Saving Infants

Between the 1960s and the 1980s, two presidents expressed their commitments to saving infants in very different ways. One of them, John F. Kennedy, was interested in expanding research and providing services to address infant and maternal outcomes; the other, Ronald Reagan, focused on a moral mandate that translated into a policy of saving that many viewed as punitive.

In 1961, President Kennedy noted during a speech that, since 1950, the United States had slipped from sixth to tenth place among the advanced nations of the world in saving infant lives (Kennedy 1962). Although the US rate of infant mortality dropped precipitously from the 1900s to the 1950s, between 1950 and 1964 the decrease slowed down. To address the issue, in 1961 President Kennedy requested a dramatic increase in federal funding for basic research into child health problems and for the expansion of maternity and infant programs (Meckel 2015, 228). Kennedy also championed the provision of prenatal care as a strategy to reduce birth defects (Paisley-Cleveland 2013). Even after Kennedy's death in 1963, Congress continued to support his commitments and in 1964 provided funds for prenatal care to reduce infant mortality, to help children with disabilities, and to expand Medicaid to include early and periodic screening, diagnosis, and treatment.

In addition to the embarrassingly high rates of negative birth outcomes, a number of other factors likely precipitated President Kennedy's commitment to maternal and child health services that led him to authorize the appropriation of $2 million to assist in the provision of prenatal care. First, Kennedy understood that a federal approach would facilitate the development of research projects concentrating on the needs of infants whose mothers are racial minorities. Racial minorities, "particularly 'inner-city' Blacks, had less chance of surviving than did their white counterparts" (Meckel 2015, 229). Embarrassingly, in 1964 the United States had the highest rate of infant mortality among "11 advanced industrial nations" (227). The racial gap was revealing: between 1960 and 1984, the Black infant mortality rate ranged from 16.5 to 20.7 per 1,000, whereas for whites, the range was from 8.8 to 9.8 per 1,000 (Centers for Disease Control and Prevention 1987).

Second, the Kennedy family was invested in how prenatal and maternal care intersected with intellectual disability and development. Their concerns resulted in broad advocacy for research. Drawing on the expertise of their family physician, Dr. Robert E. Cooke, who chaired a task force on the health and well-being of children, the Kennedy family became advocates of maternal and child health. The task force's report, submitted to President Kennedy, pointed out that research into the physical, intellectual, and emotional growth of children was sorely lacking. It also acknowledged that research efforts were seriously curtailed by the absence of a central coordinating point. The report led to the development of the National Institute for Child Health and Human Development (National Institute for Child Health and Human Development 2016).

Simultaneously, as attention on premature babies and the high rates of infant mortality increased, funding was directed to enhance hospitals' capacity to handle infants' medical needs. National interest in neonatal care can be traced, in part, to the death of Patrick Bouvier Kennedy, the newborn son of President and Jacqueline Kennedy. Patrick was born prematurely and died thirty-nine hours later. Although Patrick was a healthy weight, as he was born at thirty-seven weeks, he had difficulty breathing and was transferred from Otis Air Force Base, where he was delivered, to Children's Hospital Medical Center in Boston. He was put in a hyperbaric chamber that used air pressure to facilitate his ability to breathe oxygen. However, Patrick developed hyaline membrane disease, also known as respiratory distress syndrome, which is caused by a lack of surfactant in the lungs, which limits air exchange. Patrick's death was also a critical event that advanced the president's interest in the survival of premature infants.

NICUs proliferated between the 1960s and the 1980s. Indeed, in the 1970s the number of hospitals in the United States with NICUs was estimated to be about 600 (Budetti et al. 1980). These units provided technologically sophisticated interventions for low-birth-weight babies. According to the March of Dimes, currently there are nearly 1,800 NICUs in the country.

The development of NICUs afforded doctors new opportunities to intervene in the lives of neonates. Early on, though, those interventions generally resulted in having to make the medical choice of letting a baby live or die (Frohock 1986). In addition, investment in hospitals and the implementation of Medicaid facilitated access to the growing private medical system in the 1960s through the 1980s. Access to technology and resources resulted in a decline of 45.2 percent in infant mortality. Although the decline impacted all races, with the overall rate dropping from 12.6 to 6.9 deaths per 1,000 live births between 1980 and 2000, it was greater for whites than for Blacks. Over this same period of time the Black-white ratio of infant mortality increased 25.0 percent, from 2.0 to 2.5 (Centers for Disease Control and Prevention 2002).

The Baby Doe Infants

The effort to save babies found a public audience when the nation turned its attention to two white babies. In 1982 and 1983, a political microscope resulted in a national focus on the birth of two infants—not because of technology but due to a moral impetus, one that was different from the Progressive Era movement centered on the "right to life." Right-to-life activists were still reeling nearly a decade after the passage of *Roe v. Wade*, which legalized abortion. Though *Roe v. Wade* centered on women's access to abortion, embedded in the legislation was the idea that women were self-determining agents. This assertion, of course, was laden with many contradictions because the idea of self-determination and choice was stratified; only some women with access to money were able to choose abortion. Backlash against abortion was strident, and an adjunct to right-to-life advocates' efforts to overturn *Roe v. Wade* was to elevate and prioritize fetuses over women. Thus, lines that had been drawn in the sand about conception, abortion, and parental rights became moving targets, and "saving missions" geared to neonates became a political volleyball about life, death, and handicapped babies.

The first Baby Doe case concerned "John," who was born in Indiana on April 9, 1982, with Down syndrome and tracheoesophageal fistula, an abnormality of the throat. The obstetrician who delivered the baby told the parents that their newborn had a 50 percent chance of surviving, and if he did, the child's quality of life would be compromised. The parents declined consent to repair the newborn's tracheoesophageal fistula. However, two other physicians did not agree with the prognosis and sought legal intervention to prevent the child's death. Indiana courts chose to defer to the parents' wishes. While advocates were preparing to go before the US Supreme Court, Baby John Doe died at six days old. Surgeon General C. Everett Koop heard of the decision and was outraged. Surgeon General Koop was key in formulating policy for treating newborn infants, based on his beliefs as a conservative Christian and his experience of a 100 percent success rate operating and repairing tracheoesophageal fistula.

In response, President Reagan's administration developed a set of rules issued to prevent perceived child abuse or neglect. Health care providers were threatened with the loss of federal financial assistance if they did not protect newborns with health issues such as Down syndrome. To facilitate the implementation of this edict, the Department of Health and Human Services (DHHS) created "Baby Doe Hotlines" and mandated the posting of notices in all hospital nurseries that included the edict. The DHHS invoked Section 504 of the Rehabilitation Act, which forbade discrimination on the basis of disability. The "Doe Directives," as they were called, required all nurseries to post a federal toll-free hotline telephone number to encourage reporting of infant abuse, which included withholding food or treatment; hospitals that were not in compliance with the directive jeopardized receipt of federal funding (White 2011). While federal officials descended upon nurseries in response to these calls, they seldom found actual instances of abuse.

Eighteen months after the birth of Baby "John" Doe, Baby "Jane" Doe was born in 1983 in Port Jefferson, New York, and was diagnosed with spina bifida. Although she was under medical management at Stony Brook Hospital, her parents determined that there should be no intervention in her care after they received what some said was conflicting medical information. A call to a "Baby Doe Hotline" precipitated Koop's interest in using court action to compel intervention, although he did not succeed. The American Academy of Pediatrics, the American Hospital Association, and the American College of Obstetrics and Gynecology viewed the regulations as a threat to medical autonomy.

Lee McFarland, the labor and delivery nurse whom we met earlier, remembered this time in the 1980s, calling it "the Baby Doe regime." She recalled how hospital personnel were afraid they would be reported if they did not do everything to save an infant:

> We did everything. Once, I watched a neonatologist intubate a twenty-two-weeker. Back then, we didn't have ETs [endotracheal tubes] small enough for a newborn that size, so we used the smallest one we had; it was 2.5 centimeters, which is just over one inch in diameter. A tube that size was not nearly small enough for a twenty-two-week-old infant. We all watched as the doctor ruptured the baby's esophagus trying to intu-

bate the baby with that tube. It was gruesome, but doctors were panicked that they would end up in jail for not doing everything because the baby weighed over 500 grams. We did not judge him, and only the people in the room saw what happened. We looked in each other's eyes, knowing that we had been driven by this policy. It was so brutal.

Lee also said that the "saving culture" meant that nurses and doctors would code, or resuscitate, babies for an hour. They saved the babies long enough to send them to the NICU, where they would subsequently die—but at least they did not die in the labor and delivery room.

While this discussion of Reagan's saving policies may seem unrelated to the issue of race, it is in fact illustrative of a paradox. During the 1980s, while extolling the sanctity of life and deploring discrimination against disabled infants inside the nursery, the Reagan administration made dramatic and unprecedented cutbacks in funding for programs that would have support disabled infants outside the nursery (Anspach 1993, 171). Undermining its supposed interest in saving all babies, the administration reduced or froze funding for maternal and infant programs, including the Women, Infant, and Children (WIC) program. Advocacy groups feared that such cutbacks would result in a slowdown of declining infant mortality rates. Their fears came to pass, and the saving "agenda" was marred by a racial fallout. There was an increase in the number of Black infants with low birth weight and a rise in the neonatal mortality race ratio. That is, the ratio of neonatal deaths between Blacks and whites rose for Black infants, which, according to Meckel (2015) was attributed to the decline in funding and the imposition of programmatic restrictions.

The Rise of Technological Interventions

Some premature babies are born with immature lungs and develop what is known as respiratory distress syndrome (RDS), the syndrome that caused Patrick Kennedy's death. At the time of Patrick's death, unbeknownst to many doctors, an answer lay in the research of Drs. Mary Ellen Avery and Jere Mead. In the 1950s, Dr. Avery, who was named the first female physician in chief at Boston's Children's Hospital and revolutionized the pulmonary treatment of newborns who were dying because they could not breathe, made the crucial discovery that premature babies lacked a foaming, soap-like coating in their lungs—surfactant—which develops in the lungs around thirty-four weeks in utero. The discovery of surfactants provided the solution to RDS.[2] Between 1959 and 1965, Dr. Avery published numerous papers on hyaline membrane disease, also known as infant respiratory distress syndrome (IRDS), neonatal respiratory distress syndrome (NRDS), or surfactant deficiency disorder (SDD).

During her research on the lungs of infants who died of RDS, Avery (2000) found that before birth, babies did not need surfactants because they were not using their lungs for ventilation. But after birth they were unable to retain the air in their lungs, impeding the lung's ability to re-inflate. Put more simply, surfactant is a substance that facilitates the air exchange of oxygen and carbon dioxide by allowing the lungs to glide, so they do not collapse after every breath.

Although Avery published on the discovery of surfactants in 1959 (Avery and Meade 1959), their significance was not fully understood as an intervention for premature infants until the 1980s. Once the use of surfactants was understood, they revolutionized the field of neonatal medicine (Jorgensen 2010, 10). By 2002, fewer than 1,000 babies per year died of respiratory distress. Since the 1980s, surfactants have become one of the most important advancements used to save infants with immature lungs, even those as young as twenty-three and twenty-four weeks.

According to some researchers, prematurity alone does not determine RDS. Researchers have investigated RDS and suggest there are gender, maternal health, and racial differences in the disease's etiology. It is likely that the latter of these claims has contributed to the perception that Black infants are hardy, as discussed in an earlier chapter. A study analyzing data from 1968 to 1973 showed that among 54,064 infant deaths, RDS was the primary cause (Farrell and Wood 1976). Infant mortality rates by race showed that while white infants are more likely to have RDS, Black infants are more likely to die from RDS. However, some research suggests that the racial disparity is neutralized after accounting for gestation, birth weight, and gender (Thomas 2011). Another study explored the racial dimensions of RDS. Using a different data set of 2,295 preterm infants delivered vaginally between 1982 and 1987 (Hulsey et al. 1993), researchers found that hyaline membrane disease occurs less frequently, is less severe, and is accompanied by fewer related complications in Black preterm infants. More recently a meta-analysis of studies analyzed factors associated with respiratory disease and found that in some cases, when compared with white newborn infants, there was a lower incidence of fatal RDS in Black preterm infants (Jo 2014).

Race and lung function have quite a perverse history, with one of the more curious aspects being how race has been used to assess the lung capacity of Blacks. For example, the fact that research suggests that Black infants born early or with immature organs succumb to a lesser degree to the consequences of RDS essentially transforms Black premature infants into specimens of hardiness. In contrast, historian Lundy Braun's inquiry into the spirometer—an apparatus that measures lung capacity—demonstrates that in the mid-nineteenth century, adult Blacks were believed to have a smaller lung capacity than whites and that these spurious beliefs continue to be ingrained in racialized lung capacity calibrations (Braun 2014). While Lundy's analysis is in contrast to the studies described earlier, the intersection of lung function and race simultaneously reveals the flexibilities of race, in which Blacks make a smooth transition from one extreme to another—from being hardy to being weak—but always in ways that exist outside of white normativity.

NICU Technology

On the cover of the June 2, 2014, issue of *Time* magazine is an image of a newborn, David, who is white, with tubes coming out of his nose. David is tiny—only slightly longer than the fully open hand and part of the forearm holding him, and his fragility tugs at one's emotions. The article's title, though, leads us to assume that the infant has been cradled to safety and ushered into infancy through the use of technology. "Saving," in the *Oxford English Dictionary*, is defined as to keep safe or to rescue from harm or danger; to prevent from dying; to keep and store up for future use. The article, "Saving Preemies," flags each of these definitions, implying both a rescue mission and a declarative statement.

Jeffrey Kluger, the article's author, details the private and rarely seen world of the NICU through the story of David Joyce, who was born in a Milwaukee hospital at twenty-nine weeks. Kluger praises the Milwaukee NICU, noting its extraordinary success in saving neonates, the official term for babies from birth to thirty days—after which point they are referred to as infants. This level IV NICU has what Kluger calls a SWAT team consisting of 300 caregivers, including "nutritionists, pharmacologists, gastroenterologists, ophthalmologists, pulmonary specialists, surgeons, nurses and dietitians and, for when the need arises, a pair of chaplains" (2014, 26). His discussion of the saving technology both impresses and causes concern as he tells of the onslaught of "sensory insults," such as tubes, needles, tape, and masks, that infants must bear. The story concludes triumphantly: David has been kept safe from death, he is alive, and his parents will—theoretically—enjoy him in the future because now he *has* a future. NICU technology saved David. But what if the infant on the cover had been Black? Could we have assumed a similar future?

As spectacular as David's story is, this article obscures at least two issues. First, it does not mention the racial disparity in premature birth rates that is so prominently in attendance in the reproductive lives of Black (specifically African American) women in the United States. Second, there are no disavowals or conflicts concerning the technology and saving practices used on premature infants—not one person indicates any trepidation about the emotional or moral cost that accompanies saving. The rewards of rescuing weak patients through technological intervention overshadow other forms of addressing premature birth and the fact that some of the resources devoted to neonatal intensive care could be used toward prevention (Muraskas and Parsi 2008).

NICU technology is but one example of how biotechnologies have provoked reconsideration of clinical care (Mattingly 2010). Embedded in these technologies are notions of democracy based on the supposition that they are uniformly available and capable of saving those who require them (Haraway 1997; Rose 2007). Yet, the care for premature infants is less effective for Black neonates than for white neonates. In 2017, a group of doctors reported on the quality of care administered to more than 18,000 very-low-birth-weight infants in 134 NICUs between 2010 and 2014 (Profit et al. 2017). Their findings pointed to significant racial or ethnic differences in the quality of care between and within the NICUs under study, with African American and Hispanic infants more likely to receive low-quality care. Other examples of stratified care included the finding that, in comparison with whites, Black and Hispanic infants were less likely to receive steroid treatments that help speed up lung development, which provides a better chance of survival. Black and Hispanic infants were also less likely than white infants to receive a timely retinopathy exam, which can reduce the threat of functional or complete blindness. In the long run, Black and Hispanic infants were more likely to acquire health care–associated infection, such as the one Yvette's son had.

Trying to save or improve the health of premature infants is a sobering endeavor because premature birth has consequences even after saving interventions are applied. The technologies can both increase survival and complicate an infant's clinical condition. For instance, the mechanical ventilator provides support for infants with respiratory failure but can also cause chronic lung injury. Such outcomes have led to questions about how we save.

"What Are We Doing?"

Saving technologies are ensconced in our everyday lives, so much so that we barely give them a second thought. The technology used to save David went unquestioned, as it was presumed to be the proper intervention. Presumably, there is little need to critique saving rationales; doing so may be viewed as a threat to notions of progress (Kleinman 2005). Saving premature infants operates on slippery racial terrain evidenced by one study in New York that found that the likelihood of death and consequences of premature birth later in life—such as lung, eye, and intestinal problems—are greater among very preterm Black and Hispanic infants than among very preterm white infants (Howell, Janevic, and Herbert 2018).

Conversations with NICU nurses and March of Dimes administrators revealed that NICU technology is not always viewed as triumphant. In a far-reaching conversation, Clara St. Cyr, a nurse originally from Haiti, who began working in an NICU in 1971, described some of the complexities of saving. When we spoke in 2014, Clara, sixty-seven, had just retired as an NICU nurse in a Florida hospital. Clara was the first nurse I interviewed, and when asked how she felt about working in the NICU, she responded:

I have a lot of concerns about what we are doing. Saving these kids. I mean, are we really justified in doing some of the stuff we do? I mean, saving a twenty-two-weeker? Should we be doing that? Saving a twenty-two-weeker, a twenty-three-weeker, these kids are born with such serious complications. There are a lot of questions about that, you know? Sometimes we are just prolonging agony, prolonging the parents' agony. And they say, "Do everything to save my child." We [Clara and other nurses] talk about it. It doesn't stop us from doing what we do, but we question . . . when you see a child—a three-pounder with one hundred and fifty thousand tubes coming out of them, and you have a machine pumping this in them and pumping that in them. You're thinking, "What is their life going to be like in the long run?" Some of the things we do, it's like taking medication for a headache and then you get a stomachache. So, I mean, you question yourself: "Are we really doing something here?" You question that. At the end one was lucky enough to be 95 percent intact, and you see another one that was 5 percent intact. You ask yourself, "What are we doing?"

When I asked Clara about who she saw in the NICUs, she told me it was mostly Black infants. "They are young and low-income. I wonder how they manage?" At this point in the research I had not interviewed any parents, so I did not think to ask Clara how she knew they were low-income and if she ever cared for the infant of a mother who was not low-income. Clara's concern, though, about NICUs as a saving strategy is that it results in moving the limit of fetal viability, which intersects with race, class, and the postrelease complications that can accompany premature birth. Other nurses felt similarly.

Six months after interviewing Clara, I met Ellen Bolton, a forty-six-year-old white NICU nurse who has worked in various Louisiana NICUs since 1998. We sat in the nurses' lounge for our interview. This interview began with a different question from the one posed to Clara. I asked Ellen what she found satisfying about her work. Ellen responded practically before I finished asking the question: "Seeing a baby that goes home without any special equipment." Ellen's demeanor changed somewhat when I asked her how NICUs had changed. She noted, "Ten years ago, you would have never thought to save a twenty-two-weeker. But now we are seeing that some survive. They may have more handicaps, obviously, but we have better therapies."

Having better therapies, however, was not the panacea to the larger problem that Ellen understood to be associated with the challenge of prematurity. Although she and Clara were both concerned about prematurity, the locus of their concerns differed. Whereas Clara focused on problems facing newborns, Ellen focused on the trials that parents and siblings may face after bringing a premature infant home. "The babies were not so much the challenge," she said, and then continued:

It is the families. Because, for instance, you get that twenty-two-weeker that already has a grade 4 intracranial hemorrhage. The chances for recovery are not that great. But then you have the parents that want us to do everything for this baby even though there might be periods where the baby's oxygen saturations don't get to 40 for the whole shift. They just don't want to hear any of the options. Then when the baby ends up with a trach or a g-tube or both, they blame us. I've never been put in that position personally. I have three healthy children. I don't know if I could make that decision either. . . . The nurse in me is, like, "Look, your life is not going to be the same. You have other children. Their life, as they know it, is now going to the beach on the weekends, going to the movies on Saturday afternoon. That is going to be over because now you have a child that has all these needs." And then the kids start having some resentment . . . your life is never the same after that.

Ellen and Clara were referring to the consequences of premature birth. Some children have absolutely no consequences, and others have outcomes that can range from mild to devastating. Mild associated factors include asthma, attention-deficit disorders, or visual problems. More complicated outcomes include blindness, deafness, cerebral palsy, and the need for special education (Hack et al. 2005). The potentially long-term struggle that comes with having a child with special needs can drain a family financially, emotionally, and sometimes physically. Knowing that these are the consequences, I asked Ellen whether she ever had second thoughts about her job. She said that while she may not necessarily agree with parents' decisions about "saving a child," that does not prevent her from doing her job.

Neither Ellen's nor Clara's feelings should be interpreted as their not caring about the babies they worked with and cared for. In fact, their assessments should be interpreted based on the fact that nurses are often much closer to the families they serve than are neonatologists—literally and figuratively. They see the outcomes of premature birth more so than neonatologists, whose professional input ends after the discharge of the child. Many nurses, on the other hand, may live in neighborhoods near the families whose children were admitted to the NICU, as I learned during my conversation with Clara and while sitting with nurses Sonia, Jacqueline, and Tiffany. Sonia and Tiffany mentioned that they see the kids that they cared for with their parents in the supermarket or at malls, years after the infant was admitted to the NICU. Others nurses see the children and parents at what some hospitals market as annual "preemie" reunions. Or parents stay in touch with NICU staff, writing letters with progress updates or sending cards and photographs. Thus, the nurses have a sense of what life is like for the child and the family long after the child has been discharged. Consequently, the nurses interviewed evaluated the success of NICU technology based on infants' discharge status and their subsequent development. Nurses are able to make this assessment because they are often privy to the baby's development outside the medical environment because their social worlds are in closer proximity to the parents than the physician's.

Let us return to David, the white infant whose image was on the cover of *Time*. While David represents the potential of saving through the use of NICU technology, we saw that earlier technologies of saving had racially disparate outcomes. For the two nurses interviewed, the disparities congealed alongside issues of race, class, viability, potential family disruptions, and possible future complications for the premature neonate. Yet David's image holds so much promise and led me to investigate race and representation of infants in NICUs on websites.

To do so, I conducted a content analysis of 177 NICU websites across seventeen states. Of the 177 websites, 158 sites had images. Of the sites with images, 86 percent of the images of infants were white, and 14 percent were not white. The images revealed a racialization of the NICU as white, intensified by near absence of Blacks in the imagery. Race was not only curated in the imagery, gesturing toward whiteness or perceived whiteness, but it also suggested who is worth saving.

The absence of Black babies was curious, so I asked medical personnel if there were particular groups that tended to be admitted to the

NICU. Whether at private or public hospitals, the doctors and nurses indicated they mostly see African Americans and Latinos. In Louisiana, Dr. Shane Anderson told me that at their hospital the racial demographic was "mixed. But more African Americans and Latinos, and there are three or four really, really poor white folks and their babies." Sara Roberts, the Black NICU nurse from Minnesota, said most of the babies at her hospital were Black. Dr. Leah Kalin, the neonatologist at a New York–based Hospital, responded, "Well, it's not an unknown fact that, um, Black and Hispanic babies are born prematurely at a higher rate, particularly African-American babies."

Despite the fact that Black infants are more likely to be in an NICU, their absence in online depictions of NICUs reveals what I call "illusory prejudice." Illusory prejudice exists when imagery is used that facilitates framing an issue differently than the fact of the issue. I draw on historian Barbara Duden's (1993) astute observation of the inaccuracy of drawings of the fetal form among seventeenth- and eighteenth-century anatomists in Germany. Their anatomical depictions were unrealistic—showing fetuses that actually looked like three-month old babies–even though they knew what the fetal form actually looked like. She termed this "optical prejudice." The art of depicting fetuses as children, Duden suggests, really points to the desire to show the "child-to-be," in other words, to show a future. I suggest that the technologies of saving—be they of the past or present—gesture that the child or infant worth saving is white.

The Paradox of Saving

Saving newborns was a point of departure for my conversations with former or current administrators and executives at the March of Dimes. Initial conversations centered on NICUs, in part, because the March of Dimes developed the Family Support Program to help families during their baby's time in the NICU. The program also educated NICU staff about the best ways to support babies, families, and each other. This hospital-based program included having a nurse or social worker who guided families through what they could expect when having a child in the NICU. The program also involved organizing a transition to a home situation for the family of a premature infant. And while that program was not necessarily for African Americans, one administrator commented that since a greater percentage of preterm births occur among African Americans, probably a significant proportion of those families were part of the program.

Interestingly, most administrators pointed out that the primary intervention of addressing prematurity through NICU technology, while important, is ironic, given that NICUs can save infants but do not *prevent* prematurity. NICUs also redirect resources away from other approaches—an observation made by Dr. Anderson of Louisiana, Dr. Angliotti, the chief of the NICU at a hospital in Connecticut, and two of the March of Dimes personnel. In many ways, NICUs provide rationales for hospitals to focus on intervention because if one is able to achieve what one would want to from a public health perspective—which is to *prevent* preterm birth—NICUs would lose income. Prevention disrupts the flow of capital to the medical system, so the question becomes, how do you compensate for that loss of income? And, do you reward hospitals or the public health system for doing the right thing in preventing preterm birth?

One staff person said that, when visiting some of the NICUs across the country, it was clear our society accepts that the NICU can fix everything. "We're not really as concerned about *preventing* preterm birth, because we can fix it . . . but then we're not addressing this issue with the urgency and seriousness that we need to, because medicine can take care of everything." In other words, the technological advances that address many of the complications of premature birth are not a panacea for *preventing prematurity*. Another executive clarified this point even further:

> I happen to think that part of the reason we're in the trouble we are, around preterm birth in this country, is the NICU. We are seduced by technology, and being Americans, we will always be seduced by technology. We saw the rate of preterm birth going up, it didn't strike us that it was a problem because we had these NICUs that were doing wonderful things and could save the tiniest of babies. I think they are wonderful and they do amazing things. But . . .

The executive's voice trailed off for a moment, followed by a declaration that beyond investing in technology we also need to "resource," or fund, various approaches to address the racial disparities of premature birth.

The point was that since NICUs save smaller and smaller babies, and provide a dizzying array of medical interventions, they are obviously necessary. But what about prevention? How do we close the racial disparity gap if we continue to direct accolades and funding toward high-tech technologies of saving more than toward the lower-tech approaches of prevention? Importantly, do saving infants and the programmatic interventions speak to the ways that racism has compromised and is likely to continue to compromise the care Black women experience? In the previous chapters, we learned about the interactions between mothers and medical personnel. Some of those encounters involved lapses that, from the mothers' perspectives, resulted in their pregnancy or birth going awry. As an intervention, saving is important, but it does not address the racism that many women described. Therefore, a critique of interventions can be generative.

Theorist Lauren Berlant suggests that it is worthwhile to critique the idea of compassion. However, doing so is a gamble, and one takes the chance of "demeaning its [compassion's] authenticity and centrality to social life" (2004, 5). The same may be said of saving: to critique technologies of saving runs the risk of demeaning their authenticity and contribution to biomedicine. However, following Berlant's logic, scholarly critique does not nullify the value or importance of a topic. To critique the saving technologies used to address prematurity does not seek to diminish the importance of those strategies. Rather, the critique is being utilized in the service of questioning the dynamics of exclusion—racial exclusion in particular—from the purported success of saving.

Saving has racially differential outcomes, as evidenced by the types of saving strategies used throughout the nineteenth and twentieth centuries. And the concept of saving is fraught with tension, as we have seen reflected in conversations with nurses and March of Dimes administrators, in part because it does not address issues of future disabilities or racism. The critiques, though, open up opportunities to decenter the reverence accorded to saving interventions. In so doing, we can think through not just saving but also other mechanisms to address premature birth rates, which are the subject of the next chapter.

5

Narrowing the Gap of Black Women's Burden

Birth outcomes among Black women are at crisis levels, and the March of Dimes seeks to reduce that crisis. Narrowing the gap of premature birth between Black and other women has been central to the work of the March of Dimes since 2000. This chapter turns attention toward the organization and its approach in raising public interest and awareness about the racial dimensions of birth outcomes. Why the March of Dimes? Because it funds research in the field of premature birth more than any other charitable organization in the United States. The only entity that directs more resources to understanding and addressing premature birth is the federal government.

The March of Dimes has a long history of addressing issues related to pregnancy and infant and childhood health that overlap with race. This chapter considers how a national nonprofit organization contends with race and adverse birth outcomes and traces how it came to focus on premature birth as part of its mission. The history sheds light on how race has factored into the March of Dimes' commitment to improving infant and maternal health. Documenting the organization's early attempts to tackle birth-related illness provides insight into a public health strategy to intervene in racial disparity. By focusing on how concern about racial disparity is "given life" through the March of Dimes' efforts, we can see the tension between acknowledging race as a problem and the way identifying the problem differs from the experience of racism described in earlier chapters.

A Brief History of the March of Dimes

Originally, the March of Dimes was called the National Foundation for Infantile Paralysis (NFIP). Founded by President Franklin D. Roosevelt in 1938, the NFIP began in response to the polio epidemic that killed or disabled thousands of Americans (including Roosevelt himself), mostly children. Polio is a virus that spreads from person to person, attacks the nervous system, and can lead to paralysis. The NFIP's sole purpose was to find a polio vaccine and to provide support for polio patients.

During its first seventeen years, the organization funded the research of many scientists, including Dr. Jonas Salk, who developed the first effective vaccine against polio, which is considered to be one of public health's great achievements. After the Salk vaccine (and later a vaccine developed by Dr. Albert Sabin, also with funding from the organization) proved to be effective, it was widely adopted; the result was that polio was drastically reduced. Ultimately, polio was eliminated in the United States.

The first president of the March of Dimes was Basil O'Connor, a former law partner of President Roosevelt.[1] He is credited with creating the organization's structure: a network of local chapters—thousands of them—across the country. The chapter model resulted in the American public providing significant support to the March of Dimes, raising money and delivering aid to those affected by polio. This strategy was unique and made the organization a pioneer in the annals of American philanthropy. It differed from other philanthropic organizations in the early part of the twentieth century, when the most significant charitable organization type was the private foundation supported by wealthy families and individuals. But the March of Dimes became "the people's foundation," supported by millions of average Americans, even children, who cared about the fight against polio.

Polio, like premature birth, was entangled with racial politics. Whereas the March of Dimes takes the issue of race seriously in its efforts to end premature birth, that was not originally the case with polio. Initially, there were few attempts to address the needs of Black people with polio. The decision to forgo attending to the impact of polio on the Black community was related, in part, to the dominance of racial science at the time, in which Blacks were viewed as differently—if at all—affected by the disease. Some experts did not believe that "primitive" races could contract the same kinds of diseases that "civilized" people of northern European heritage contracted. As early as 1917, George Draper, who directed Roosevelt's therapies, argued that there were racial differences in terms of who was susceptible to polio. In his text on polio, Draper wrote that it was "well-grown, plump, White, native-born children with widely spaced upper front teeth and 'delicate' teenagers who filled hospital beds and doctors' offices during polio outbreaks" (1917, 59). Meanwhile, "Negroes" were supposedly strong and immune to such illness, an argument similar to ideas about hardiness (Hoberman 2012) discussed in earlier chapters.

Bolstered by the research of Paul Harmon, the Chicago public health officer who, like Draper, contributed to the idea that Blacks were immune to polio, logics of racial hierarchy were widely accepted, and white susceptibility was prioritized over Black susceptibility to the disease. Harmon (1936) made the question of race central to his investigation of polio by analyzing the number of Black, white, and "Oriental" polio cases. In his final analysis, Harmon concluded polio was not common among the "colored race." History of medicine scholar Naomi Rogers (2007) argues that the idea of a white child's proclivity to contracting polio as a consequence of race compared with a Black child's immunity fit well within the assumption about biological differences between Blacks and whites. In the case of polio, the science of difference converged with the politics of racial segregation, such that rehabilitation programs available for whites with polio were denied to Blacks.

In the 1920s, Roosevelt founded the Georgia Warm Springs Polio Rehabilitation Center, which admitted only whites (Rogers 2007). This policy reflected both the reality of race-segregated health facilities and scientific arguments that asserted Black people were not predisposed to polio (Harmon 1936). However, Black people did in fact contract polio; for example, Wilma Rudolph, a track and field Olympic gold medalist, contracted it in 1944 (M. M. Smith 2006). Not only did Blacks deserve access to medical treatment and places of respite such as Warm Springs; Blacks had been contributing to and were an important part of the fundraising efforts for a rehabilitation center (Rogers 2007). Political and emotional tempers flared as the Black community fought against being denied access to resources to combat polio.

More than twenty years after the founding of Georgia Warm Springs, the March of Dimes funded a similar center in 1941 for Black people— the Tuskegee Infantile Paralysis Center. The center's opening was the result of a political calculus that sought to relieve the embarrassment of Georgia Warm Springs maintaining a whites-only admission policy (Rogers 2007). The Tuskegee Infantile Paralysis Center had two purposes: "One was to treat Black children with polio and the other was to serve as a research and training base for Black health care professionals in the ongoing battle against polio" (Turner 2012, 5). This center began the organization's engagement with the racial dimensions of health.

In his role as a board member of Tuskegee, Basil O'Connor was familiar with the research and provision of health services at the John A. Memorial Hospital associated with the Tuskegee Center. O'Connor knew of and respected John W. Chenault, an orthopedist and director of orthopedics at the hospital. In 1941, Dr. Chenault was named director of the Tuskegee Infantile Paralysis Center. Chenault, who wrote articles challenging the susceptibility argument, did so in the vein of what literary scholar Britt Rusert (2017) calls "fugitive science," namely, those nineteenth-century projects in which African Americans crafted sophisticated claims against scientific racism, although most of them were not scientists. Even though Chenault was a scientist, his writing fits within the category by virtue of the fact that he, like fugitive scientists, was explicitly writing against racism.

With Chenault at the helm of the Infantile Paralysis Center, two researchers at Tuskegee, Russell V. Brown and James H. M. Henderson, investigated the science of polio. Brown and Henderson led a team who mass produced HeLa cells, the first line of human cells to survive in a test tube. The cells were named after Henrietta Lacks, an African American woman, from whom the tissue samples were taken. Among the many uses of those cells was the development of the polio vaccine.[2]

O'Connor also met Charles Bynum, who was the assistant to the president of the Tuskegee Institute. Bynum was at the center of medical knowledge as a result of his affiliation with Tuskegee, which was essentially the CDC for Black people, and ultimately he was hired in 1944 to direct the NFIP's interracial activities division, which he did for almost three decades. Bynum, who was the head of a department called Negro Activities, made the case that polio care was also a civil rights issue. He was instrumental in connecting the organization to issues of race, rights, and health. He conducted outreach to African Americans with polio in the United States and helped to ensure that Black children and adults received proper treatment during polio epidemics (Mawdsley 2010). Bynum traveled throughout the United States to develop patient care programs for African Americans with polio and also organized fundraising efforts and promoted the inclusion of African American children in campaigns.

Polio was a disease that required massive funding for research and targeted education. The March of Dimes utilized promotion and images of children with braces and using crutches as the linchpin of its campaign. Throughout the 1950s, funding from the NFIP supported the research of both Albert Sabin, who developed an oral vaccine from weakened strains of the virus, and Jonas Salk, who developed an injectable vaccine from a killed virus. Often lauded as successful, ending polio was not an endeavor without consequences and compromises. In his book *Selling Science: Polio and the Promise of Gamma Globulin* (2016), historian Stephen E. Mawdsley argues that various publics had been "sold the science" of polio treatments that facilitated the development of federally sanctioned immunizations. Charting the "first large clinical trial to control polio using healthy children" (Mawdsley 2016 12), Mawdsley shows how science trumped ethics by testing gamma globulin on 50,000 children and details the coercion used to experiment with this particular polio prevention treatment. A second lesser-known story about the polio vaccines is that the efficacy of different experimental vaccines was tested on premature African American babies born at Philadelphia General Hospital in the 1950s (Wadman 2017, 112).

After the development of the polio vaccine, the March of Dimes turned its attention to addressing birth defects caused by rubella, also known as German measles. Initially, rubella was not viewed as a dangerous disease. Then, in 1941, an Australian ophthalmologist, Norman Gregg, discovered there was a relationship between mothers who had been infected with rubella during pregnancy and infants born with cataracts. Rubella became a public health issue in the 1960s because while the symptoms were mild in adults, the infection could be detrimental to babies. In fact, a woman infected with rubella had a 90 percent chance of giving birth to an infant with congenital rubella syndrome. Among the complications linked to rubella infections were deafness, enlarged spleens, congenital heart disease, and death. Between 1964 and 1965, more than 10 million people were sick, and a *New York Times* article reported that thousands of babies would be born "bearing the mark of their mothers." Part of the prevention effort included a test to determine if a woman had been infected and "thus permit the consideration of therapeutic abortion" ("German Measles" 1965).

In the 1960s, Dr. Stanley Plotkin of the Wistar Institute in Pennsylvania played an important role in the development of rubella vaccines. But, according to science reporter Meredith Wadman, as the vaccine was being developed, it was tested on some infants who had been born at St. Vincent's Hospital for Women and Children in Philadelphia and were later transferred to the Home for Children. These orphaned infants had not been placed with foster families and often were Black or of mixed race (Wadman 2017, 176). Plotkin had received permission from Philadelphia's prelate to study his new RA 27/3 rubella vaccine in the children—another example of the experimental uses of the Black body. What Plotkin failed to tell the archbishop was that the vaccine had come from an aborted fetus of a woman in Sweden (Wadman 2017, 6), clearly a moral failure.

Once the vaccine was developed, rubella immunizations required public education campaigns and media coverage. This health education approach for rubella focused on prenatal testing, and by 2004, rubella was all but eliminated. It was not that much of a stretch for the March of Dimes to shift from rubella to prenatal care in the mid-1980s when prenatal care campaigns took center stage. However, in the process, according to Leslie J. Reagan, a historian of American medicine, societal ideas about maternalism shifted from mothers being viewed as nurturers to mothers being viewed as a risk. On the heels of illnesses such as crack addiction, Black mothers were constructed as criminals (Ortiz and Briggs 2003) and dangerous. These same ideas about dangerous mothers and dangerous pregnancies made their way into March of Dimes campaigns as the organization transitioned from a focus on rubella to addressing prenatal issues such as prematurity. For example, the "Mommy, Don't" campaign showed expectant mothers receiving advice from a talking fetus (Reagan 2010). The campaign's goal was to educate women about the dangers of drugs, smoking, alcohol, and taking unprescribed medication while it simultaneously depicted women as "potential threats to the babies they carried" (Reagan 2010, 229). Basically, danger marked mothers' reproduction, and often, according to Reagan, the images used in promotional materials perpetuated that idea that Black women, especially, were dangerous—a theme discussed earlier—and a potential threat to their children.

* * *

This overview of the March of Dimes' history brings together some of threads that shaped the organization's attention to issues of race, gender, and reproduction and is a backdrop against which the March of Dimes took up the pressing issue of premature birth and racial disparities. By 2003, the March of Dimes had launched its national prematurity campaign to address the high rate of preterm birth in the United States. Gradually, the prevention of premature birth was integrated into the organization's official mission in 2005. This expanded focus led to a name change in 2007 to the March of Dimes Foundation, whose stated mission is to improve the health of babies by preventing birth defects, premature birth, and infant mortality.

The Premature Birth Campaign

While I was interviewing executives at the March of Dimes, all of whom were white, Dr. Lori Woodson's name came up often. Whenever I asked, "At what point did the March of Dimes begin to integrate a race analysis into its work around prematurity?" those with whom I was speaking responded, "When Dr. Woodson was here." Initial attempts to contact her failed, but ultimately, I was able to conduct an interview. Dr. Woodson is an African American physician trained as an obstetrician and gynecologist, and she holds a master's degree in public health. She began consulting at the March of Dimes in 2003, just as the organization launched its new prematurity campaign. At that time, the premature birth rate was 12.1 percent (March of Dimes 2009). Dr. Woodson has been credited with guiding the March of Dimes toward addressing the racial dimensions of premature birth.

The organization's focus began with a campaign that had two goals: to raise public awareness of the problem of prematurity and to decrease the rate of premature birth in the United States. To meet those goals, the organization developed (and continues to use) these seven strategies:

1. Fund research to identify the causes of prematurity.
2. Encourage investment of public and private research dollars to test promising interventions.
3. Educate women about risk reduction strategies and the signs of and prevention of preterm labor.
4. Provide information and emotional comfort to families.
5. Advocate for the expansion of health care coverage.
6. Help health care providers improve risk detection and address risk factors.
7. Generate concern and action around the problem.

It is the last goal that is the centerpiece of this chapter.

Since 2005, the March of Dimes has achieved some milestones related to its goals with respect to premature birth. The organization has funded research and projects, and successfully shepherded the Prematurity Research Expansion and Education for Mothers Who Deliver Infants Early (PREEMIE) Act into law. The act, which became law in 2006, authorizes increased federal support for research and education about prematurity. As the rate of preterm birth in the United States steadily rose, peaking in 2006, the organization emphasized reducing the racial/ethnic disparities in these rates. In 2008, it set the goal of achieving a premature birth rate of 9.6 percent by 2014. The agency also implemented initiatives to facilitate meeting the goals that have included reducing preventable preterm birth such as elective deliveries (that is, when women choose deliveries by C-section, before thirty-nine weeks' gestation). Although early elective deliveries are medically unnecessary and pose maternal and infant risk, they have been supported by some physicians who view them as a choice issue. The surgery was common enough that the March of Dimes developed the "Healthy Babies Are Worth the Wait" campaign, whose goal was to end the practice.

By 2013, the March of Dimes had secured the support of seven major health organizations that urged hospitals to reduce or eliminate early elective deliveries. Evidence that the March of Dimes realized some success in reducing premature birth was that it met the 2008 goal of achieving a 9.6 percent preterm birth rate by 2014. Consequently, the board established a new target of 8.1 percent to be achieved by 2020.

Among the approaches the March of Dimes has deployed to address prematurity is supporting transdisciplinary research. Within this research model, interdisciplinary investigators participate in uncovering multiple possible causes of premature birth, with the rationale being that the more lines of inquiry that can be pursued, the better chance researchers will have of finding solutions. A range of disciplinary specialists, including physical scientists, cardiologists, pediatricians, obstetricians, orthopedic investigators, and reproductive scientists, contribute to collaborative thinking and the development of approaches to understand and prevent premature birth. This work is conducted within Prematurity Research Centers (PRCs), which receive approximately $20 to $25 million in grants each year, with the March of Dimes offering strong oversight. What distinguishes the PRCs is that they are not like a standard grant investigator initiative, which typically involves one or two scholars conducting research. Instead, scholars across a number of fields at a university are encouraged to collaboratively investigate themes and share their knowledge and data to enhance one another's perspectives in solving the causes of prematurity.

Mobilizing resources was fundamental in order to drive policy changes, including policies that reduce racial/ethnic disparities in preterm birth rates. And under Dr. Woodson's guidance, the March of Dimes shifted its focus from "just" prematurity, to prematurity and race.

The Meaning of Race

Understanding and acknowledging the racial dimension of premature birth has been high on the list of the foundation's priorities. Circling around the racial dimension of prematurity is the question of whether Black women's risk is based on an inherent biological difference. When I posed the question about a genetic predisposition to adverse birth outcomes, directors and administrators at the March of Dimes rejected the purely biological explanation—that there is something about race or being Black that causes women to give birth prematurely. Rather, they said, it is the interaction between biology and the environment, including race, ethnicity, economics, and education, that offers the best explanation and is a topic of interest. One director commented that the

March of Dimes needs to better understand how those factors—social determinants—are biologically expressed. "We need more science on that. And that can lead us to ask how we can intervene." But, according to the director, there are other ways of looking at the question of why Black women have higher rates of prematurity; these concern their health during their reproductive years and ensuring that women access the interventions that are known to be effective. A second director noted:

> We need to make sure [Black women] are as healthy as possible, and what we're seeing in our population is that is not happening. There is more obesity, hypertension, diabetes, and higher smoking rates. All of those are conditions that affect women's health in pregnancy. But, we need to look at the whole life cycle of women in reproductive age—to make sure they are as healthy as possible. We need to look at the intentionality of pregnancy. Half the pregnancies are unintended, and it is up 70 percent or more when you get to poor women. So, we really need to factor in reproductive planning for women so that they can become intentional in their life about when they become pregnant—so it doesn't drive them into poverty. Access is what we need to work on. Prenatal care is an access issue. But there is also the issue of . . . many women not coming for prenatal care. We can unpack all that too, about trust of the health care system. But we also need to make sure that they're getting all the interventions that we know work. And that's not happening. We're not seeing drug and alcohol screens happening. With a history of preeclampsia, we're not seeing the use of aspirin. So, often, the interventions that we know work, women are not getting.

Seemingly, the point of the administrator's discussion is to move beyond the biological argument as an explanation for Black women's higher rates of premature birth by shifting to more individual factors that influence carrying a pregnancy to term. Yet, he describes a group of racialized health characteristics such as obesity, hypertension, diabetes, and smoking, which serve as proxies for biological causes and, he suggests, occur more often among Black women. Interestingly, a study funded by the March of Dimes found inconsistencies in the effects of obesity on pregnancy, and it is not necessarily related to factors in preterm birth of obese Black women relative to obese white women

(Shaw et al. 2014). The administrator then replaces biological markers that influence birth outcomes with a behavioral or personal decision marker—focused on intentionality—which is then linked to class, access, and birth outcome.

Other administrators deftly incorporated evidence to contradict biological explanations of racial differences in premature birth by discussing scientific studies. On several occasions, when I asked how race factors into understanding premature birth, administrators referred to studies that challenge this perspective. Administrators mentioned a Minnesota study that explored birth outcome differences between US-born Black women and African-born Black women who have given birth in such countries as Cameroon, Ethiopia, and Somalia, among others (Minnesota VitalSigns 2013). Interestingly, in the United States, immigrant Somali women have birth outcomes that rival the rates of white women, and researchers are investigating the possible protective factors among these women. What happens over time, the longer Somalian women live in the United States? Does the protective factor change? Do the rates worsen? In other words, will the toxicity of US racism have an adverse effect on the birth outcomes of future generations of these Somali women?

During conversations, interviewees mentioned the Intergrowth 21st study, which offered evidence against the biological explanation for premature birth outcomes among Black women ("Intergrowth 21st" n.d.). The study looked at women on all the major continents except for Antarctica and in the region of Oceania—they were women of optimal reproductive age who had optimal health, good social conditions, and higher educational attainment. Each woman received standard prenatal care, and there were similar outcomes across all the continents, races, ethnicities, and nationalities: preterm birth rates of 4.5 to 5.5 percent.

Of course, the implication of the Minnesota study is that the biological rationale does not hold up if Black women from African countries have good birth outcomes. The Intergrowth 21st study demonstrated the *lack of genetic cause* because women of different races, ethnicities, and nationalities had similar outcomes. When educational attainment, as a measure of class, is the dominant lens through which to understand prematurity, the analysis is confounded by the fact that educated African American women of a high socioeconomic status still have higher rates of preterm birth and infant and maternal morbidity and mortality than white or Asian women of that same socioeconomic status in the United States. So, when we tease out the social determinants, race remains. But what does race mean to the March of Dimes?

The March of Dimes staff and directors I interviewed agreed that race is a sociopolitical construct. Operationally, the March of Dimes uses the CDC's definition of race. In a Morbidity and Mortality Weekly Report that is published by the CDC on the use of race and ethnicity in public surveillance, the preface states that "while race may have some biological basis, its significance is mainly derived from social arrangements. Thus, race should be viewed within public health surveillance as a sociological phenomenon. Race and ethnicity are not risk factors—they are markers used to better understand risk factors" (Morbidity and Mortality Weekly Report 1993, vii). Another administrator, in describing race as a marker for the experience of racism, said:

> We think of the way someone looks . . . their skin color is a marker for the racism they experience. That's only sort of true because it also depends where they are. . . . To me the link between the color of skin and the health outcome is how people perceive that person. Then [that leads to] how they treat that person and either the interpersonal, institutional, or historical racism they've been subjected to or their ancestors have been subjected to.

This comment underscores the complex understanding that this administrator has about what racism means. For her, racism begins with race, which begins with skin color and the way other people interpret the meaning of skin color. According to this explanation, the perception of race is a reaction, from either individuals or systems. And from there, the cumulative effects of all those experiences of racism become part of a person's subjugation. This, then, becomes the risk that generates racial disparity. However, to state that racism begins with race is to assume race is real and detracts from the idea that racism produces race (Balibar 2005).

In another conversation, the response to a question about how the March of Dimes defines and understands racism in terms of its impact on prematurity was, "We talk about institutional racism as part of the cause of these differences. But, we tend not to talk about racism a whole lot. We acknowledge it, but we don't use that terminology. We'd like to solve the problem rather than polarize the problem. And, we have to raise money from everybody." While the term "racism" might be polarizing, the March of Dimes staff used terms such as "health equity" and "intersectionality" that are much more palatable. Another executive explained what health equity means:

> Health equity, to me, is preferable to use to talk about disparities because it's aspirational. It's something that we haven't achieved but we need to strive for. So that's why we use health equity and that of course means that everybody achieves their full potential or health . . . everybody has the opportunity to achieve their full potential or health.

The March of Dimes staff I interviewed were very conscious of the racial politics that informed how the organization views its work toward reducing racial disparities. The administrators I spoke with sought to analyze the problem of racial differences in premature birth by using what they call an intersectional analysis. Intersectionality is a concept that illuminates multiple factors that influence Black women's lives. Instead of examining independent factors, such as race *or* gender, one must consider how experiences come together, sometimes simultaneously, to shape outcomes (Crenshaw 1989; B. Smith 1983).

I took the statements of the two administrators with whom I spoke regarding intersectionality to mean that they examine more than one aspect of a problem, peeling back the layers of a situation and not relying on just one dimension to understand the complexities of Black women's lives. For instance, a woman's medical circumstance is not reducible to one demographic characteristic such as race, class, or gender. A situation must be analyzed from a vantage point that considers all of those characteristics.

To illustrate, one of the directors described the distribution of 17 alpha-hydroxyprogesterone caproate, a drug also known as 17HP or 17P, which costs between $225 and $385 per week, or between $2,250 and $3,850 for a full course of treatment, which is ten weekly doses that must be administered by a doctor (Abbott 2017). If a woman has previously experienced a preterm birth, 17HP decreases the chances of having another preterm birth by 30 percent (Abbott 2017). The March of Dimes administrator told me that the North Carolina Division of Public Health had invested in and promoted 17HP for eight years, but only slightly more than half of the African American women who were eligible actually received it. That is not surprising, given that a similar rate holds true for nearly any medical treatment. An analysis showed there were three barriers to administering 17HP: first, doctors often did not recommend it; second, when it was recommended, women did not accept it; and, third, some women accepted the drug but then did not complete the course. This administrator went on to provide an intersectional analysis:

> You can look at the data and you can say, "bad doctors," they're not doing something they should. But when you actually drill down, it is impossible to preauthorize 17HP. You have to order the ten doses. If a woman doesn't show up, after the first dose, you "eat" nine doses of a $2,250 drug. Or, you can also look at the women and say they are noncompliant. An intersectional analysis goes further and requires you to think "Well, wait a minute, you have to go for a weekly shot in your doctor's office." If you are somebody who works in the service industry and don't have sick time or don't have time off, you can't take two to three hours a week for ten weeks to go to a doctor's office for a shot!

However, this same administrator also told me that in Puerto Rico, the administration and delivery of 17HP to women was successful. When 17HP was introduced in Puerto Rico in 2008, it was through a public-private partnership between the Puerto Rico Department of Health and the Vita HealthCare Company. They developed a preapproval model for insurance for each woman. Nurses were also dispatched to convenient locations to facilitate women's ability to receive shots, even in their homes, which eliminated the problem of potential hours lost at work. There was what appears to have been a successful education campaign between 2008 and 2013, and the preterm birth rate dropped from 20 percent to 14 percent. A private company in close proximity to the physician's offices conducted trainings on the importance of 17P for medical professionals (ASTHO 2016).

Comparing these two scenarios, we can see that an intersectional framework redirects a potentially stereotypical assessment of a patient who is presumably low income (although the administrator did not explicitly state that was the case, it was implied by the reference to the patient having a job in the service industry). Rather than stereotyping a patient as being "noncompliant," one needs to consider the life conditions that may prevent a woman from coming in for treatments—even though she may want to. I was told "that this is a kind of filter, it's not necessarily a racial filter, but it's a social determinant–type filter."

The administrator described a low-income Black woman's situation to explain intersectionality. It is not that this was inaccurate, but the explanation ended up making a question about how racism is defined into an example of the barriers that prevented her from receiving treatment that might decrease the possibility of giving birth prematurely, without mentioning racism. Importantly, the response did not consider the possibility of medical racism. Indeed, the "bad doctor" was absolved. There was no indication that the behavior of the medical professionals may have factored into why women did not return for the full course of 17HP.

Although the March of Dimes executives I spoke with seemed to understand race and racism as structural and systemic, racism does not easily translate into a campaign in the fight against racially disparate birth outcomes. Racial disparity, however, is a consequence of racism, and it is a measure that depends on historically constructed categories. In response to the question "How do you define racial disparity?" one administrator replied, "One of the challenges we face in this country is moving away from seeing health disparities as natural outcomes [of race] to recognizing that they aren't genetically based outcomes." "The problem is," he continued, "that systems advantage some people while disadvantaging other people. That, to me, exemplifies racism and the result is racial disparity, which places an unfair burden on a population that causes a difference in outcomes in health."

Accomplishing the goal of reducing racial disparity involves using numbers to demonstrate the depth of the racial disparity of premature birth, which in turn exposes how racially advantaged groups, such as whites, continue to secure advantages in the US health system. However, I found that discussing racism is not as easy as discussing race or racial disparity, particularly as the organization depends on funds from philanthropists and foundations, which typically do not seek to have their grants used to address racism.

Racial Disparity

Driving the March of Dimes' research, advocacy, programmatic interventions, community-based programs, patient education and resources, and work with state departments of health and local chapters are data and statistics. Statistics can be very appealing. When relied on as facts, statistics and data are capable of indexing alarm and animating program development and policy initiatives. Considered to be a trusted partner of the federal government, according to one director, the March of Dimes' Perinatal Data Center receives its information from government agencies and organizations. The director described the center's role as seeking to "acquire and analyze maternal and infant health data, and to interpret this information for the March of Dimes and for health professionals, research groups and organizations external to the March of Dimes" (March of Dimes 2016). Data for the Premature Birth Report Card are derived from the National Center for Health Statistics (NCHS), a group within the CDC, which collects vital statistics data from birth and death certificates. When the Perinatal Data Center receives information from the NCHS, it does not just accept the information as is but works with it, massaging numbers and developing ways to present it. One administrator explained the role that numbers play in the organization's mission as follows:

> Look, last year [in 2016] there were 381,000 babies born term in the US. That represents 9.6 percent of all babies born. What is important to me, what is important to us, is that every single number is a baby. Every single one has a family. In putting those numbers out there, we are telling their story, and that is our responsibility. It is our responsibility to make sure we're telling their story in the best way possible. You know there is a technical definition of prematurity, but these are people. And, to me, it's really important that we keep that in mind when we go out and present these statistics. If we're presenting data on disparities, or we're presenting on outcomes, or risk factors . . . we're talking about real people. It's not just that 10 percent of pregnant women smoke. It's that they are real people.

When the Perinatal Data Center developed the Premature Birth Report Card in 2008, the card reported the preterm birth rate by state. By

2013, race and ethnicity data were included in the report card. However, the director of the Perinatal Data Center said that staff thought something more was needed. They wanted to hold states accountable for what they were doing to address health disparities. The idea behind the Health Disparities Index is that it provides a way of looking at progress toward decreasing racial disparity, essentially by looking at and assessing each state's progress toward that goal.

According the Dr. Woodson, the subject of racial disparity was initially raised by organizations with which the March of Dimes had been collaborating. Members of the collaborative posed questions such as, How was the March of Dimes dealing with preterm birth? How was it planning on addressing the disparities in birth outcomes for African American women? Dr. Woodson said, "At the time there really was no answer to the question. We did not know how we could go about making a difference in that population. But it was important to at least raise awareness in the community, that this issue does disproportionately affect African American women. So probably the best approach was to think about preventive ways." During our conversations, Dr. Woodson told me that group members wanted to explore the impact of racism on individual health and how that environmental factor translates into physical manifestations that impact health. Initially, simply listing preterm birth rates by race was the extent of the information the March of Dimes provided the communities it was working with. Then around 2010 or 2011, the Perinatal Data Center searched for ways to focus on the issue a little differently because, although the national preterm birth rate had dropped, there were still significant racial and ethnic disparities. That change came in the form of a number: the Racial Disparity Index.

The Racial Disparity Index

On November 1, 2016, for the second year in a row, the March of Dimes posted its Premature Birth Report Card for the United Sates with an accompanying Racial Disparity Index. The report card assigns grades to each state based on the three-year rolling average of premature birth rates in that state. The states are then compared to the March of Dimes goal of reducing prematurity to less than 8.1 percent by 2020. The report card also provides race and ethnicity data for specific counties to highlight "areas of increased burden and elevated risks of prematurity." Take the example of California, which received a grade of B because its preterm birth rate was 8.5 percent. But the state's racial disparity is wide: whereas the white preterm rate is 7.7 percent, the Black preterm rate is 11.9 percent.

Overall, the United States received a grade of C because the preterm birth rate was 9.3 percent, higher than the March of Dimes' goal of 8.1 percent. The 2016 rate rose for the first time in eight years and represented widening differences across race and ethnicity. According to Dr. Jennifer Howse, president of the March of Dimes at the time, the report card revealed an unfair burden of premature births among particular racial groups: specifically, the burden is born by Black women, *whose rates were nearly 49 percent higher than those of white women* (March of Dimes 2016). The news about the racial disparity was startling, but not inconsistent with what is known about historical demographic estimates—that Black women's rates for premature birth and infant mortality are, and have been, persistently higher than those for any other group *since the time of enslavement in the United States* (Haines 2008; Berry and Alford 2012).

When the March of Dimes prepares the report cards, the Perinatal Data Center staff uses the overall preterm birth rate in a state, which represents every baby born in that state. The numbers are not a sample, and they are not estimates of the preterm birth rates for that state. Data exist for every single baby and for every single baby born prematurely, which allows the Perinatal Data Center staff to calculate a percent from that data universe. The federal government puts those numbers out, and those are the numbers the March of Dimes uses to determine the overall preterm birth rate for each state. States are then graded. The state of Washington, for example, received an overall grade of A because its preterm rate was 8.1 percent, which is equal to the target goal (Figure 5.1).

Among the white population, the rate was 7.8 percent, and the Black and American Indian/Alaska Native rates were 10.0 and 12.1 percent, respectively. These rates show quite a range of disparity. While the state of Washington's overall grade takes into account the racial and ethnic distribution, the fact is that the majority of babies born in Washington are born to white mothers. What we see is that regardless of how large or small a racial/ethnic population is in different states, there are differ-

2016 PREMATURE BIRTH REPORT CARD

	Preterm Birth Rate	Grade
Washington	8.1%	A

The March of Dimes Prematurity Campaign aims to reduce preterm birth rates across the United States. Premature Birth Report Card grades are assigned by comparing the 2015 preterm birth rate in a state or locality to the March of Dimes goal of 8.1 percent by 2020. The Report Card also provides county and race/ethnicity data to highlight areas of increased burden and elevated risks of prematurity.

COUNTIES

Counties with the greatest number of births are graded based on their 2014 preterm birth rates.

County	Preterm birth rate	Grade
Clark	8.3%	B
King	7.8%	A
Pierce	8.1%	A
Snohomish	8.3%	B
Spokane	9.3%	C
Yakima	8.4%	B

RACE & ETHNICITY IN WASHINGTON

The March of Dimes uses a Disparity Index score to measure and track progress towards the elimination of racial/ethnic disparities in preterm birth. The score represents the average percent difference in the preterm birth rate across all groups compared to the group with the lowest rate in the state. Index scores range from 0 (achievement of equity) to 44 (highest score in 2016).

Percentage of live births in 2012-2014 (average) that are preterm

Disparity index
25
State rank
#27

In Washington, the preterm birth rate among American Indian/Alaska Native women is 49% higher than the rate among all other women.

For details on data sources and calculations, see Technical Notes.
For more information on how we are working to reduce premature birth, visit www.marchofdimes.org.

marchofdimes.org/reportcard

march of dimes
A FIGHTING CHANCE FOR EVERY BABY™

Figure 5.1. Premature Birth Report Card, 2016

ences in the risks by racial and ethnic groups. The index is an average risk across the groups. The rate is in relation to the March of Dimes' goal, which again, in 2016, was 8.1 percent. Overall, across the entire state, Washington achieved the goal, but the disparity index shows particular groups' rates, giving a better sense that the disparities need to be accounted for.

It should come as no surprise, a staff person confessed, that some March of Dimes chapters wanted to do away with the Racial Disparity Index. Objections included the assertion that the March of Dimes staff in the field offices would not understand the index. The response from executives was "Then we'll do webinars!" There was also push-back from state health departments, which objected that, on the one hand, a state could look good by having a "good grade," but on the other hand, its disparity index, which does not weight for populations, might look bad. Some states resisted the index by arguing that they did not have a large population of the group carrying the burden of disparity. Such comments reflect resistance to change. But the response of one staff person was to ask, "So, does having a small number of 'X' group mean that group is not important?"

The desire to adjust, control for, or weight race and ethnicity data is erroneously linked to ideas of fairness and the desire to compare states to one another. If you have a state like Louisiana or Mississippi that has a very high proportion of its births born to Black women, how can you compare that to Washington State, Oregon, or Vermont, where the majority of babies are born to white women? While it may seem like a fair question, adjusting for race and ethnicity means that a state is not responsible for narrowing the gap of a racial disparity. In developing the Racial Disparity Index, the idea was that the emotional impact of numbers would make people accountable. That the disparity exists in the first place should motivate a desire for change, which in turn should generate the will to reduce the disparity.

Why is it that people believe numbers can achieve change, especially when it concerns narrowing the racial disparity gap in premature births? Because numbers possess degrees of power. They are presumed to be a rational representation of truth and often are used to prove that a problem exists. The power of numbers is that they can lead governments, policy makers, and the public to care enough to enact change. This power is similar to the "magic of intervention" that Tess Lea, a former bureaucrat and current policy researcher in Australia, describes in her ethnography *Bureaucrats and Bleeding Hearts: Indigenous Health in Northern Australia* (2008). When Lea uses the term "magic," it is an effort to explain the passion of people working to intervene in a public health or social problem. Sometimes, when looking at bureaucrats, that effort is invisible, but still they continue to have faith in the interventionist tools they develop. Lea convincingly argues that people working in bureaucracies really do seek to address Indigenous people's health issues. But her cogent description of the humane interests that drive bureaucracy is cautious. It is also inflected with a critique of the professionals—including administrators—who carry out the state's mission to help Indigenous people in Australia.

To be clear, I am not arguing that data should not be collected. Numbers tell us the scope of a problem. But what do data tell us if the focus is on the numbers rather than the experience? As anthropologist S. Lochlann Jain argues in her book *Malignant: How Cancer Becomes Us* (2013), numbers not only count what is already out there; they also become a basis of evidence for arguments about an issue—in this case, prematurity—by virtue of the preset categories for data collection.

Of course, the March of Dimes is not the state, but administrators with whom I spoke utilized the state's data to generate compelling arguments that could ultimately motivate local health departments and community-based organizations to address the racial disparity of prematurity in their areas. While there was, and is, broad institutional recognition about racial disparity at the March of Dimes, it was the Perinatal Data Center staff who first proposed that a disparity index be developed and distributed. The point was to successfully narrow the racial disparity of prematurity lies with deploying data effectively based on the idea that in data lies the possibility of improvement.

Narrowing the Gap

To reduce the burden that Black women bear with higher rates of premature birth, the March of Dimes also supports alternative models of prenatal care. Prenatal programs, according to the March of Dimes, hold a lot of promise. Dr. Woodson lauded such programs because they often helped lower rates of preterm birth. One the most memorable programs for her was the March of Dimes–funded Honey Child Prenatal Education Program, a faith-based program in Atlanta, Georgia ("Honey Child" n.d.). Honey Child is a free prenatal program that explicitly works to help African American women carry their babies to full term. The group-centered sessions, which meet monthly and include up to fifteen people, offer information to help prevent premature birth, birth defects, low birth weight, and newborn deaths.

Dr. Woodson and other staff and administrators discussed the success of CenteringPregnancy, a popular prenatal project in which participants meet in a group rather than being seen individually by a physician. More time is dedicated to patient education and how to manage self-care, such as checking heart rates and blood pressure. Women compare notes and create a sense of community that extends beyond the pregnancies, enhancing their social networks. Sharon Schindler Rising—a certified nurse-midwife who developed CenteringPregnancy in 1993—offers it as an alternative model for delivering prenatal care (Theilein 2012). It brings together women with similar due dates to participate in ten group sessions led by the same doctor or nurse practitioner at each session. It is a way for expectant mothers to be more actively engaged in their own care.

Getting African American women to participate in group prenatal care programs can be difficult, conceded Dr. Woodson. In fact, she said, studies show that "African American women are more guarded in group prenatal settings, they are less inclined to discuss their personal life and some of the personal, emotional, and mental health challenges they face during pregnancy. This is in contrast to Latino women, who absolutely flourish in those kinds of settings."

Admittedly, it took a lot more engagement and a lot more time to get African American women to feel supported enough so that they could talk about some of the issues that may be impacting their lives, their health, and their pregnancy outcomes. But all the administrators at the March of Dimes agreed that providing strong preventive health services offers the best opportunity to impact health outcomes.

One of the most successful organizations, as part of the Healthy Start program, has been the Northern Manhattan Perinatal Partnership, located in Harlem, New York. Dr. Woodson praised its success in coordinating services for its pregnant patients, making referrals and follow-up appointments, and offering on-site case management. This program's model of care resulted in dramatic decreases in the preterm birth rate among the African American participants.

Dr. Woodson shared a sentiment that was held by all the administrators I interviewed: the medical system has to do a better job of integrating public health and clinical care, and looking at issues such as the social determinants of health in those neighborhoods that are socioeconomically depressed. It is difficult to get a woman in for prenatal care if she is homeless, experiencing domestic violence, or living in poverty. All those factors—the physical, emotional, and environmental—must be taken into account when you are trying to improve health outcomes. Yet, as we have seen, the outcomes are similar across socioeconomic status.

The March of Dimes, as the largest national nonprofit organization seeking to address premature birth, does so with a commitment to narrowing the disparity between Black and white women's rates of prematurity. The organization's health education approach is certainly attuned to racial disparity, and its public education efforts use numbers to make the issue "come to life." In so doing, they create a measure of intolerance so that state and local governments and community-based organizations will be motivated to narrow the gap in premature birth rates.

* * *

I came to the title of this chapter as the result of a mistake: I asked one of the March of Dimes administrators how the organization sought to close the racial disparity gap. He quickly corrected me, stating, "We are not closing it, but we will narrow the gap." I was reminded of how much caution is required when attempting to fix a problem: overstating a goal or success is very risky. But there is something about imagining the end of premature birth that seemed to keep the people I spoke with committed to thinking about how to secure broad-based support to pay attention to the issue of race. But that may be part of the problem.

We have seen how the March of Dimes grapples with science, data, and communicating messages that will, hopefully, continue to make an impact on reducing prematurity. However, there are tensions associated with depending on numbers as part of an intervention. Numbers become a way in which we *understand and mark* a problem (O'Neil 2016).

Relying on numbers or data sets, as anthropologist Shaka McGlotten (2016) argues, can also result in the negative construction of particular groups of people, subjecting them to further marginalization. Additionally, numbers and data also tend to neglect other aspects of the very problems that they seek to clarify. Numbers that reveal racial disparity do not explain what the disparity may feel like, or what role racism plays in how women assess the care they receive. What constantly emerged was how, in addressing the racial disparity, the organization did not see addressing racism as its mission.

While the March of Dimes pays attention to race and disparity, that may not quite be enough. Returning to the questions I asked, it was apparent that they were talking about race and racial disparity, but they were not talking about how to address racism because the March of Dimes is not a racial justice organization.

So, who is addressing Black women's adverse birth outcomes and taking into account medical racism in prenatal encounters? The next chapter explores how birth advocates attend to racism as part of their understanding that Black babies and mothers matter. Birth advocates, who are often part of racial and reproductive justice movements, do some of the work to ameliorate the benign and explicit forms of racism that Black women experience during medical encounters.

Many birth workers attempt to circumvent reproductive injustices such as Ashley's concerns about her high blood pressure during her pregnancy not being addressed; to Veronica's interpretation that her partner was treated with indifference due to his race; to Sherry, feeling slighted because she wanted her newborn to be given breast milk but was made to feel that she was being demanding; to Yvette's high-risk pregnancy being ignored by her doctor, then being treated dismissively in the ER. Part of what the practice of birth advocacy addresses is the issue of medical racism. Birth advocates, doulas, and midwives engage in care and support that attend to not only preventing negative birth outcomes but also ameliorating the racism that many Black women perceive in their interactions with medical personnel and believe influence their birth outcomes.

6

Radical Black Birth Workers

She just flew. Collected every bit of life she had made, all the
parts of her that were precious and fine and beautiful, and
carried, pushed, dragged them through the veil, out, away,
over there where no one could hurt them. Over there. Outside this place, where they would be safe.
—Toni Morrison, *Beloved* (1987)

There has never been a time when Black women's reproduction was
treated respectfully in the United States. Ideologies and racist practices
have permeated the content of Black women's reproductive lives. Black
women have been mistreated, misdiagnosed, derided, pushed aside,
and erased. These practices have a long history, extending back to the
antebellum period, and have made their way into the contemporary
experiences. The state, as well as medical institutions that are monitored
by the state, ostensibly provides health care for its citizens. However, as
the past is reinvented or reasserted, the state and its institutions offer
care that is truncated. In the case of Black women's reproduction, the
traces of earlier forms of racism are difficult to eradicate. And yet, the
impenetrable wall segregating Black from white women's birth outcomes
has never prevented Black women from picking up the shards of a medical system structured on racism to try to create better and more caring
ways of having a pregnancy reach term and giving birth with dignity.

This chapter explores the role of radical birth workers, who include
reproductive advocates, doulas, and midwives. Radical birth workers
draw on ideas of justice and see reproduction as a site where the inalien-
able right to have the kind of birth one wants should exist. Although I
do not suggest that every birth worker is sensitive to the issues discussed
here, the radical birth workers I interviewed did connect the history of
Black women's reproductive exploitation to current medical practices.
They viewed their role as one that involved supporting birthing par-

ents in their decision to have the kind of birth they want, with or without medical intervention. Most important, radical birth workers seek to ensure that birthing parents are treated respectfully and understand the consequences of the procedures to which they might be subjected. Along with working toward facilitating informed decisions, they actively engage in advocacy, care, and medical practices that seek to shift adverse birth outcomes.

Radical birth workers engage in birth work that may be characterized as biological citizenship, biosociality, or bioactivism. Biological citizenship was first defined in the anthropological literature by Adriana Petryna, in her book *Life Exposed: Biological Citizens after Chernobyl* (2002). Petryna argues that after the Chernobyl nuclear reactor exploded in what was then the Soviet Ukraine, citizens made moral and political claims for the right to health services from the government. The concept of biological citizenship, or biocitizenship, is that people become political actors in relation to biomedical processes, such as testing and making diagnoses in an attempt to maintain health.

Biosociality is the formation of social relations and the production of identity based on genetic conditions (Rabinow and Rose 2006). It involves providing support, raising public awareness, and serving as a networking site as group members take their care into their own hands at the same time that group members seek to influence the direction of research. Although polio is not based on a genetic condition, Charles Bynum, discussed earlier, engaged in a form of biosociality in the 1950s when he organized around the issue of polio in the Black community. He focused on raising awareness, and ultimately the March of Dimes was compelled to address the needs of the Black community, which shared concerns about the transmission of the polio virus (Mawdsley 2010). Some may call this bioactivism, which is when principles of solidarity exist among patients with a disease, who demand a collaborative approach to research (Woods 2016). Somewhere coursing through these three concepts—biocitizenship, biosociality, and bioactivism—are Black women who are birth workers, sometimes operating within the medical system and other times not, who typically critique the medicalization of birthing and attempt to protect Black women from medical racism. Their contestations differ from biocitizenship, biosociality, and bioactivism in that for some birth workers, the state is not dependable enough to look to for care. Indeed, these birth workers believe that birth should be decoupled from the state apparatus and want to limit the medicalization of birth, such as supporting expectant peoples' decision to decline Pitocin and discussing the implications of being connected to a fetal monitor, which restricts movements during labor. Given the regularity with which such interventions are used, to recommend abstaining from them is a form of contestation, which has a long tradition in Black communities.

Black people have a history of contesting medical segregation and medical racism, and of necessity have had to develop their own spaces in which to provide care for their communities, such as building their own hospitals and medical training schools (Gamble 1995). For instance, nineteenth- and twentieth-century midwives saw themselves as important liaisons between poor Black women and white health professionals. In the 1920s, the Black women's club movement created health institutions in Black communities to ameliorate the lack of services (S. L. Smith 1995, 20). Lay care providers have often sought to make the medical system responsive to Black women's needs. Historian Susan L. Smith describes a situation in 1939 in which a midwife, Estelle W. Christian, who was Black, reported to a white nurse about a pregnant woman with sores. Her intent in telling the nurse was to ensure that the woman would receive medical attention because it was likely that she had syphilis. In describing this situation, Smith notes that "the cumulative effect of such actions by midwives improved poor women's access to medical services" (1995, 140). A final example is that the Black Panther Party established free clinics to ensure medical services, with women as the backbone of the effort (A. Nelson 2011; Bassett 2016). In other words, Black women have facilitated access to social and medical services.

Clearly, Black women have been at the vanguard of both negotiating for and providing care to the Black community at large, and Black women in particular, when, due to discrimination and segregation, US society failed to do so. Following in this same tradition, the radical Black birth workers who were part of this research project—advocates, midwives, and doulas—see their role as fundamentally important in the prevention of both prematurity and infant and maternal mortality.

The term "doula"—which in Greek means "woman who helps"—was first used by anthropologist Dana Raphael in her theorization of primate and mammalian behavior, which offered a window into the supportive needs of nonhuman and human mothers. Research showed that supporting, "or aunting," among primates facilitated the primate mother's ability to lactate (Raphael 1969, 1973). Concerned with issues around breastfeeding, Raphael termed a person who provides positive and supportive behavior to a mother a "doula" and argued that successful breastfeeding is often stimulated and triggered by caretaking. Her point is that doulas can be instrumental to maternal success because they "surround, interact with, and aid the mother at any time within the perinatal period" (Raphael 1973, 24).

Being a trained doula or midwife is one way to support women and trans people through pregnancy, labor, and birthing, as the preventive mechanism to stem high prematurity and infant and maternal mortality rates in the Black community. By no means are all radical birth workers limited to assisting Black women, but as a form of reproductive justice, their work is often linked to other justice movements because they understand that the politics of racism has led to negative health outcomes among Black women, regardless of class. Women who utilize doulas and midwives have rethought how they want to give birth and have embraced strategies for doing so. What does a praxis of resistance look like when Black women seek to shift the likelihood of their own adverse birth outcomes or those of other Black women?

Decolonizing Birth

Entering Stuyvesant Mansion in Brooklyn, New York, on a Saturday in September 2016, I heard a woman say: "Thank you, thank you . . . it is up to us to really take the reins, we have issues in our own neighborhoods that we have to navigate every day." Once inside, though, I was unable to see the person speaking because people were gathered in front of the doorway leading to the room where the speaker was.

Walking toward the check-in table, I noticed the faint smell of sage wafting through the air: wanting to know its source, I turned to the right and saw a children's play space and noted a sign directing attendees to a relaxation room upstairs. After checking in and glancing at the conference packet, I realized that Khiara Bridges, the keynote speaker, had left. Silently lamenting having missed Bridges, I was interrupted by the voice of the woman I heard when I first arrived: I caught her comment midsentence:

Don't wait . . . don't say, "Oh my goodness what I am going to do?" If you are sitting here in this space; this space was created to decolonize birthing. It was created so that women of color and people of color could have their voices heard. So often we come to these spaces and we don't have a space in which to share how we feel.

I moved toward the larger room hoping to find a seat, but it was clear that there were none. There was a sea of mostly brown faces, a few white women and men, along with quite a few babies, infants, and toddlers. As conference attendees sat on the floor and in chairs, I scanned the room and caught a glimpse of a Black woman holding an infant in a baby carrier. She moved around the front of the room, her hands choreographing the urgency of her comments. "I charge you to speak about the injustices you see." Standing on the side of the room, I could feel the body heat of the nearly seventy-five people listening in rapt attention and the group responded in agreement: "Mmm, hmmm." Then the woman proclaimed, "I am going to create the spaces, so that people who look like me, who when they want to come they can feel safe and they can have those spaces."

This was the second day of the "Decolonizing Birth Conference" organized by Ancient Song Doula, a group that "reclaims the ancient principles of birthing"—in other words, prioritizing natural child birth practices. Participants were there to support and learn about how communities of color could be strengthened through kinship and "innerstanding"; to address the issues that make pregnancy, birthing, and parenting complicated, and even dangerous. The voice I had heard was that of Chanel Porchia-Albert, the founder of Ancient Song Doula, which has been in existence since 2008 and provides low-cost, quality doula services to women of color and low-income families. Chanel, a mother of six, recalled that the first person she knew who told her about pregnancy was her sixth-grade teacher. When Chanel asked about her pregnancy, her teacher told her that she had a C-section; Chanel recalled, "That was the first birth story I remember hearing." Then, when her sister gave birth at seventeen, Chanel was a documentary filmmaker, and she recorded the entire birth. She zoomed in and saw the placenta come out. When the nurse took it, Chanel asked what they were going to do with it. The response was "Throw it away," and Chanel thought, "That isn't right."

The memory of that moment was one of two that led Chanel to rethink the birthing process. She later began offering birth education in her home after the birth of her own children, and she wanted to have a program centered in the Black community. Reminiscing, Chanel said:

> Between 2009 and 2010, it was in my house. I was doing trainings in the living room. By 2011, what became Ancient Song Doula had so many people coming through that I had to find another space and engaged in a space-sharing process. But a fire made that space uninhabitable, but the community came together and raised money for us. Then in 2017 we moved to our current space.

Ancient Song trains doulas and midwife assistants in a curriculum that focuses on community engagement and advocacy around preventing infant and maternal mortality ("Ancient Song Doula" n.d.). These birth workers are part of the birthing justice movement, which falls under the broader category of reproductive justice, a term that was created in 1994 in response to increasing governmental efforts to control and manage women's sexual and reproductive health. A group of thirteen African American women attended a Chicago conference sponsored by the Ms. Foundation for Women and the Illinois Pro-Choice Alliance.[1] During the meeting, there was an impromptu caucus in which women of color expressed concern that they were not included in the plan for universal health care that was being proposed by the Clinton administration. The development of the reproductive justice framework arose out of the caucus and sought to move the conversation about women's reproductive health from a focus on individual rights or freedom of choice to an expanded conversation about women's human rights and the need for greater social and economic support for women and children (Bond-Leonard, personal communication, October 8, 2014). Reproductive justice activists "maintain that reproductive safety and dignity depends on having the resources to obtain good medical care and decent housing, to have a job that pays a living wage, to live without police harassment, to live free of racism in a physically healthy environment" (Ross and Solinger 2017, 56).

Birthing justice, one aspect of reproductive justice, "refers to the right to give birth with whom, where, when and how a person chooses" (Ross and Solinger 2017, 262). A central concern of birth justice advocates is the quality of caregiving and ensuring that women have knowledge about their bodies, the politics of reproduction, and the ability to plan for births and reproductive services. Birthing justice also serves as a point from which organizing can occur, but it is not a movement, although it brings birth workers to the reproductive justice table. And that is what happened in September 2016 at the "Decolonizing Birth Conference." Mothers, doulas, midwives, health professionals, men, and children attended the conference seeking like-minded people concerned with the reproductive health of Black women who give birth prematurely, have children die, and die themselves. Many attendees were part of other movements such as the Movement for Black Lives, which is a coalition of groups across the United States that maintain political focus on the needs of Black communities in particular, organizing around community concerns such as police killings.

The deaths of seventeen-year-old Trayvon Martin and twenty-five-year-old Freddie Gray precipitated a movement that sparked a national conversation and organizing about race and policing. In 2012, Martin was killed by a neighborhood watch person in Florida, George Zimmerman, who says Martin had a weapon, which turned out to be a bag of Skittles. Zimmerman was acquitted. Freddie Gray of Baltimore, Maryland, died in 2015 as a result of spinal injuries after being in police custody. Additionally, the unjust treatment of Marissa Alexander, who had been incarcerated for protecting herself and her children from her violent husband by using a gun in the stand-your-ground state of Florida, was another example of the need to connect social justice to reproductive justice because "the right to have children, not have children and to parent the children we have in safe and healthy environments" is a mandate of the reproductive justice framework (Ross and Solinger 2017). Nonprofit groups such as Ancient Song Doula and the International Center for Traditional Childbirth believe that Black families require empowerment to facilitate the reduction of adverse birth outcomes and view those outcomes as being linked to social issues.

Ancient Song Doula, birthing organizations, and the growing number of home birth and practicing midwives across the country exemplify the burgeoning grassroots movement of women of color creating strategies to transform birthing. They are part of a long tradition of Black women who have formed the backbone of the Black health movement (S. L. Smith 1995), which has roots in "granny midwifery" work (G. Fraser 1998). In the United States, "granny midwives," most of whom were Black, were an integral part of the community during the colonial and antebellum periods, attending to most pregnant women, both Black and white. According to sociologist Alicia Bonaparte (2015), granny midwives' earliest role on plantations was to help maintain the labor force by providing both care for enslaved people who became sick and childbirth care.

Reproductive Justice in the Afterlife of Slavery

During the era of slavery, reproductive slavery began at the moment of capture; those of reproductive age were exposed to sexual assault and forced pregnancy and went through labor and childbirth while shackled on ships bound for various ports of call. Reproductive slavery was sustained through slave owners forcing sexual relations between enslaved people and sexually exploiting enslaved peoples—all toward increasing property and potential earnings ("Born in Slavery" 1936). Women's value lay in their fecundity, "and traders made projections based on their 'future increase'—their appraisals linked to their ability to reproduce" (Berry 2017, 11).

We know the role that forced reproduction played in the plantation economy, "increasing the wealth of slave-owning whites" (Ross and Solinger 2017, 15). To keep that economy thriving, reproductive health care was structured in such a way that population control "made the fertility of the enslaved woman into the essential exploitable, colonial resource. Her pregnancies, whether the result of rape or love, or something else," engorged the holdings of her owner (18). Midwives were an effective part of this reproductive circuit, providing abortions and orchestrating the spacing of women's pregnancies—despite slaveholders' financial interests. Until the nineteenth century, the vast majority of births occurred at home, under the supervision of traditional midwives who provided reproductive and general health care to enslaved peoples. Midwives also provided contraceptive care and abortions and delivered babies for both Black and white women. A granny midwife "was a woman, often a mother and wife, but her special calling allowed her to transgress the rules and expectations of what a woman should be and do" (G. Fraser 1998, 43).

Whereas midwives were once the dominant care providers for pregnant women in the mid-nineteenth century, medical practitioners increasingly attended to the medical issues of enslaved women. Physicians, medically trained nurses, and white nurse midwives in the South came to control pregnancy and childbirth, casting both of these as medical events in need of supervision. Ultimately the power of childbirth was wrested away from women as reproducers and as assistants in the birthing process (Craven 2010). Plantation owners deployed physicians' expertise to manage the health of their property. By the early twentieth century, midwives were increasingly vilified, due to the competition they posed for doctors. The professionalization of medicine subordinated midwifery to medical science, and many came to see midwifery as providing substandard care (Craven 2010). Between 1900 and 1940, health officials and medical doctors depicted granny and other forms of midwifery as unsafe and illegitimate forms of health care by citing egregious mortality rates as well as racialized claims about Black midwives not being "far removed from the jungles of Africa" (H. Mathews 1992, 65). Midwives were viewed as primitive and outmoded: the campaign against them worked. In South Carolina, for example, the number of registered midwives decreased from 197 in 1900 to 124 by 1920 (Bonaparte 2015, 27). Physicians utilized their professional journals to denigrate midwives. One example was Dr. Allen W. Freeman's castigation of midwives in response to an essay written by Dr. W. P. Manton on obstetric medicine in an article in the *Journal of the American Medical Association*:

> There is no doubt that tens of thousands of women are being absolutely murdered by ignorant midwives. Everyone who has ever practiced obstetrics knows how filthy and dirty, how officious and meddlesome these women are. . . . We must tell the people how many women these midwives are killing, and how much illness they are causing. (Manton 1910, 174)

Freeman's perspective was common and contributed to the medicalization of pregnancy and childbirth. Both the history of medicalizing pregnancy and the medicalization of birth have been well documented (Davis-Floyd 1992; Rapp 1999; Duden 1993; Rothman 1993). Anthropologist and activist Robbie Davis-Floyd argues that the medicalization of pregnancy met with resistance between the 1970s and 1980s as the natural childbirth movement in the United States fought for "humanistic rights [such as] the right to the supportive presence of family, friends and doulas; to more comfortable environments for labor and birth; and to breastfeeding support" (Davis-Floyd 2005, 37). Although there have been feminist critiques of reproduction's medicalization, few have centered on Black women's resistance (Brubaker 2004). Yet health activism has been important for Black women around reproduction, pregnancy, and birthing. This activism was galvanized when the American welfare state was expanding and Black rights were decreasing. Many Blacks saw their struggle for improved health conditions as part of a political agenda for Black rights, especially the right to equal access to government resources (S. L. Smith 1995).

Among the health concerns impacting Black women were maternal and infant mortality. The CDC reports that from 1980 to 2000 the infant mortality rates for Blacks declined from 22.2 to 14.0. Comparatively, white infant mortality rates declined from 10.9 to 5.7, making the disparity twice as great for Blacks versus whites (Centers for Disease Control and Prevention 2002). In the 1980s, one young woman responded to this crisis and initiated a program to help arrest the high Black infant and maternal mortality rates. The Birthing Project became a model for helping Black women to bring their pregnancies to term. Following in the footsteps of health care organizers from the antebellum period through the twentieth century, it exemplifies a form of resistance promulgated by Black women on behalf of other Black women.

The Birthing Project

A long tradition of maternal activism among middle-class Black women prompted cross-class and gender/ethnic solidarity among Black women activists in the 1980s and 1990s, according to sociologist Katrina Bell McDonald (2004, 4). One such project that drew on Black women's volunteerism was the Birthing Project, founded by Kathryn Hall, now Hall-Trujillo. The project confronts the epidemiological crisis of Black infant mortality through the provision of maternal support to Black women. This activist mothering or other-mothering, is a translation of traditional African principles and involves a complex practice of biological mothering or community other-mothering, and political activism (Collins 1991).

I met Kathryn Hall-Trujillo, who lives in New Mexico, through a midwife who used to work with the Birthing Project. Becoming fast friends, we settled into a phone check-in routine much like sisters and spoke weekly. Kathryn spends a good deal of time on planes traveling to cities and meeting with health department officials to develop plans that address high prematurity and infant and maternal mortality rates. Occasionally, our check-ins took place during her travels and we Skyped. Kathryn explained how the Birthing Project began. In 1988, she was the fiscal administrator with the California State Department of Health. Kathryn told me, "The point of the Birthing Project was to try to reduce the cost, the financial burden of taking care of babies that were born drug exposed." In trying to figure out how to confirm data about Black women's birth rates, and to identify the root cause of adverse births, Kathryn contacted the CDC. She recalled:

> They said, "Whatever the number is for the general population in any city, you can always just double that, it will be correct, because you can always expect Black babies to die two to one." That was an assumption I never expected—our babies to die two to one. When I asked why, the gentleman on the phone said because "Black people don't have strong families." And that gave me an idea. That is when the Birthing Project went from volunteers to sister/friends. That was our strength.

Kathryn thought that drawing on the skills of public health nurses, who had always been the Health Department's foot soldiers, was a good idea. At that time, California had lost about 30 percent of its public health nurses. Her idea was to bring together birth mothers with public health nurses—who could serve as the eyes and ears of the Health Department. She developed a project that drew from the past and from a community care model. From her perspective, Black people "always took care of each other," even when they did not speak the same language. "That was our saving and grace—making family. And that became the Birthing Project's structure."

The Birthing Project is a prenatal program that asks mentoring women to connect with one pregnant woman and be her "sister" throughout the pregnancy and the first year after the birth of the baby. Women taking care of women and providing support was part of Kathryn's own history, as she comes from a family who understood that their lives were entwined with the lives of others in their community.

Kathryn Hall-Trujillo was born in Moscow, Arkansas, and raised in the nearby town of Pine Bluff, in the far southeastern part of the state. The oldest of nine children, Kathryn lived with her maternal grandmother and also spent time with her paternal grandmother, both of whom lived in Arkansas, and also with her mother and stepfather in California. Both her maternal grandmother—Miss Dorothy—and her grandmother's sisters, and her father's side of the family had a tremendous impact on her about the importance of social justice. Although Kathryn spent a lot of time with her maternal family, she also spent time with her paternal family. Miss Viola, her father's mother, had another son, Ben. Her Uncle Ben Grinage, was the project director for the Student Non-violent Coordinating Committee (SNCC) in Arkansas (US Congress 1963, 1314). Privy to the SNCC's organizing tactics, Kathryn says when she was in the tenth grade she overheard SNCC members planning demonstrations and marches, as they sat at the table in Miss Viola's kitchen.

Kathryn's most poignant memory of her maternal grandmother, Miss Dorothy, was when the two of them walked all over Pine Bluff. "We would walk all over town. And she would just say 'How do' to people on their porches. We would fish, cook, and listen to music at the local juke joints. Some of my fondest memories are of me sitting under the table at a juke joint, eating ice cream and listening to her laugh."

Her grandmother's death was, in part, what drove Kathryn to develop a model of helping other women. When her grandmother died, Kathryn says she "damn near lost my mind." Continuing, Kathryn said softly, "I could not believe it. I could not imagine life without my grandmother. She died, I believe, from food poisoning. She might have been forty-nine." Kathryn's family was informed that when Miss Dorothy got sick, she died because the white doctor didn't come to the Black neighborhood after dark. "I was driven by that. It was a great injustice," Kathryn said.

The Birthing Project, which has been replicated in more than 100 communities in the United States, Canada, Central America, and Africa, assists young women through their pregnancies and decreases the risk for low birth weight and infant mortality. "Big Sisters" (and in one case a "Big Brother") undergo training and learn to support their "little sisters." She or he should be prepared to serve as an advocate on the little sister's behalf. The project creates a sense of belonging and connection among Black women. As Kathryn explained, "It reestablishes a collective witness to Black births in order to legitimate children's existence."

Evaluations of the program are limited. However, one evaluation of the Birthing Project in Tennessee reveals the promise of the project. Lillian Q. Maddox-Whitehead is the director of the Adolescent Pregnancy, Prevention, and Parenting Program of the Metro Davidson County Nashville Public Health Department in Nashville, Tennessee. In a study she authored, she describes the program's efficacy. Her findings show that from 2003 to 2008, 96 percent of the Birthing Project babies in the Nashville program were born at term. Moreover, the infant mortality rate was zero (Maddox-Whitehead 2008).

Within a year after the Birthing Project began, it secured an office. The project staff decided that they needed their own clinic and developed models of care that seemed intuitive. For instance, one of the programmatic actions they implemented was turning the waiting room into a living room. Women talked to each other there, "just like you might do during family time," Kathryn stated. That was where childbirth and parenting education took place. They "did it in a circle, because people think they are the only ones who are going through something. But we had to stop, because one of the licensing people from the Department of Health, who I knew, said I was violating confidentiality. So, I had to stop it. But now it is like the centering models they use." Kathryn was referring to the CenteringPregnancy model, the group prenatal program that Sharon Rising started and trademarked in 1993, discussed earlier in the previous chapter.

In the 1980s, group prenatal care was a new idea to help women manage their pregnancies in the company of other women. However, a review article comparing prenatal group care to traditional care both undermined group prenatal care and then said it worked. The article was contrary to the praise often bestowed upon this model: it found "no significant difference in the rate of preterm birth in group compared with traditional care" (Carter et al. 2016, 558). Ironically, the same article also noted that in a subgroup analysis, *the rate of preterm birth among African Americans participating in group care was significantly lowered.* Despite being a positive prevention model that improves the birth outcomes of African American women, its impact was written off as insignificant. Viewing the success of a preventive project that helps Black women's birth outcomes as "insignificant" is tied to antiblackness. Research of this type, that seemingly privileges the medicalization of prenatal care and childbirth while downplaying the potential of a model of care that can be beneficial to women of color, is an extension of medical racism.

The Birthing Project used group prenatal care as a support mechanism. Additionally, the model embraced a perinatal access initiative; that was how it received funding. Such initiatives provide coordinated services such as supportive services, information, and resources to prevent and reduce infant and maternal illness and death. Some of the indicators that Birthing Project advocates examined to understand problems that pregnant women faced included the number of prenatal visits made and kept, well-baby care visits, and well-woman care visits. The project found that the average woman in the group did not receive a well-woman visit. Nor, did she make a visit before getting pregnant. This led the group to decide it was going to support women. Kathryn told me, "We decided we would support mothers. Women need to know that they are cared about. And sometimes they need someone to affirm their intuition." In her opinion, women may not follow their instincts because they are not supported.

Throughout this book, we have seen numerous examples of women having instincts about their health that are dismissed, such as Ashley's saying she knew something was wrong with her pregnancy because of her high blood pressure, yet no one paid attention to it, and Yvette knowing that her pregnancy was high-risk, but her instincts that she needed to be monitored were dismissed by her physician. Both cases illustrate Kathryn Hall-Trujillo's point about women having instincts regarding their health but being written off. She said, "I can't tell you how many women get sent home, even though they know something is wrong."

Highlighting Kathryn Hall-Trujillo's thirty-year-old Birthing Project, which has successfully reduced adverse birth outcomes for African American women, is important in addressing the birthing disparities of Black women's pregnancies compared with whites. Using a prevention model, Kathryn Hall-Trujillo created a space to address a public health problem and was successful in doing so, yet her work is largely absent from the research on preventive approaches to address premature birth and infant and maternal mortality. What Hall-Trujillo started thirty years ago resonates with what Black women training as radical birth workers and advocates are doing today: helping women to plan what kind of births they want and how they want to do it, in an effort to minimize the medicalization of the process. In other words, birth planning is an empowering act that seeks to disrupt the medicalization of birthing that tends to diminish women's autonomy.

Birth work is not limited to prenatal care and labor. Advocating for women across the reproductive spectrum is a fundamental aspect of what radical birth workers do. For instance, among the midwives and full-spectrum doulas I interviewed, they provide care for a range of reproductive experiences that include abortions, prenatal care, postnatal care, menopause, and loss. Shortly after completing the first draft of this book, I entered a doula training program whose curriculum includes learning about supporting families, including single, queer, and straight families; breastfeeding support; the physiology of labor; relaxation techniques; and how to assist during home births. Importantly, the training included the history of Black women's reproduction in the United States. Many doulas and midwives are radical because they see the connection between Black women's reproductive history, the services they provide, and their role as advocates and activists. Those connections are woven into the justice work in which they participate, which calls for a radical transformation of practice and care for people giving birth.

Birth Workers and the Racial Politics of Pregnancy, Labor, and Birthing

Efe and I were supposed to speak for an hour, which turned into two and a half hours, which turned into more frequent interactions as we attended doula workshops. Efe is young, in her twenties, and is a full-spectrum doula. Her practice includes working with heterosexual families, queer families, and families with multiple spouses. Born in the United States to Nigerian parents and raised in the South, Efe has been a doula since 2014 and had assisted with more than forty births, when we met in 2016. As a doula and doula trainer, in her birth work Efe focuses on sharing with her clients the role that racial politics has played in Black people's reproductive lives, although Black people are not the only group she serves. Efe identifies as a radical Black doula, which to her means understanding the history and politics of reproduction and racism in the United States from prior to enslavement to the present. Making linkages between the practice of birth justice to broader justice movements takes the form of developing and building relationships with the community in which one is working and responding to injustice. Barbara Katz Rothman (2016) rightly notes that in birthing movements, people seek change through individual education, and the focus on effecting change in this manner is precisely how Efe sees her role.

Of course, I wanted to know what Efe thought of the impact of radical birth work, to which she responded, "People are not paying attention or concerned with young Black doulas and what we are doing. But I feel like we are shifting the birth work. We are infiltrating, we are going in to health departments and hospitals." To take one example: each month, she meets with a group of birth workers to discuss organizing strategies to address the kinds of racist injustices they see in medical settings.

Efe is among the birth workers whose politics are very clearly enmeshed with reproductive and racial justice. Organizations such as Trust Black Women have emerged in solidarity with Black Lives Matter to promote the value of Black women and families and respect the decisions Black women make to determine their own lives. This includes having access to abortions, economic resources, and the ability to have or end pregnancies. Trust Black Women, created in 2010, and the Black Lives Matter movement, created in 2012, joined ideological and political forces because the lives of Black people were in peril. Both organizations grew out of the need for self-determination and liberation of Black people and did so under the leadership of Black women.

Catching Babies

Jennie Joseph, aged fifty-nine, is arguably one of the most famous Black midwives in the United States. She is of West Indian descent, born in England, and has been practicing as a midwife in Orlando, Florida, for nearly thirty years. Jennie says she was called to midwifery when she was sixteen; she knew she wanted to be a midwife after seeing a row of incubators in a hospital. In one of the incubators was a baby, and Jennie was in awe that it was just a few hours old. Jennie attended midwifery school and remarked to me that in all the time she practiced in London, there was only one maternal death at her hospital, and it resulted from the mother having a blood- clotting disorder. Later, after she arrived in the United States, she reentered midwifery after experiencing what she described as medical racism.

Jennie had endometriosis, and a doctor she was working for offered to treat it. He performed laser surgery and multiple laparoscopies, which resulted in Jennie needing to have a hysterectomy and removal of both ovaries. "I did not understand the politics of reproduction back then. I feel like I was taken advantage of because I was a Black woman, my ova-ries were dispensable and so was my uterus. That doctor made money off of me with those multiple surgeries, and I ended up with surgically-induced menopause at age thirty." As a result of that experience, Jennie decided to open a home birth practice, which grew into a thriving birth center, and she was determined to offer services to women of color. The birth center provides continuity of care combining support, education, health care, and system navigation—essentially a comprehensive care model. If a woman choses to have a hospital-based birth, as a midwife, Jennie sees her role as an intermediary, one who negotiates between the medical structure and the woman. Jennie does this work, she says, be-cause the system is capitalist; it does not center the patient, and it is not set up to do what is right by women. When I asked how she made this determination, Jennie replied, "Because an entire shift of nurses can be on staff and yet something still happens, particularly to people of color. There really is no accountability; not for doctors or anyone who is on the hospital staff, the institution protects itself first and foremost, leaving the patients to fend for themselves." And, she said, it is not just a class issue. "It is racism, classism and sexism, all three!" Jennie concluded by saying that she is overwhelmed that the United States has no impetus to make broad-based change for practices that leave women feeling that they have been exploited and treated badly. "Institutional racism is sanctioned, and it truly is a matter of life and death."

Sakina O'Uhuru (2013), another Black home birth midwife, who is fifty-six, began her journey toward midwifery because she felt that African American women were not provided a sacred place give birth. Many years ago, she said, "I saw women were having medicalized births that were 'owned' by someone else. I thought it was possible to have a birth outside of a hospital setting." Sakina had a home birth practice for fourteen years and, like Jennie, has delivered close to a thousand babies. Jennie's and Sakina's outcomes have been extremely positive. Between them, there have been no more than three adverse outcomes with either the mothers or the babies they "caught."

Catching babies is what midwives call what they do when a baby is birthed. The craft or art of birthing is one that midwives prepare for, and one of the most prized attributes they possess is that they "do not rush births, they do not rush women in to cesarean sections when laboring goes slowly" (Rothman 2016, 16). Midwives do not risk births, as medical sociologist Barbara Katz Rothman (2016) argues; they have skills and are part of movements that work on social systems, offering checks and balances to the biomedical industry. Being uneasy with the medicalized options that are available for birthing, midwives and birth workers are responding to the desire for less commodified births.

Two other birth workers of color, Tamika Middleton and Cara Page, also view birth work as an extension of political work and are part of movements to decommodify birthing, especially for Black women.

* * *

As I approached Tamika Middleton and Cara Page in the lobby of the hotel where Tamika was staying, they greeted me with broad smiles and open arms. I had never met Tamika before but immediately felt a connection. I was thrilled that we were going to spend time together conversing about birth work and reproductive justice. Tamika had flown up to New York from Georgia to do a training session for health care professionals with her reproductive justice training partner, Cara. If the past was any indication, I had no doubt that the training was fantastic, because I had seen Cara lead one of most extraordinary workshops on the medical-industrial complex at a reproductive activists' conference. During the session, she had used an entire wall to create a timeline, using Post-it notes that summarized various examples of medical exploitation. It was stunning to see a visual expression of medical atrocities.

Tamika is a thirty-three-year-old doula and midwife in training. Her relationship to birth work is completely integrated with the other forms of social justice work in which she is engaged, including food and environmental justice. As a child, Tamika wanted to be an obstetrician. She recounted that when she was seven years old, her mother was pregnant with twins. "One passed away in utero but they did not know that. The other was strangled in the cord. It was traumatic. It was a very heavy experience for me." Then, when her brother was born, her mother almost died. "I wanted to do something so that it wouldn't happen again."

After Hurricane Katrina devastated parts of Texas and Louisiana, Tamika moved to Atlanta to attend graduate school. Just a few weeks into grad school, Tamika, who had no health insurance, discovered she was pregnant. The hospital closest to her school was a public hospital where she went for prenatal care. Tamika told me that her experience was one of humiliation: "I felt thoroughly degraded by the experiences I had there. Hospital staff held assumptions about my age, marital status, education level, and class status because I was uninsured. That is when my friend recommended a home birth midwife." The home birth midwife, in her opinion, "was powerful," and it was that experience that led Tamika to do birth work.

Cara, a forty-seven-year-old justice worker who identifies as Black of mixed ancestry, said she came to birth work and reproductive justice as a result of the racism surrounding her own birth. Nearly fifty years ago, Cara's mother—a white woman—gave birth to Cara, and for three days the nurses kept mother and child separated and tried to convince Cara's mother to put her baby up for adoption because she was Black of mixed heritage. Her mother refused to be intimidated and demanded to see her child. Informed by that past, Cara developed a nuanced understanding of the medical-industrial complex and its control of Black people's lives. Cara told me that she does not "want any part of that kind of journey." She and her partner, who is trans, are a queer interracial couple. They are planning to have children, and Cara does not want to be separated from their child for any reason, especially not due to race or gender.

Both Tamika and Cara, like other birth workers, see that the racial politics of birth work is manifest at the intersection of racism and medicalization, which combined to denigrate Black people's worth. Thus, as Cara pointed out, another aspect of the racial politics of birth work "centers on mobilizing against the medical-industrial complex, the scientific racist state, and private and corporate practices." For example, according to Cara, physicians/surgeons built the ob-gyn industry off of enslaved African women's reproductive capabilities. Both the medical-industrial complex and scientific racism have informed policy and legislation, which, she argues, "facilitates population control that negotiates our lives only as labor or objects to be sold." To understand the exploitation of Black people in the realm of reproduction, we can refer back to J. Marion Sims and other medical men who experimented on enslaved Black women, as Cooper Owens (2017) describes in her book on the origins of American gynecology. These experimentations represent one form of exploitation to which Cara referred. We might also consider that tests such as amniocentesis and ultrasounds are income generators for the medical industry. While they are the standard of care, that does not shield such tests from being overused. Or, as we saw earlier, Dr. John Lantos described the yield that NICUs provided for hospitals in the 1990s. More recently, an article in *Business Insider* pointed out that premature infants' admission to an NICU can account for 50 percent or more of the total clinical revenue base for a hospital (Halperin 2014). In other words, the capital generated by NICUs is invaluable—perhaps worth more than preventing prematurity itself. Cara drove home her final point: "When we think about medical care and race, we have to think about the relationship to the profit-driven medical industry. We have to think about the construct of race within a medical industry that is rooted in the preservation of cis, white, male, straight, able-bodied Christian concepts of wellness and existence."

Black women and people lose because the medical and caring economies have little investment in their well-being, safety, and value. That is the reality against which reproductive justice advocates fight. As a movement, reproductive justice seeks to identify racism and disparity where they exist and to effect change. Another option is to reduce dependency on medical systems, which some of the birth workers I interviewed see as one reason for the rise in out-of-hospital births. Births at birthing centers and home births, as well as the inclusion of a birth team, can ensure that Black births matter in ways that center dignity, the right to birth, and the right to feel safe no matter one's gender, race, and/or class. Radical birth workers help to create that safe space by supporting women's autonomy and treating people who are pregnant with dignity. Radical birth workers are trained to provide support both throughout the pregnancy and after the birth of the baby. This is precisely what Crystal and Keely, whom we will meet later, imagined for their respective pregnancies, labor, and birthing experiences.

Crystal's Birth Story

Crystal Rainey was excited to share her birth story, which included having a doula. Crystal is a twenty-eight-year old Black woman who is married and has one child. Although she looks like she may have just graduated from college, Crystal actually graduated with a bachelor's degree in psychology when she was twenty-two years old. She made sure to tell me that has only been pregnant one time. Stressing this fact was a fundamental signpost of her story, as proof that she did not fit the stereotype that young Black women have lots of children.

When she became pregnant, Crystal did not have health insurance, but that was fine with her because she had hoped for a home birth with a midwife. Instead, she had a doula and planned to be at a midwife-staffed birthing center. Her choice was an accommodation she made because her husband, James, had apprehensions about an out-of-hospital birth. As Crystal told me:

> Having a doula was a compromise. If I had done things my way, I would have had the baby at home. I would have taken all of my money out of my 401k and had a midwife. But my husband was concerned. The compromise was I would go to the birthing center, and if something happened I could go to the hospital. It was the first time he had heard about home births. So, I thought, "OK, this is your kid too" [she laughs], and I wanted to be fair.

Antiblackness influenced Crystal's decision to have a doula—a decision that was calculated based on the devaluation of Black life in US society. The social and political climate in which we live was of great concern to Crystal, who told me, "Black men are not valued; Black children are not valued." "You have Trayvon Martin," she continued, "and that brought me a lot of anxiety." When I asked her to explain, Crystal said, she thought that if she gave birth to a little girl, "she might not have a father, since Black men are killed by police. If I have a son, then I might not see him grow up; he would either be killed or incarcerated." Therefore, Crystal wanted a positive birthing experience. Fear of losing a child or family member to police violence holds many Black women emotionally hostage. As we have seen, studies reveal that racism creates particular stressors that disrupt Black women's pregnancies. Indeed, one report found that pregnant African American women are stressed about the likelihood that their children will someday have negative encounters with police (F. M. Jackson et al. 2017). Crystal was unquestionably right to be concerned.

Crystal was also resolute in her desire to use the least amount of medical intervention possible during her labor. This included not wanting an epidural, the pain reliever that numbs the back during labor. Epidurals have a host of effects, including that they may slow labor, and thus require the use of Pitocin, which speeds up labor. Both these drugs increases the chances of a C-section.

Researchers have studied the racial differences in pain management by medical professionals and found that nonwhite patients are less likely to receive pain management (Staton et al. 2007; K. M. Hoffman et al. 2016). However, white women are more likely to receive epidurals in labor than women from other racial and ethnic groups, due to perceived fragility. Yet, a 2014 study found that women of color were more likely to face pressure to *accept* epidurals but then experience pain medication *failure*. The failure is accompanied and complicated by the fact that medical professionals may not adequately listen to their patients and take their pain and anxiety seriously (Morris and Schulman 2014). This is yet another egregious example of medical racism, and the failure to manage pain is likely rationalized by the obstetric hardiness syndrome.

* * *

Crystal found and worked with a doula in order to assume as much control over her labor and birth as possible. She said:

> I was determined to have a peaceful birth. I thought that if the birth was peaceful, then everything from there on would be peaceful. I just imagined that the birth would be representative of the rest of our relationship [between her and her child]—that it would set the precedent for the rest of our lives.

Crystal was at forty weeks when she began laboring on a Monday. She called her doula and went to the birthing center, but due to meconium aspiration, she had to be transferred to a hospital.[2] When Crystal arrived at the hospital, she had already been in labor for a day and a half, and she was tired. But her doula was present, which helped. "When medical staff asked me questions, my doula, Adowa, would reframe open-ended questions as yes or no, so that I would not have to expend so much energy." Or, her doula would say, "Can you give her a minute?" This was the kind of support that Crystal, like other women who had doulas and midwives, craved—someone to manage the medicalization of their labor and birthing, if they had to have a medical birth at all. Crystal ended up having a C-section, in the presence of her doula and husband, which made her feel better.

The birth did not go the way Crystal planned. She did not want an IV or an epidural. She wanted to have skin-to-skin contact when the baby, Junior, arrived. In fact, she only saw Junior, who was named after his father, briefly after he was born. She said, "It was frustrating. But my doula was there with me and she was helpful. They showed Junior to me and they were like 'OK, he has to go to the NICU because meconium is present.'" Crystal believes that the hospital kept Junior in the NICU longer than necessary in retaliation for her wanting to have a birth of her choosing. For example, after two days, she found out from an NICU resident that Junior's lungs looked clear. Crystal's suspicion that Junior was not released for five days as punishment for her forthrightness was affirmed by both her husband and her doula.

I asked Crystal why she had wanted a doula in the first place, and she told me, "You know, I thought about the politics of having children. I wanted to control my pregnancy." Crystal took pride in what she had

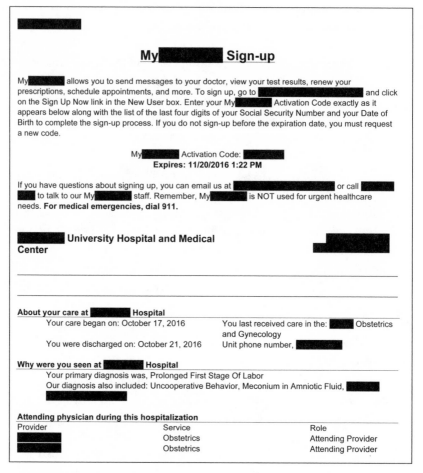

Figure 6.1 Discharge papers

accomplished in terms of knowledge acquisition and having developed a birth plan. But then, when she was in the hospital, all the work she had done to prepare her birth plan went out the window. She said she became a little depressed because she was made to feel that it was inconvenient, even wrong, to ask for what she wanted. And, for reasons that were unclear to her, her discharge papers indicate that she was admitted to the hospital because she was uncooperative (Figure 6.1). Crystal was stunned because Junior was in the hospital for five days. She and her husband drove there every day to see him. NICU staff would not permit her to feed him on demand, she said, but would make her return later. So, she acquiesced to the doctors and nurses mostly because she "did not want to be labeled as being a bad mom. I did not want to end up having my child taken away from me." She was made to feel that her desires were unimportant. Regardless, Crystal said, "I wasn't fighting by myself. My doula was there to make sure I was OK."

Keely's Birth Story

Keely, who was thirty-eight years old at the time of our interview, and identifies as Black-biracial, was born in Kingston, Jamaica. She holds a bachelor's degree and works part-time as a legal secretary. The mother of two sons, Keely and her younger son Caleb, who was eight months old at the time, met me at the Brooklyn Library at Grand Army Plaza on a rainy June afternoon. We met through Efe, who was Keely's doula and had asked her if she wanted to be interviewed. Keely was happy to oblige.

Keely began her birth story by telling me how she came to want a doula in the first place. Her first pregnancy was so horrific due to serious medical complications that she feared getting pregnant a second time, waiting thirteen years to have another child. Besides her first son having meconium aspiration syndrome and being admitted to an NICU, Keely also had a C-section and was put in a medically induced coma due to excessive bleeding. For her second pregnancy, Keely was determined to have a midwife and doula because she did not want to go through another experience like the first.

Efe introduced Keely to prenatal yoga and offered nutritional advice. When Keely was frustrated with being pregnant because she was "so big," Efe provided emotional support. They were in touch two to three times a month throughout the pregnancy, and in the last month they made contact weekly. Although she was just past term, Keely wanted to labor at home as long as possible, which she did with Efe's encouragement.

When Keely went into labor, she was admitted to the hospital when she was dilated eight centimeters. The doctors offered her an epidural, which Keely declined. Efe was present throughout the labor; she dimmed the lights and made sure Keely was comfortable. She massaged Keely's back and helped her through the labor by reminding her of the breathing techniques they had practiced. By the time the doctors came in, they said it was time to push and she did. She recalled:

> So, I pushed for about eighteen minutes, and he came out! I could not believe that he came out after two big pushes. At one point, there were about eighteen medical students in my room. Most of the women at the hospital that night, who were in labor, had epidurals. I was the only one that night who had a vaginal birth. They wanted to see it! But Efe told them to get out!

The other important contribution Efe made toward Keely's labor and birth concerned Keely being at forty weeks. In the last week or so of Keely's pregnancy, every time she went to the doctor, she was encouraged to have labor induced by Pitocin. Emily Martin observed in *The Woman in the Body* (1987) that Black women are given Pitocin more often than other women, which often leads to the need for a C-section. Keely completely rejected Pitocin, and Efe worked with her to maintain the integrity of her birth plan, which included giving birth free of medication and laboring at home as long as possible. Keely was at forty weeks and did not want a labor induction, and each time she was pressured to do so, Efe supported Keely's decision to return home. Because she rejected the medical advice on each visit, Keely had to sign a waiver acknowledging that she had gone against the physician's recommendation.

At forty weeks, instead of being manipulated into being induced, Keely depended on Efe to share various strategies to initiate labor. At Efe's suggestion, Keely walked, gently bounced on a birth ball that pregnant women use to relieve pelvic pressure, and ate fresh pineapple. Although there is no research proving the efficacy of these natural strategies, fresh pineapple does contain the enzyme bromelain, which is believed to contribute to cervical ripening. In less than twenty-four hours after eating the pineapple, Keely went into labor.

It is possible that Keely would have gone into labor even if she had not eaten the pineapple. But the larger point is that she labored on her own, at home, and with no medical intervention. Had she been administered Pitocin, her labor would have conformed to a medical schedule rather than to that of her own body.

* * *

Sitting on the floor, at 8:00 on a Sunday morning, were almost twenty women, mostly Black and Latinx, along with some Asian women and white women. They were young, many in their late twenties or thirties. We were all there for the doula certification class. The first day focused on the politics of reproduction and how enslavement and settler colonialism set a precedent for the way Africans' and Native Americans' reproduction was colonized. I moved around on the floor trying to find a comfortable way to sit on pillows. For most of us, the only thing that eased the discomfort was that our attention was completely focused on the trainer, Chanel. Chanel, whom we met earlier, is the founder of Ancient Song Doula. Birthing justice is her passion. She left a corporate job to start Ancient Song Doula and is sincere about the role doulas can play in decreasing premature births and infant and maternal mortality. Conducting trainings and being a doula is Chanel's full-time job. Her commitment to preventing adverse birth outcomes among Black women has led to her being a consultant to the New York City Department of Health, and she is active in national efforts to train other organizations that want to start doula programs. Many other radical doulas work two jobs so that they can offer their services to people regardless of their ability to pay.

The doulas and birth workers I interviewed believed that their work was essential in addressing and ameliorating the larger political forces that shape maternal and child health care. Supporting women through pregnancy, labor, and birth is a way to navigate structures of oppression within the medical environment and to shift the ways that care is provided. As Tamika recounted the birth work she had done, she mentioned that several people she has worked with have described how it felt to make self-determining decisions about their births in partnership with a support person. They intentionally chose fewer interventions— such as epidurals or Pitocin—and avoided surgeries, making a significant difference in their birth experiences and subsequent recovery. The benefits of doula care are increasingly being accepted as social support during labor and even some medical professionals and policy makers recognize that doula care is an important component of birthing (Meyer, Arnold, and Pascali-Bonaro 2001). Recent research shows that it is cost-effective and also helps to reduce preterm births. Doula support is associated with "lower cesarean rates and fewer obstetric interventions, fewer complications, less pain medication, shorter labor hours, higher infant Apgar scores, and also shows the potential for reducing racial-ethnic disparities" (Kozhimannil et al. 2016, 21). Recognition of the importance of prevention through other models of care is expanding. On a small scale, state Medicaid programs and managed care organizations are reimbursing for nonmedical assistance from a doula.

Doulas and midwives can have very intense interactions with their clients as they get to know each other and develop birth plans. Upon first meeting with a doula, some mothers want to talk about their lives. Some want the doulas to talk to partners and family members, inviting them into the conversation and planning. Sometimes the first conversation may not even relate to the pregnancy. Efe told me that she has gone on prenatal visits that lasted for three hours and there was no mention of the pregnancy. The point is to build a friendship. In doing this, the doulas offer childbirth education; they inform parents about racial disparities in childbirth and in maternal and infant mortality rates; and prepare them for what a medical relationship can be like when a woman goes to the hospital.

Kathryn, Efe, Jennie, Sakina, Tamika, Chanel, and Cara are all radical Black birth workers who understand that birth support is a right for people in all communities. And they understand how race, class, sexuality, and gender identity impact pregnancy outcomes. One of their goals is to bring together reproductive health and social justice. As for many other birth workers, the point of their work is to curtail negative birth outcomes.

Birth workers committed to the tradition of justice work and movement building are not solely helping to navigate a birth. They are part of a rich history of Black activism. They are engaged in the labor of caring and advocating for Black people's right to reproduce (or not) and seek to eliminate or reduce people's feelings of being manipulated and disrespected. Generally, birth workers I spoke with were opposed to the medical structure that does not respect people's desires to assert their right to have a pregnancy and birth in the way they choose. But even when birth workers oppose medicalization, they may still practice in medical spaces because they are there with clients who may have chosen to be in a medical setting. Or, they had to be in that setting for reasons related to a birth complication. In the end, wherever they are, midwives engage in skills-based practices, and doulas provide care that can shift the terms of the medical commodification of birthing, by offering an alternative to the systems that may perpetuate racism. While doulas and midwives may serve as a bridge in laboring and birthing processes, many believe that they should also participate in transforming the systems that place women and their children at risk.

Conclusion

Throughout my research, people regularly sent me articles, blog posts, and videos that took up the issue of race, racism, premature birth, and infant and maternal mortality. They posted items on my Facebook page and tagged, instant messaged, or e-mailed me. Even people I interviewed sent me sources. Every article or video I received made the emotional work of researching Black women's medical encounters harder to bear. Each article or video was a devastating reminder of the societal failure to address Black women's reproduction. For instance, a former student sent me an article that appeared in *Bitch Media* by journalist Vanessa Mártir (2017), who explores the many challenges Black women face during their pregnancies and after the birth of their infants. Then there was the woman who urged me to listen to the TED Talk by Miriam Zoila Pérez (2016), a doula who became a journalist and gives talks about the intersection of race, class, and illness. Her solution to the problem of racism and women's birth outcomes looks to the provision of radically compassionate prenatal care. In an article entitled "Why Black Birth Matters," Jamilla H. Webb (2016), writing for the Black Women's Blueprint—an organization that seeks to empower women of African descent to erase gender, race, and other disparities—argues that Black women are on the cusp of a crisis. She says that despite advances in medical innovation, Black women continue to have the most deplorable health outcomes in the United States. Her recommendation centers a synergistic approach that involves self-care, as well as participation by other Black women in the caregiving process. Another article that appeared in BabyandBlog made its way to my inbox. "It Takes a Village: Resources for Black Moms to Advocate for Healthy Childbirth" describes one Black woman's experience with medical providers. This blog post offers suggestions about contacting the hospital's ombudsman to make complaints (Mathis 2015). *The Root* published a piece by Dr. Joia Crear Perry (2016), on Black maternal mortality rates. Dr. Perry, an ob-gyn, situates the issue as a domestic and international crisis.

Of all the articles, reports, and videos I received, the February 15, 2017, issue of *The Nation* made an especially strong impression. The cover read "Black Births Matter" and the articles inside were by Zoë Carpenter (2017) and Dani McClain (2017). Carpenter examines how racism puts Black mothers and their children at risk for mortality, and McClain shares the story of own her pregnancy and the fight to give birth to a healthy baby. What drew me in was the front cover image (Figure 7.1). Cover images can do a lot of work to illuminate a topic, and the image of the mother and child, by artist Louisa Bertman, captured my attention, reminding me of the carved wood Baule masks from Côte d'Ivoire. The mother's embrace was so captivating because it was both tender and desperate. She held on to her child as if for dear life.

Dear life.

Dear life somehow seems related to afterlife. To me, the phrase is an iteration of the afterlife of slavery. Bertman's image called to mind both a historical and a contemporary reproductive vulnerability. It visually and viscerally represents what I have written about in this book—the aftereffect of slavery, the impact of medical racism, the desperation of vulnerability, and the hope of receiving prenatal and postpartum care differently.

In the preceding chapters, I have tried to analyze the perceived impact and meaning of race and racism for Black women based on their interpretation of interactions they and their family members had with doctors and nurses while their infants were in the NICU. I demonstrated the persistent crisis of premature birth, pregnancy, and birth outcomes by contextualizing what I learned about those subjects using historical documents that explicate the racial and racist dimensions of medical care. I accomplished this task only partially, by speaking and spending time with a number of people whose professional work centers on maternal and child health. There are others who could have been part of this project, such as pregnant women and their obstetricians. I could have spent time with them to see how racism *emerged* in the context of the medical care they received. However, as Rayna Rapp so cogently points out, "Complex cultural objects—and I would add subjects such as pregnancy, prematurity, race and racism—have no theoretical or methodological boundaries" (1999, 306). These subjects have so many possible entry points. In the end, I came to understand from parents, doctors, nurses, public health workers, and birth workers some of the

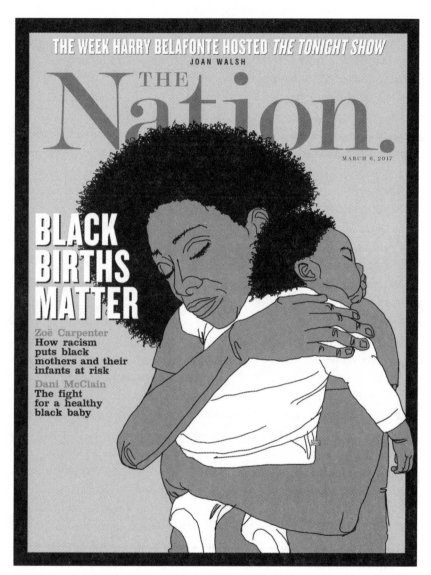

Figure 7.1 "Black Births Matter," in *The Nation*

cultural specificities of medical interactions. Those who were part of this project and the paths I took offered a unique look at how class cannot be so easily segregated from race when thinking about prematurity and what medical racism feels like.

One of the major points this book has made is that the distance between poor, low-income, and middle-class and professional Black women's birth outcomes is a short one. The class structure in US society is ostensibly a strategy for accessing sets of privileges that supposedly transcend race and racism. Of course, we know that is not the case. To believe that one's educational attainment and insurance coverage will serve as a protective mechanism against adverse birth outcomes in an anti-Black society is ideological pablum and offers a false sense of security. I wish this statement was less true, but time and again parents' social positions and recollections affirmed its veracity.

Investigating the content of Black women's medical interactions with nurses and doctors was somewhat unexpected, as I mentioned earlier. However, listening to women and birth advocates discuss mistreatment, neglect, or dismissal revealed quite a bit about how medical racism appears. When medical racism is interpreted by those who have been at the receiving or witnessing end (as often happens with doulas and midwives), the circumstances under which racism is expressed are haunting. This book has shown that medical racism has traveled through time, and the vestiges of its practice continue to show up. It also appears in discourse and data, and through deflection and redirecting blame.

Drawing on the concept of the afterlife of slavery as a biopolitical project, I have shown how earlier forms of medical racism, with origins in Black women's treatment during the era of slavery may influence the treatment and even outcome of Black women's reproductive health today. I demonstrated the temporality and intersection of adverse birth outcomes and race, and I situated the relationship between these subjects in the context of scientific racism of the 1800s. I used documents to shed light on how earlier histories of ideology and practice are mirrored in contemporary medical racism. Taking the position that medical racism is an example of the afterlife of slavery, various chapters reiterated racism's grammar. Thus, regardless of when a medical encounter took place, the stories—from historical sources and interviews—reflected uncanny resemblances even across more than a hundred years, in shacks, excellent hospitals, public hospitals, or clinics. These uncanny resemblances remained regardless of where or when women lived.

Medical racism operates through discourse and data. Risk data deploy statistics and numbers to legitimate differences or risk factors between groups of people. That legitimation rests on spurious assumptions about the Black body. Medical practice, research data, and public policies are replete with racist discourse about the pathology of the Black body, and all are instances of the afterlife of slavery. Conversations with March of Dimes staff revealed the inadequacies of a public health approach that indexes racial disparities as a strategy to generate moral outrage against racism, which is the cause of racial disparity.

Finally, this book found that medical racism operates in many forms. We can see that in some instances, racism takes on the form of deflection, which occurs when medical professionals and researchers suggest that Black women's adverse birth outcomes are the result of self-destructive behaviors, such as smoking. Despite research challenging these presumptions, Black bodies are tethered to the etiology or cause of giving birth prematurely.

My interviews indicate that Black women must contend with what anthropologist Christen Smith, in her discussion of the politics of blackness in Brazil, calls "repertoires." The repertoires of racism include "gestures, looks, glances, and movements" (2016, 12) that women perceive as disrupting the care they receive during and after their pregnancies. The repertoires of racism exist in the crevices and creases of a conversation, in the space between a comment and a pause. If doctors and nurses give dismissive looks or make a woman feel unworthy, that also constitutes a repertoire of racism. It may involve stereotyping a patient, which can lead to a misdiagnosis, or setting aside a woman's concerns about the fears she has for her health, her newborn's health, or the treatment of her partner.

For many of the women in this book, racism is the explanation for why during their pregnancies doctors did not address their health concerns, even when the women insisted that something was wrong. The repertoires of racism are etched onto Black women's reproductive lives and serve as reminders that the care Black women receive in the medical system is attenuated (Berlant 2011) through what I view as diagnostic lapses.

Diagnostic lapses are an outcome of medical racism in which professionals make or neglect to make medical decisions, thus exacerbating the vulnerabilities of a racially or ethnically marginalized group. A diagnostic lapse is flexible and can also operate in other contexts, such as ones that stem from sexism. Such lapses occurred in the care of many women whose stories appear in the pages of this book. Examples of diagnostic lapse can also be found in media accounts. For example, African American tennis star Serena Williams experienced a diagnostic lapse when she insisted that she needed to have a scan and have heparin administered after she had a C-section. She knew her body well enough to recognize that something was awry, but a nurse dismissed her concerns, thinking she was foggy from having just given birth. As it turned out, Williams had several blood clots in her lungs. Medical personnel at the highly regarded hospital where she had given birth made a lapse by neglecting to take her seriously (Haskell 2018).

Conceptually, diagnostic lapses serve another purpose. They offer an alternative to the social determinants explanation so often used to answer the question, why do Black women have such high rates of premature birth? "Social determinant talk" refers primarily to low-income people with poor health and results from structural discrimination such as high rates of incarceration, economic instability, and lower educational attainment (Focus for Health 2017). However, social determinants, like any framework, cannot explain every bad outcome. They certainly do not explain all the outcomes of the women who are part of this research, which makes the social determinants argument less convincing.

Indeed, this book points to a necessary revision in the risk profile associated with prematurity and other birth outcomes. The emphasis on class—specifically poverty—as the cause of Black women's unfavorable birth outcomes suggests that class mobility is the intervention that will result in more favorable births for them. By contrast, I have argued that Black women's birth outcomes starkly testify to the outcomes of medical racism, and that to avoid having to deal with the issue of racism, public health and medical professionals deploy the social determinants argument in much the same way as the neonatologists I interviewed skirted discussions of race—as a deflection.

Yet, as we know, avoiding talking about or naming race does not preclude the existence of racism, particularly since Black women's pregnancy, labor, and birthing is one medium through which medical racism is carried out. Certainly, in the case of Black women's pregnancy and birth, we find the discourses of risk formed within discourses of race.

Of course, my inquiry begs the question, how do we address Black women's birth outcomes? Quite possibly, we can start by making more options available for prenatal care and birthing. We can draw on the cultivated wisdom of those who have studied the craft of childbirth. As sociologist Keisha Goode (2014) suggests in her work on midwifery, one way to address adverse outcomes is by broadening prenatal care and birthing options to create a culture that embraces home births, birthing centers, and the inclusion of skilled birth workers and advocates. In other words, we can rethink models of care that might transform how we approach pregnancy, labor, and birth. Some birth workers suggested that having a certified midwife or a home birth is preferable to medicalized births. Thus, we can increase the number of birth centers, support home birth, and promote and develop more collaborative models of hospital-based care. According to retired obstetrician Dr. Leslie Farrington, a woman who is low-risk and wants less intervention usually is better off seeing a midwife for prenatal care and delivery. Although, Dr. Farrington pointed out, even some low-risk women may prefer anesthesia and having a C-section, which requires being in a hospital setting.

Given that we know outcomes are better when comprehensive care is provided to childbearing people, we might also consider reframing pregnancy so that it is viewed not only as a risk but as a life event—unless, of course, there is an actual risk. Because radical birth workers take reproductive justice seriously, and many see their role as preventive, they operate strategically and skillfully to increase successful birth outcomes and survival of Black women. The birth workers in this study believe in comprehensive care, which depends in large part on listening to their clients. One might argue that more gynecological and obstetric professionals should embrace this approach. In her book on having cancer and moving through the tumultuous world of testing and therapies, S. Lochlann Jain quotes physician and author Rachel Ramen: "Perhaps the most important thing we ever give each other is our attention" (2013, 217). Parents, birth workers, and Dr. Farrington stressed the importance of having doctors and nurses pay attention to women's concerns. Dr. Farrington argues that it is important for there to be good communication between patients and their clinicians because that communication is key to partnering in the care process: "If a medical professional—be they a physician or a midwife—is dismissive of patient concerns, or unwilling to hold a dialogue or participate in shared decision-making, it is usually in the best interest of the patient to find a clinician who takes into account their values, needs, and preferences. Seeking recommendations from their community will be important in that search."

Dr. Farrington's advice to seek out care that is indeed "caring" and attentive may help to stave off problems before they arise, making it possible to rely less on interventions that are deployed after the fact to correct wrongs that took place during initial care, such as diagnostic lapses. Intervening, whether through NICU technology or public health initiatives, is not enough to address racism. Indeed, there are two core problems with an intervention-only approach. First, interventions are an after-the-fact approach and overshadow the importance of prevention. Second, and most germane to this book's focus, is that interventions are unable to address racism. NICUs do not address racism; charts showing racial disparities do not address racism; health promotion campaigns focused on patients' behaviors and habits do not address racism.

Therefore, how do we address racism and undo the history that has rendered Black bodies so different through the medicalized approach to pregnancy, labor, and birthing? Is it necessary to look at each Black woman and size up her pregnancy as a potential risk, or to use the power of medicalization to control her birth, deny her symptoms, and then make the risk of an adverse birth outcome an actualized event?

My goal in writing this book was to understand how Black women interpreted the care they received during their pregnancies and during labor and birth. My study has shown that, in terms of pregnancy risk, racism can be conjured up by the medical system's past. It is thus fundamentally important that medical and health care professionals who have been trained and work in that system be willing to take responsibility for their own behaviors and biases. *They* must look racism in the face and question the ways that the system within which they work might contribute to racist outcomes, draw from racist discourse, or perpetuate racist ideas. To move closer to reproductive justice, we must address medical racism. It is in fact possible, if there is the will. Hopefully this book has provided some insights to guide that process, helping to improve the health and safety of Black mothers and their babies.

ACKNOWLEDGMENTS

Generally, I believe that when you walk down a path, the unevenness of the road and possible detours represent opportunities to engage with choices, move barriers, and possibly break falls with your hands or your heart. The world looks different when there is a roadblock. It looks different when you have fallen; you may look up to see life from below or may look down and see it from above. You may look from side to side, but the field of vision is quite different from when you are three feet higher. So, typically, I embrace all those vantage points. This same sentiment encompasses how I feel about people, those who move in and out of my life, offering new ways of seeing the world. My tendency has been to walk closely with the people I have met. We become kindred, even if only for a while, and I almost always remember some extraordinary moment we shared. The intent of this acknowledgment page is to express my sincerest gratitude for all the people I have met on the path to here. Many of you held my hand and walked with me, or very near, as I tried out new ideas and engaged with new fields of study—science and technology, medical anthropology, and history—for which I am grateful.

To every parent whose child was born prematurely or with a congenital disease and was admitted to a neonatal intensive care unit, I am honored that you relived those moments with me and entrusted me with your stories. I hope I have done them justice. Every doctor, nurse, social worker, and birthing advocate, please know that you opened my field of vision about the problem of prematurity and the place where some of its consequences are, or are not, resolved—the NICU. You took the time to show me around and to discuss your frustrations and joys, for which I am so grateful.

Sometimes you have a dream, and the primary reason you understand it is because somebody catches the dream with you. I have many dreamcatchers in my life, but the first three who wove the beautiful web that allowed me to hold on to the idea of this project were Vanessa Agard-Jones, Monica Casper, and Annie Menzel. Each one of them had faith that I could do this work and convinced me to push forward—even when what I was doing was unclear to me. Another group of dreamcatchers was the Race, Politics, and Reproductivities Working Group. It has been an honor to be in dialogue with such amazing women—Christa Craven, Risa Cromer, Daisy Deomampo, Nessette Falu, and Natali Valdez. I also thank Karen Baird, Sean Brotherton, Melissa Checker, Zeynep Kubilay, Yanique Lowe-Williams, Jeff Maskovsky, Brenda Murphy, Ashanté Reese, and LaKisha Simmons for their support and brilliant insights. Chris Danguilan, Shaka McGlotten, Andrea Queeley, Abigail Rabinowitz, Rayna Rapp, Wendi Schnaufer, Evans Valerie, and Margot Weiss listened as I thought this project out, providing constructive engagement at various stages. A special thanks to Elizabeth Chin, whose friendship and final read made this a much better book.

Now and again, you meet people and have no idea what role they will play in your life. One such person was Lisa Guido, an avid movie- and theatergoer and a person for whom fun times are a fine art! Thank you for introducing me to Gina Braun, who became my "smoother of the way." Gina, you are fierce—so very, very fierce.

Michelle Fine, Mark Schuller, and Oneka LaBennett—each of you invited me to give lectures early on in this research. This allowed me to share and learn from audiences whose intellectual generosity inspired new avenues for me to consider.

After years being away from the reproductive justice movement, Toni Bond helped me find my way back to doing reproductive justice work. Toni, along with Lynn Roberts, Andrea Williams, and Andrea Queeley, are sister/friends who have made the world a much better feminist place.

I am fortunate to have worked with three amazing graduate assistants. Yasemin Ozer, Brenna McCaffrey, and Lee Gensler worked on various stages of this book, and I am grateful for their commitment and care.

When I think back over the years, to the people who have been the rocks of my life, I would say that Elizabeth Chin, Christa Craven, Sue Hyatt, Antoinette T. Jackson, Jeff Maskovsky, Shaka McGlotten, and

Leith Mullings have kept around me a circle of comradeship and love like no other. I admire and adore each of you.

In writing this book, I received many gifts. The first was meeting new colleagues who have similar visions of justice. I consider myself fortunate to have been in the company of amazing scholars whose work has influenced my thinking. Laura Mauldin, Laury Oaks, and Samuel K. Roberts, I am so glad that I took whatever path I did that led me to each of you. Another gift I received was the wisdom of the reviewers. Thank you for your careful and considerate reading of the manuscript. I appreciate your thoughtful critiques. My gratitude goes to NYU Press and to my editor, Jennifer Hammer. Jennifer saw the value of this book and took it under her wing. I thank you for your tremendous support, and many thanks to your assistant, Amy Klopfenstein, Alexia Traganas, and the copy editor, Susan Ecklund.

One day I took a chance and cold-called the March of Dimes. A wonderful woman answered the phone and connected me to the administrators with whom I ultimately spent nine months in conversation. Thank you to those who gave of their time and acknowledged the importance of working work with a social scientist.

To my family: Mom, Ricci, Sadan, Deirdre, Dan, India, Liz, Alex, Ethan, Susana Fried, the Jacksons, and Uncle Max/Myron Kalin—thank you for being the family you are.

Antoinette Jackson, you read these chapters repeatedly. You listened as I talked incessantly about this project and, with love, helped shape this book. You held me close when I needed to stop or rest. And then you urged me to keep going. I am blessed that we stand beside each other.

If you do not see your name here, it is not because I do not consider your influence in my life important. Do not take it as a slight: I am older, and I forget names. But I never forget the feeling we probably shared. Just know that you walk with me, and I, with you. Always.

Finally, this book is dedicated to Dalgis. Dalgis, it is not likely I will ever see you again, but you were born just a few weeks after the 2016 election. Your parents generously gave me permission to witness your birth, and your mother's nurse/midwife asked me to do some small tasks that I interpreted as assisting in your birth. Because I was allowed to stay in the birthing room, I saw how much your parents love you. Witnessing your birth gave me hope at a moment when the world was reeling in the face of many manifestations of racism, sexism, anti-immigrant sentiment, and antigay backlash. But when you emerged with that last miraculous push, I remembered once again that what we do in this world may seem small and insignificant, but we must keep pushing. Your birth gave me a renewed sense of purpose. Gracias, mi querida.

Aché

NOTES

PREFACE

1 All names are pseudonyms to protect the confidentiality of participants, except where noted.

2 I conducted this search on July 6, 2017, entering the term "Black women premature birth" for the specific dates 01/01/2007 to 07/01/2017 and using "All Types" for the result type. Results included articles on infant mortality, preterm births, and NICUs.

3 I refer to labor and birth or birthing rather than delivery when describing women's experiences. To deliver is to take and hand over or to set free. To birth is an act or process that signals a greater degree of autonomy.

INTRODUCTION

1 "Prematurity" and "preterm" are often used interchangeably. However, some scholars and researchers delineate between the two, noting that "preterm" refers to giving birth prior to thirty-seven weeks, and prematurity is when an infant is born before the organs are sufficiently developed. Among some of my informants the distinction was a professional one: "preterm" was associated with obstetrics, and "prematurity" was addressed by neonatologists. Like the March of Dimes, I use "prematurity" and "preterm" interchangeably to describe a birth prior to thirty-seven weeks, which may or may not include lack of functional maturity.

2 When working on my first book, *Battered Black Women and Welfare Reform: Between a Rock and a Hard Place* (Davis 2006), I faced a similar conundrum. In the interest of contributing to policy changes about the perils of welfare reform, I wrote about Black women's lives and their being battered. I often omitted some of the more disturbing details. In both cases, for that project and this one, women implored me to share their stories, hoping to elucidate the nuanced ways that they experience racism to a broad audience in order to effect change.

3 I intentionally capitalize "Black" because it refers to people of the African diaspora, who constitute both a cultural group and a condition. Although I use the terms "African American" and "Black" interchangeably, I am referring to both US-born Black women and those born in other countries. In so doing, I do not mean to imply that all members of the African diaspora are as likely to have the same birthing outcomes as US-born African American women. Where individuals used the term "African American" or "Black" to describe themselves, I do so as well.

4 All Kids is the program that Illinois offers to children who require comprehensive and affordable health insurance; it also covers prenatal care.

5 Magnesium sulfate is a tocolytic, which slows contractions. Its stated purpose is to address the pregnancy-induced hypertension that results from placenta previa. However, there are conflicting data about the association between placenta previa and hypertensive disorder in pregnancy. See, for example, Yin and Liu 2015.

6 Ultrasounds are considered to be standard prenatal care. Ashley said that she was concerned about her pregnancy and requested a second ultrasound. Her request for another one was refused, which is unusual in part because ultrasounds can be used in the evaluation and management of placenta previa (Jodicke et al. 2012).

7 Across the reproductive spectrum, African American women also have higher rates of contracting sexually transmitted infections and, along with Latinx women, account for 80 percent of reported female HIV/AIDS diagnoses (Center for Reproductive Rights n.d.). African American women are three times as likely as white women to have an unintended pregnancy (Center for Reproductive Rights n.d.).

8 The story of Kim Anderson, featured in the episode "When the Bough Breaks" from the documentary series *Unnatural Causes* (Strain 2008), is emblematic of Black middle-class women's similar birth outcomes to low-income women's outcomes. The documentary reveals what has increasingly become one accepted cause of prematurity—the stress caused by racism and its influence on the adverse birth outcomes of non-Hispanic Black middle-class woman. In terms of adverse birth outcomes, the lines between poor or low-income women and middle-class Black women are not so rigid; in fact, they are porous.

9 Two other texts are important to mention in relation to this book. Social welfare scholar Lisa Paisley-Cleveland (2013) and anthropologist Janet Bronstein (2016) have published on Black infant mortality and preterm birth, respectively. Paisley-Cleveland's *Black Middle-Class Women and Pregnancy Loss: A Qualitative Inquiry* focuses on middle-class and professional Black women's loss and analyzes infant mortality that goes beyond the "poverty paradigm." While Paisley-Cleveland focuses on middle-class Black women, her goal is to *transcend* the poverty narrative. Stated differently, Paisley-Cleveland depicts middle-class women's experience of pregnancy and loss as a counternarrative to the experience of poor and low-income women. In contrast, this book does not position professional and educated Black women in contradistinction to poor or low-income women. Professional and educated Black women are not being cast as exceptional or different. The point is that there are similarities between Black women across class. Janet M. Bronstein's *Preterm Birth in the United States: A Sociocultural Approach* (2016) explores prematurity by examining the social, institutional, and cultural contexts in which preterm birth exists. However, no original ethnographic evidence contextualizes her description of preterm birth. Bronstein bases her discussion on an analysis of "large data sets accumulated for other purposes, such as paying insurance claims, recording births and deaths or monitoring hospital use in particular

states" (xiii). For example, data sets showing higher rates of prematurity among Black women run the risk of interpreting Black women as reproductive failures. Thus, data require stories for context.

10 Cross-disciplinary engagement with the afterlife of slavery has included historians, such as Leroy (2016); scholars of education (Wun 2015); and comparative literature scholars (Womack 2017).

11 SisterSong was founded in 1997. At that time, sixteen organizations, made up of women of color, joined together to take on the role of representing themselves in terms of reproduction and the needs of their communities. Their goal is to advance policies and systems that benefit and impact the reproductive lives of women of color (http://sistersong.net).

12 Freud's concept of "the uncanny" is useful for talking about memories and feelings when revisiting the past. The uncanny is that which is thought to have been buried and may remain as such, but instead has been brought to the surface, creating a dynamic link between the past and the present (Freud [1919] 2003; A. T. Jackson 2016).

13 Throughout the book, I refer to a pregnant, laboring, or birthing parent as a woman because that is how interviewees identified themselves. In chapter 6, however, I intentionally use some derivative of the category "person or people." I do so in recognition of the fact that not all those who become pregnant, labor, and give birth identify as women but also because some of the birth workers I interviewed provided care and services to trans men.

CHAPTER 1. PREMATURE PREDICAMENTS

1 I am struck by Jacobs's bravery and agency in choosing to escape from her owner and tormentor. Other interpretations narrate Jacobs's escape as a form of self-authorization. See, for example, Weheliye 2014; Barrett 2014. While everyday forms of resistance must be accounted for (Scott 1985), we may caution against situating all forms of resistance equally as expressions of rebellion. This is particularly the case when those resistances are actualized in the face of accepting an established order (Gutmann 1993). An equally compelling example of resistance is the *very fact* that Harriet Jacobs wrote the book as a catalyst to support abolition.

2 Prior to 1989, the race of a newborn was attributed based on the race of the infant. Since then, race has been calculated based on the race of the mother.

3 The Children's Bureau was created in 1912. From 1912 through 1968, all the bureau chiefs were women. The first was Julia Lathrop (1912–21), followed by Grace Abbott (1921–34), Katharine Lenroot (1934–51), Martha May Eliot (1951–56), and Katherine Oettinger (1957–68).

4 There was a racial politics to registering births in the early twentieth century. During this time, midwives were required to report the race of both parents on birth certificates. For Black midwives attending births of mixed-race couples, that was dangerous because they either incriminated Black men in their community or risked imprisonment themselves if they did not report the race (G. Fraser 1998).

5 Shifts in the meaning of prematurity and viability have implications for thinking through the politics of abortion and the position that life begins at conception.

6 In the 1940s, Dunham wrestled with how to medically manage premature birth while simultaneously needing to draw attention to the scope of the problem. To address the latter, she had to determine the prevalence of the problem and made estimations about the rate of premature birth based on a Children's Bureau study published in 1925. In that study nearly 23,000 live births were recorded in eight cities (Woodbury 1925). According to that study, 5 percent of the births occurred prior to eight months—which was an indicator of premature birth. To estimate the incidence of premature births in 1944, Dunham relied on the 5 percent rate from 1925. Thus, for 1944 she estimated that of the 3 million live births that occurred that year, 150,000 births—5 percent of the 3 million live births—were premature (Dunham 1948, 11). Race was also calculated. That estimate was based on a John Hopkins study that put the incidence of live premature births at 10.7 percent; 60 percent of those births were of Negroes (Dunham 1948, 11).

7 A study published by the Institute of Medicine delineates six contributing factors to preterm birth. They are behavioral and psychosocial, sociodemographic and community, medical and pregnancy, biological pathways, the interaction between genes and the environment, and the role of environmental toxins. See Behrman and Butler 2007.

8 Labor induction and planned cesarean sections increased between 1990 and 2003. By 2003, according to *New York Times* science writer Jane Brody, one in five babies was born as a result of induced labor. Most often the beneficiary was the physician, who would schedule births during convenient times. But there are health risks associated with inductions that require cesarean delivery. Of course, when there are medical indications to induce labor, such as diabetes or high blood pressure, the benefits may outweigh the risks. Brody's article (2003) also reports that consumerism is part of the reason that C-sections have increased because obstetricians are concerned that their patients will find another physician if they do not comply.

9 Relman's discussion of the medical-industrial complex did not refer to medical equipment or pharmaceuticals. However, given the proliferation of technology and technologically assisted treatments, it is not unreasonable to consider how those suppliers, at this point, are part of the complex.

10 Myomectomy is the preferred treatment for women with fibroids who want to become pregnant. It involves surgically removing the fibroids, which allows the uterus to be left in place.

11 Some of the nurses interviewed for this project indicated that magnesium can only be administered for forty-eight hours.

12 According to the CDC, the twinning rate rose 76 percent between 1980 and 2009, primarily the result of ARTs that facilitate fertility (J. A. Martin, Hamilton, and Osterman 2012).

CHAPTER 2. INTO THE NICU

1 Because all of the children of parents I interviewed survived except one, I turned to a series of parental memoirs to understand the impact of premature birth and loss. The memoirs deploy a range of rhetorical strategies, including humor and martyrdom (see, for example, Degl 2013; Kemper and Sinconis 2010; K. Mathews 2012; A. Stevenson 2010).

2 LEEP stands for loop electrocautery excision procedure. A cone biopsy is a test that rules out or confirms cervical cancer. It involves excising a cone-shaped piece of tissue from the cervix and having it tested for cancer cells. An aggressive removal of a wedge of the cervix (i.e., too large a piece) can compromise the cervix's ability to maintain the integrity of a pregnancy.

3 I did not use the term "Latinx" during interviews and general conversations, knowing that hospital-based demographic data are not captured using this term.

4 I thank Jeff Maskovsky for helping me clarify this point.

CHAPTER 3. PREGNANCY AND PREMATURITY IN THE AFTERLIFE OF SLAVERY

1 MRSA is an infection caused by a type of staph bacteria that has become resistant to many of the antibiotics used to treat ordinary staph infections.

2 No doubt some white women are also treated with disregard during their pregnancies and after their babies are born. However, the cases with which we are most likely familiar involve women who are arrested and shamed for using drugs while pregnant or for not seeking prenatal care. And punitive approaches that control pregnant women are directed most often at women who are not white.

3 Fistulas are categorized in two ways: obstetric and traumatic. Obstetric fistulas are the result of prolonged labor; traumatic fistulas are the result of violent rape. Documentation of violent rapes in the Congo in 2003 revealed fistulas as a major health concern (Nordland 2006). It is interesting that most of the analyses about the fistulas that Sims "repaired" on enslaved women rely on the presumption that they were the result of labor and birthing, not rape.

4 The Strong Baby campaign was launched in 2011 and depended on the submission of babies' images to the Strong Baby Facebook page. The point of the campaign was to promote healthy behaviors for pregnant and new mothers with the overall goal of reducing the racial and ethnic disparity of infant mortality in Milwaukee ("We're Looking for Milwaukee's Next Strong Baby!," Serve Marketing, accessed June 21, 2018, http://servemarketing.org). In the press release for the 2016 Strong Baby campaign, Mayor Tom Barrett stated that he wanted every baby in Milwaukee to be a strong baby, and that it starts at home ("Strong Baby Campaign Promotes Home Visiting for Milwaukee Families," Milwaukee Health Department, www.unitedwaygmwc.org, September 28, 2016). One photographer for the campaign, Eric Sahrmann, said in an interview that babies in the photos are not just one baby. The producers used casting calls for

babies between three months and one and a half years, then chose ten babies, photographing each one individually and then digitally merging them to create synthesized images. Younger babies were used to compile the faces, and older children are used to compile the body (Murphy 2013). This example of "composite blackness" evokes the work of French ethnographic sculptor Charles Cordier, whose focus was the North African subject and represented nineteenth-century theories of art and racial difference. Cordier "professed himself to work from many models towards a racial type" (C. A. Nelson 2010, 23). It is interesting to consider the temporal consistency of this earlier form of "making" Black people and the production of blackness using composite images in the Strong Baby campaign.

5 Research shows that infants born to mothers who smoke during pregnancy are more likely to be born prematurely, have birth defects, or be low birth weight. Smoke is considered to be a toxic exposure that can influence birth outcomes. At the level of representation, there is often an association between race, smoking, and pregnancy. However, a number of studies contradict the assumption that Black women are more likely to smoke when pregnant. For example, in 1986, a vital statistics report showed that among nonsmoking pregnant women, the Black and white rates were the same. Among smoking pregnant women, white women were more likely to smoke than Black women (US Department of Health, Education, and Welfare, Public Health Service 1986). A 2006 study in Indiana showed higher rates of smoking among non-Hispanic whites than among non-Hispanic blacks (Rahmanifar 2006).

6 Scholar and activist W. E. B. Du Bois also experienced the loss of his son, Burghardt, who, in 1899, died of diphtheria at the age of two. Du Bois believed that if not for the dearth of medical services and facilities available to Blacks in Atlanta, his son might have lived. Du Bois documents his feelings in *The Souls of Black Folk*, in the chapter "The Passing of the First Born."

7 Historically, federal surveillance of Black people has been directed at those who are "politically suspicious." Recently the FBI developed a report to justify monitoring members of Black Lives Matter based on the presumption that they will resort to violence. The FBI believes that these individuals, who have been labeled Black identity extremists, are likely to target law enforcement officers (Federal Bureau of Investigation 2017). Monitoring Black people has been facilitated by technology applications such as SketchFactor, a crowdsourced safety mapping app. For example, residents in Washington, DC, invited users to search for or report "sketchy" behavior in a neighborhood. Nextdoor.com is another app that residents in Oakland, California, have used to register suspicious activity. Critics of both SketchFactor and Nextdoor, which have been billed as empowerment tools for community safety, say that the apps facilitate racial profiling (Marantz 2015).

8 An ileostomy is used to remove waste from the body when the colon or rectum is not working properly.

WITNESSING A BIRTH: AN INTERLUDE

1 While water immersion births are believed to be low-risk, there are some factors that raise concern. Gilber and Tooley (1999) discuss some of those risks. For example, if the mother has herpes, that can be problematic because herpes is transmitted easily in water. In addition, water immersion is not advised if preterm labor is expected, if the mother is having multiples, or if the baby is in a breech position.

CHAPTER 4. SAVING THE BABIES

1 In addition to the lack of programs for Black women, other groups had limited access to interventions. For example, in the Native American community in Montana, infants were almost three times more likely to die than whites, but the state did not have a full-time nurse on the reservations. There were also limited programs for Spanish-speaking populations.

2 Total parenteral nutrition (TPN) was also discovered in the 1960s and has been an effective intervention for premature infants. Also known as intravenous feeding, TPN is a method of getting nutrition into the body through the veins. The infusion of intravenous fluids was a turning point because the development of microinfusion pumps facilitated accurate administration of intravenous fluids to extremely preterm infants.

CHAPTER 5. NARROWING THE GAP OF BLACK WOMEN'S BURDEN

1 Entertainer Eddie Cantor coined the phrase "March of Dimes"—it was a pun on the popular 1930s newsreel known as The March of Time. The effort to raise awareness was also boosted by other personalities of the day, including Jack Benny, Bing Crosby, and Rudy Vallee.

2 Tuskegee University's Carver Research Foundation was instrumental in the development of Dr. Jonas Salk's polio vaccine. The production of the HeLa cell line involved maintaining a noncontaminating environment and the development of quality control. By 1955, the Tuskegee HeLa Project had shipped about 600,000 cultures, approximately 20,000 tube cultures per week. But "in 1954, Microbiological Associates, Inc. copied the template designed at the Carver Research Foundation and set up a large-scale cell culture factory in a former Fritos factory in Bethesda, Maryland. There, the company began mass-producing HeLa cells for global distribution, which became a multibillion-dollar biocapitalist industry. The NFIP closed down the Tuskegee HeLa cell factory due to competition from companies like Microbiological Associates" (Turner 2012, 10). This was, ironically, a cell-based instance of preventing Black reproduction by African Americans themselves, putting the control of such reproduction squarely outside the Black community.

CHAPTER 6. RADICAL BLACK BIRTH WORKERS

1 The Black women who were the founding mothers, and involved in coining the term and laying the initial framework, were Toni M. Bond-Leonard, the Reverend Alma Crawford, Evelyn S. Field, Terri James, Bisola Marignay, Cassandra Mc-Connell, Cynthia Newbille, Loretta Ross, Elizabeth Terry, "Able" Mable Thomas, Winnette P. Willis, and Kim Youngblood.

2 Meconium is the earliest stool of an infant. Meconium aspiration syndrome is a form of respiratory distress that occurs when a newborn has inhaled meconium into the lungs just before or around the time of birth.

BIBLIOGRAPHY

Abbott, Jodi Frances. 2017. "There Is Medication to Stop Preterm Births but Many Women Don't Get Treatment." *Washington Post*, October 29, 2017. www.washingtonpost.com.

Abbyad, Christine, and Trina Reed Robertson. 2011. "African American Women's Preparation for Childbirth from the Perspective of African American Health-Care Providers." *Journal of Perinatal Education* 10 (1): 45–53.

Abdou, Cleopatra M., and Adam W. Fingerhut. 2014. "Stereotype Threat among Black and White Women in Health Care Settings." *Cultural Diversity and Ethnic Minority Psychology* 20 (3): 316–23.

Adair, Fred L., ed. 1940. *Obstetrics and Gynecology*. Vol. 1. Philadelphia: Lea and Febiger.

Agency for Healthcare Research and Quality. 2012. *2012 National Healthcare Disparities Report*. Rockville, MD: US Department of Health and Human Services.

Ahmed, Sara. 2017. *Living a Feminist Life*. Durham, NC: Duke University Press.

American Academy of Pediatrics. 1936. "American Academy of Pediatrics: Proceedings, Fifth Annual Meeting. June 7, 1935." *Journal of Pediatrics* 8:117.

American College of Obstetricians and Gynecologists. 2013. "Study Finds Adverse Effects of Pitocin in Newborns." www.acog.org.

"Ancient Song Doula." n.d. Accessed February 23, 2017. www.ancientsongdoulaservices.com.

Andaya, Elise. 2014. *Conceiving Cuba: Reproduction, Women, and the State in the Post-Soviet Era*. New Brunswick, NJ: Rutgers University Press.

Anderson, Nina. 1947. "Clinical Considerations of the Premature Infant." In *Mitchell-Nelson Textbook of Pediatrics*, edited by W. E. Nelson, 260–364. 4th ed. Philadelphia: W. B. Saunders.

Ansell, David A., and Edwin K. McDonald. 2015. "Bias, Black Lives, and Academic Medicine." *New England Journal of Medicine* 372 (12): 1087–89.

Anspach, Renée R. 1993. *Deciding Who Lives: Fateful Choices in the Intensive-Care Nursery*. Berkeley: University of California Press.

Anzaldúa, Gloria. 1987. *Borderlands/La Frontiers: The New Mestiza*. San Francisco: Aunt Lute.

ASTHO. 2016. "Public-Private Partnership in Puerto Rico Leads to Increased Access to 17P and a Lower Preterm Birth Rate." Arlington, VA: Association of State and Territorial Health Officials.

Avery, Mary Ellen. 2000. "Surfactant Deficiency in Hyaline Membrane Disease: The Story of Discovery." *American Journal of Respiratory and Critical Care Medicine* 161 (4): 1074–75.

Avery, Mary Ellen, and Jere Meade. 1959. "Surface Properties in Relation to Atelectasis and Hyaline Membrane Disease." *American Journal of Disease of Children* 97:517–23.

Baer, Hans. 1990. "The Possibilities and Dilemmas of Building Bridges between Critical Medical Anthropology and Clinical Anthropology: A Discussion." *Social Science Medicine* 90 (9): 1011–13.

Baker, Jeffrey P. 1996. *The Machine in the Nursery: Incubator Technology and the Origins of Newborn Intensive Care*. Baltimore: Johns Hopkins University Press.

Balchin, Imelda, and Philip J. Steer. 2007. "Race, Prematurity and Immaturity." *Early Human Development* 83:749–54.

Balibar, Étienne. 2005. "The Construction of Racism." *Actuel Marx* 2 (38): 11–28.

Barrett, Lindon. 2014. *Racial Blackness and the Discontinuity of Western Modernity*. Urbana: University of Illinois Press.

Bassett, Mary T. 2016. "Beyond Berets: The Black Panthers as Health Activists." *American Journal of Public Health* 106 (10): 1741–43.

Behrman, Richard E., and Adrienne Stith Butler, eds. 2007. *Preterm Birth: Causes, Consequences, and Prevention*. The National Academies Collection: Reports Funded by National Institutes of Health. Washington, DC: National Academies Press. www.ncbi.nlm.nih.gov.

Berlant, Lauren, ed. 2004. *Compassion: The Culture and Politics of an Emotion*. New York: Routledge.

———. 2011. *Cruel Optimism*. Durham, NC: Duke University Press.

Berry, Diana Ramey. 2017. *The Price for Their Pound of Flesh: The Value of the Enslaved from Womb to Grave in the Building of a Nation*. Boston: Beacon Press.

Berry, Diana Ramey, and Deleso A. Alford, eds. 2012. *Enslaved Women in America: An Encyclopedia*. Santa Barbara, CA: Greenwood Press.

Bettie, Julie. 2014. *Women without Class, Girls Race, and Identity*. Berkeley: University of California Press.

Bigo, Didier. 2006. "Globalized (In)Security: The Field and the Ban-Opticon." In *Terror, Insecurity and Liberty: Illiberal Practices of Liberal Regimes after 9/11*, edited by Didier Bigo and Anastassia Tsoukala, 10–49. New York: Routledge.

Blakey, Michael L. 1999. "Scientific Racism and the Biological Concept of Race." *Literature and Psychology* 45 (1/2): 29–43.

Bolles, A. Lynn. 2013. "Telling the Story Straight: Black Feminist Intellectual Thought in Anthropology." *Transforming Anthropology* 21 (1): 57–71.

Bonaparte, Alicia D. 2015. "Regulating Childbirth: Physicians and Granny Midwives in South Carolina." In *Birthing Justice: Black Women, Pregnancy, and Childbirth*, edited by Alicia D. Bonaparte and Chinyere Oparah, 24–34. New York: Routledge.

Bonilla-Silva, Eduardo. 2002. "The Linguistics of Color Blind Racism: How to Talk Nasty about Blacks without Sounding 'Racist.'" *Critical Sociology* 28 (1/2): 41–64.

"Born in Slavery: Slave Narratives from the Federal Writers Project, 1936–1938." 1936. Georgia Narratives, vol. IV, pt. 4. Federal Writers' Project, United States Work Projects Administration.

Bowler, Isobel. 1993. "They're Not the Same as Us: Midwives' Stereotypes of South Asian Descent Maternity Patients." *Sociology of Health and Illness* 15 (2): 157–78.

Braun, Lundy. 2014. *Breathing Race into the Machine: The Surprising Career of the Spirometer from Plantation to Genetics*. Minneapolis: University of Minnesota Press.

Braverman, Paula. 2008. "Perspective: Racial Disparities at Birth: The Puzzle Persists." *Issues in Science and Technology* 24 (2). http://issues.org.

Bridges, Khiara M. 2011. *Reproducing Race: An Ethnography of Pregnancy as a Site of Racialization*. Berkeley: University of California Press.

Briggs, Laura. 2002. *Reproducing Empire: Race, Sex, Science and U.S. Imperialism in Puerto Rico*. Berkeley: University of California Press.

Brody, Jane. 2003. "As Cases of Induced Labor Rise, So Do Experts' Concerns." *New York Times*, January 14.

Bronstein, Janet M. 2016. *Preterm Birth in the United States: A Sociocultural Approach*. Switzerland: Springer.

Brosco, Jeffrey P. 1999. "The Early History of the Infant Mortality Rate in America: A Reflection upon the Past and a Prophecy of the Future." *Pediatrics* 103: 478–85.

Brown, Francis, IV. 1922. "Neonatal Death." *British Medical Journal* 2 (September): 590–93.

Browne, Simone. 2015. *Dark Matters on the Surveillance of Blackness*. Durham, NC: Duke University Press.

Brubaker, Rogers. 2004. *Ethnicity without Groups*. Cambridge, MA: Harvard University Press.

Bryant, Allison S., Ayaba Worjoloh, Aaron B. Cuahey, and Eugene Washington. 2010. "Racial/Ethnic Disparities in Obstetrical Outcomes and Care: Prevalence and Determinants." *American Journal of Obstetrics and Gynecology* 202 (4): 335–43.

Buchbinder, Mara, and Stefan Timmermans. 2013. "Affective Economies and the Politics of Saving Babies' Lives." *Public Culture* 26 (1): 101–26.

Budetti, Peter, Peggy McManus, Nancy Barrano, and Lu Ann Heinen. 1980. *The Cost-Effectiveness of Neonatal Intensive Care*. Washington, DC: US Congress, Office of Technology Assessment.

Burris, Heather H., Andrea A. Baccarelli, Robert O. Wright, and Rosalind J. Wright. 2016. "Epigenetics: Linking Social and Environmental Exposures to Preterm Birth." *Pediatric Research* 79 (1–2): 136–40.

Butler, Octavia E. 2001. *Wild Seed*. New York: Grand Central Publishing.

Campbell, Alexia Fernández. 2015. "Five Myths about Women of Color, Infertility and IVF Debunked." *Atlantic*, September 3. www.theatlantic.com.

Carpenter, Zoë. 2017. "What's Killing America's Black Infants? Racism Is Fueling a National Health Crisis." *Nation,* February 15.

Carter, Ebony B., Lorene A. Temming, Jennifer Akin, Susan Fowler, George A. Macones, Graham A. Colditz, and Methodius G. Tuuli. 2016. "Group Prenatal Care Compared with Traditional Prenatal Care: A Systematic Review and Meta-analysis." *Obstetrics and Gynecology* 128 (3): 551–61.

Casper, Monica J. 1998. *The Making of the Unborn Patient: A Social Anatomy of Fetal Surgery.* New Brunswick, NJ: Rutgers University Press.

Castanon, Alejandra, Rebecca Landy, Peter Brocklehurst, Heather Evans, Donald Peebles, Naveena Singh, Patrick Walker, Julietta Patnick, and Peter Sasieni. 2014. "Risk of Preterm Delivery with Increasing Depth of Excision for Cervical Intraepithelial Neoplasia in England: Nested Case-Control Study." *BMJ* 349 (November): g6223.

"CenteringPregnancy." n.d. Centering Healthcare Institute. Accessed February 18, 2017. www.centeringhealthcare.org.

Center for Reproductive Rights. n.d. "Addressing Disparities in Reproductive and Sexual Health Care in the U.S." Accessed January 23, 2017. www.reproductiverights.org.

Centers for Disease Control and Prevention. 1987. "Infant Mortality among Black Americans." *Morbidity and Mortality Weekly Report* 36 (1): 1–4.

———. 2002. "Infant Mortality and Low Birth Weight among Black and White Infants— United States, 1980–2000." *Morbidity and Mortality Weekly Report* 51 (27): 589–92.

———. 2013. "Factors Associated with Preterm Birth." https://stacks.cdc.gov.

———. 2015. "Births: Preliminary Data for 2014." *National Vital Statistics Reports* 64 (6): 1–18.

———. n.d. "Reproductive Health: Preterm Birth." Accessed December 19, 2016. www.cdc.gov.

Chapman, Elizabeth N., Anna Kaatz, and Molly Carnes. 2013. "Physicians and Implicit Bias: How Doctors May Unwittingly Perpetuate Health Care Disparities." *Journal of General Internal Medicine* 28 (11): 1504–10.

Children's Bureau, US Department of Health, Education, and Welfare, Social and Rehabilitation Service. 1967. *The Story of the White House Conferences on Children and Youth.* Washington, DC: US Government Printing Office.

Christie, Amos U., Ethel Dunham, Rachel Jenss, and Louis A. Dippel. 1941. "Development of the Center for Cuboid Bone in Newborn Infants: A Roentgenographic Study." *American Journal of Diseases of Children* 61 (3): 471–81.

Cocozza, Paula. 2015. "Poet Claudia Rankine: 'The Invisibility of Black Women Is Astounding.'" *Guardian*, June 29. www.theguardian.com.

Colen, Shelle. 1995. "'Like a Mother to Them': Stratified Reproduction and West Indian Childcare Workers and Employers in New York." In *Conceiving the New World Order: The Global Politics of Reproduction*, edited by Faye D. Ginsburg and Rayna Rapp, 78–102. Berkeley: University of California Press.

Collins, Patricia Hill. 1991. *Black Feminist Thought: Knowledge, Consciousness, and the Politics of Empowerment.* Boston: Unwin Hyman.

Commentary. 1897. "The Use of Incubators of Infants." *Lancet* 149 (3848): 1490–91.

Cooper Owens, Deirdre. 2017. *Medical Bondage: Race, Gender, and the Origins of American Gynecology*. Athens: University of Georgia Press.

Craven, Christa. 2010. *Pushing for Midwives: Homebirth Mothers and the Reproductive Rights Movement*. Philadelphia: Temple University Press.

Crenshaw, Kimberlé. 1989. "Demarginalizing the Intersection of Race and Sex: A Black Feminist Critique of Antidiscrimination Doctrine, Feminist Theory and Antiracist Politics." *University of Chicago Legal Forum* 140: 149–67.

Cromer, Risa. 2016. "Saving: Stem Cell Science, Christian Adoption, and Frozen Embryo Politics in the United States." PhD diss., Graduate Center, City University of New York.

———. 2017. "Waiting: The Redemption of Frozen Embryos through Embryo Adoption and Stem Cell Research in the United States." In *Anthropology of the Fetus: Biology, Culture, and Society*, edited by Sally Han, Tracy Betsinger, and Amy Scott. 171–99. New York: Berghahn Press.

Cruikshank, Barbara. 1999. *The Will to Empower: Democratic Citizens and Other Subjects*. Ithaca, NY: Cornell University Press.

Dart, Helen M. 1921. *Maternity and Child Care in Selected Rural Areas of Mississippi*. Rural Child Welfare Series No. 5. Bureau Publication No. 88. Washington, DC: US Government Printing Office.

Davis, Dána-Ain. 2006. *Battered Black Women and Welfare Reform: Between a Rock and a Hard Place*. Albany, NY: SUNY Press.

———. 2007. "Narrating the Mute: Racializing and Racism in a Neoliberal Moment." *Souls: A Critical Journal of Black Politics, Culture, and Society* 9 (4): 346–60.

———. 2016. "The Bone Collectors: Comments for Sorrow as Artifact: Black Radical Mothers in Times of Terror." *Transforming Anthropology* 24:8–16.

Davis-Floyd, Robbie E. 1992. *Birth as an American Rite of Passage*. Berkeley: University of California Press.

———. 2005. "Anthropology and Birth Activism: What Do We Know?" *Anthropology News* 46 (5): 37–38.

Degl, Jennifer. 2013. *From Hope to Joy: A Memoir of a Mother's Determination and Her Micro Preemie's Struggle to Beat the Odds*. Mahopac Falls, NY: Lemon Tree Publishing.

de Lauretis, Teresa. 1987. *Technologies of Gender: Essays on Theory, Film, and Fiction*. Bloomington: Indiana University Press.

De Lee, Joseph M. 1902. "Infant Incubation, with the Presentation of a New Incubator and a Description of the System at the Chicago Lying-In Hospital." *Chicago Medical Recorder* 22:22–40.

Deomampo, Daisy. 2016. *Transnational Reproduction: Race, Kinship and Commercial Surrogacy in India*. New York: NYU Press.

Dixon, Lydia Zacher. 2015. "Obstetrics in a Time of Violence: Mexican Midwives Critique Routine Hospital Practices." *Medical Anthropology Quarterly* 29 (4): 437–54.

Dominguez, Tyan Parker. 2010. "Adverse Birth Outcomes in African American Women: The Social Context of Persistent Reproductive Disadvantage." *Social Work in Public Health* 26 (1): 194–203.

Dominguez, Tyan Parker, Christine Dunkel-Schetter, Laura M. Glynn, Calvin Hobel, and Curt A. Sandman. 2008. "Racial Differences in Birth Outcomes: The Role of General, Pregnancy, and Racism Stress." *Health Psychology* 27 (2): 194–203.

Downey, Gary Lee, and Joseph Dumit. 1997. *Cyborgs and Citadels: Anthropological Interventions in Emerging Sciences and Technologies.* Santa Fe, NM: School of Advanced Research Press.

Draper, George. 1917. *Acute Poliomyelitis.* New York: Appleton-Century.

"Dr. Mary Ellen Avery. Biography." n.d. Changing the Face of Medicine. Accessed September 21, 2014. www.nlm.nih.gov.

Du Bois, W. E. B. 1963. *The Souls of Black Folk.* New York: Penguin Classics.

Duden, Barbara. 1993. *Disembodying Women: Perspectives on Pregnancy and the Unborn.* Translated by Lee Hoinacki. Cambridge, MA: Harvard University Press.

Dudley, Rachel. 2012. "Toward an Understanding of the 'Medical Plantation' as a Cultural Location of Disability." *Disability Studies Quarterly* 32 (4). http://dsq-sds.org.

Dumit, Joseph D., with Sylvia Sensiper. 1998. "Living with the 'Truths' of DES: Toward an Anthropology of Facts." In *Cyborg Babies: From Techno-Sex to Techno-Tots*, edited by Robbie E. Davis-Floyd and Joseph Dumit, 212–39. New York: Routledge.

Dunham, Ethel C. 1939. "The Care of Premature Infants." *American Journal of Public Health* 29: 847–55.

———. 1948. *Premature Infants: A Manual for Physicians.* Children's Bureau Publication 325. Washington, DC: Federal Security Agency, Social Security Administration.

Ehrenreich, Barbara, and John Ehrenreich. 1970. *American Health Empire: Power, Profits, and Politics.* New York: Random House.

Elliott, Sirikka, Rachel Powell, and Joslyn Brenton. 2015. "Being a Good Mom: Low-Income, Black Single Mothers Negotiate Intensive Mothering." *Journal of Family Issues* 36 (3): 351–370.

Epstein, Rebecca, Jamilia J. Blake, and Thalia González. 2017. *The Erasure of Black Girls' Childhood.* Washington, DC: Center on Poverty and Inequality, Georgetown Law.

Epstein, Steven. 2007. *Inclusion: The Politics of Difference in Medical Research.* Chicago: University of Chicago Press.

Farrell, P. M., and R. E. Wood. 1976. "Epidemiology of Hyaline Membrane Disease in the United States: Analysis of National Mortality Statistics." *Pediatrics* 58:167–76.

Federal Bureau of Investigation. 2017. "Black Identity Extremists Likely Motivated to Target Law Enforcement Officers." FBI Counterterrorism Division. https://privacysos.org.

Ferguson, Roderick A. 2004. *Aberrations in Black: Toward a Queer Color of Critique.* Minneapolis: University of Minnesota Press.

Fitzgerald, Ruth P., Michael Legge, and Julie Park. 2015. "Choice, Rights, and Virtue: Prenatal Testing and Styles of Moral Reasoning in Aotearoa/New Zealand: Choice, Rights, and Virtue." *Medical Anthropology Quarterly* 29 (3): 400–417.

Florido, Adrian. 2014. "Why Do Black Infants Die So Much More Often Than White Infants?" 89.3 KPCC, March 3. www.scpr.org.

Focus for Health. 2017. "Social Determinants of Health: 5 Key Elements You Need to Know." www.focusforhealth.org.

Foucault, Michel. 1997. "The Birth of Biopolitics." In *Ethics, Subjectivity, and Truth*, edited by Paul Rabinow and J. D. Faubion. New York: New Press.

Franklin, Sarah. 2007. *Dolly Mixtures: The Remaking of Genealogy*. Durham, NC: Duke University Press.

———. 2013. *Biological Relatives: IVF, Stem Cells and the Future of Kinship*. Durham, NC: Duke University Press.

Franklin, Sarah, and Celia Roberts. 2006. *Born and Made: An Ethnography of Preimplantation Genetic Diagnosis*. Princeton, NJ: Princeton University Press.

Fraser, Gertrude. 1998. *African American Midwifery in the South: Dialogues of Birth, Race, and Memory*. Cambridge, MA: Harvard University Press.

Frazier, E. Franklin. 1939. *The Negro Family in the United States*. Chicago: University of Chicago Press.

Freud, Sigmund. (1919) 2003. *The Uncanny*. Translated by David McLintock. London: Penguin Books.

Frohock, Fred M. 1986. *Special Care: Medical Decisions at the Beginning of Life*. Chicago: University of Chicago Press.

Fullwiley, Duana. 2011. *The Encultured Gene: Sickle Cell Health Politics and Biological Difference in West Africa*. Princeton, NJ: Princeton University Press.

Gamble, Vanessa Northington. 1995. *Making a Place for Ourselves: The Black Hospital Movement 1920–1945*. New York: Oxford University Press.

Gammage, Marquita Marie. 2015. *Representations of Black Women in the Media: The Damnation of Black Womanhood*. New York: Routledge.

Gantt, W. H. 1854. "Post-mortem Revelations of Case of Supposed Ascites or Pregnancy." *The Stethoscope: A Monthly Journal of Medicine and the Collateral Sciences* 4:336–37.

Gay, Roxane. 2017. *Hunger: A Memoir of (My) Body*. New York: HarperCollins.

Geiger, H. Jack. 1996. "Race and Health Care—An American Dilemma." *New England Journal of Medicine* 335: 815–16.

"German Measles." 1965. *New York Times*, April 25. http://query.nytimes.com.

Geronimus, Arline T. 1992. "The Weathering Hypothesis and the Health of African American Women and Infants." *Ethnicity and Disease* 2 (3): 207–21.

Gertz, Michelle. 2013. "'Why Do Our Mothers and Babies Die?': The Progressive Approach to Reducing National Rates of Infant and Maternal Mortality, 1909–1936." PhD diss., Sonoma State University.

Gilbert, R. E., and P. A. Tookey. 1999. "Perinatal Mortality and Morbidity among Babies Delivered in Water: National Surveillance Study." *British Medical Journal* 319 (August): 483–87.

Gilmore, Ruth Wilson. 2007. *Golden Gulag: Prisons, Surplus, Crisis, and Opposition in Globalizing California*. Berkeley: University of California Press.

Ginsburg, Faye D., and Rayna Rapp. 1995. *Conceiving the New World Order: The Global Politics of Reproduction*. Berkeley: University of California Press.

Giroux, Henry A. 2003. "Spectacles of Race and Pedagogies of Denial: Anti-Black Racist Pedagogy under the Reign of Neoliberalism." *Communication Education* 52 (3–4): 191–211.

———. 2006. "Reading Hurricane Katrina: Race, Class, and the Biopolitics of Disposability." *College Literature* 33 (3): 171–96.

Glenn, Evelyn Nakano, Grace Chang, and Linda Rennie Forcey, eds. 1994. *Mothering: Ideology, Experience, and Agency*. New York: Routledge.

Golden, Janet. 2001. *A Social History of Wet Nursing in America: From Breast to Bottle*. Columbus: Ohio State University Press.

González-Lopez, Gloria. 2011. "Mindful Ethics: Comments on Informant-Centered Practices in Sociological Research." *Qualitative Sociology* 34 (3): 447–61.

Goode, Keisha La'Nesha. 2014. "Birthing, Blackness, and the Body: Black Midwives and Experiential Continuities of Racism." PhD diss., Graduate Center, City University of New York.

Goodman, Allan. 2000. "Why Genes Don't Count for Racial Differences in Health." *American Journal of Public Health* 90 (11): 1699–1702.

Gould, Stephen Jay. 1978. "Morton's Ranking of Races by Cranial Capacity." *Science* 200 (4341): 503–9.

Guillemin, Jeanne Harley, and Lynda Lytle Holmstrom. 1986. *Mixed Blessings: Intensive Care for Newborns*. New York: Oxford University Press.

Guitiérrez, Elena R. 2008. *Fertile Matters: The Politics of Mexican Origin Women's Reproduction*. Austin: University of Texas Press.

Gurr, Barbara. 2015. *Reproductive Justice: The Politics of Health Care for Native American Women*. New Brunswick, NJ: Rutgers University Press.

Gutmann, Matthew C. 1993. "Rituals of Resistance: A Critique of the Theory of Everyday Forms of Resistance." *Latin American Perspectives* 20 (2): 74–92.

Hack, Maureen, H. Gerry Taylor, Dennis Drotar, Mark Schluchter, Lydia Cartar, Laura Andreias, Deanne Wilson-Costello, and Nancy Klein. 2005. "Chronic Conditions, Functional Limitations, and Special Health Care Needs of School-Aged Children Born with Extremely Low-Birth-Weight in the 1990s." *JAMA* 294 (3): 318–25.

Haines, Michael. 2008. "Fertility and Mortality in the United States." *EH.Net Encyclopedia*. Edited by Robert Whaples. http://eh.net.

Haldane, J. B. S. 1923. *Daedalus, Or Science and the Future*. London: Kegan Paul.

Hall, Stuart. 1980. "Race, Articulation, and Societies Structured in Dominance." In *UNESCO Sociological Theories: Race and Colonialism*, 305–45. Paris: UNESCO Press.

Halperin, Alex. 2014. "Prematurity Rates Are Too High—And Children's Hospitals Are Cashing In." *Business Insider*, June 4. www.businessinsider.com.

Haraway, Donna. 1997. *Modest_Witness@Second_Millennium.FemaleMan_Meets_OncoMouse: Feminism and Technoscience*. New York: Routledge.

Harmon, Paul H. 1936. "The Racial Incidence of Poliomyelitis in the United States with Special Reference to the Negro." *Journal of Infectious Diseases* 58 (3): 331–36.

Harris, Seale. 1950. *Woman's Surgeon: The Life Story of J. Marion Sims.* New York: Macmillan.

Hart, Tanya. 2013. "Can Numbers Lie? Race, Data Collection and Black and Italian Infant and Maternal Health Care in Early Twentieth Century New York City." *Western Journal of Black Studies* 37 (3): 169–82.

———. 2015. *Health in the City: Race, Poverty, and the Negotiation of Women's Health in New York City, 1915–1930.* New York: NYU Press.

Harwood, Robin, Stella Yu, and Laura Kavanagh. n.d. "Remembering Our Past, Building the Future: 100 Years of the Maternal and Child Health Research Program." Accessed October 29, 2016. www.essaydocs.org.

Haskell, Rob. 2018. "Serena Williams on Motherhood, Marriage, and Making Her Comeback." *Vogue.* February. www.vogue.com.

Henderson, M., and J. Kay. 1967. "Differences in Duration of Pregnancy." *Archives of Environmental and Occupational Health* 14:906–11.

Hess, Julius, II. 1922. *Premature and Congenitally Diseased Infants.* Philadelphia: Lea and Febiger.

Hill, Shirley A. 2016. *Inequality and African-American Health: How Racial Disparities Create Sickness.* Bristol, UK: Policy Press.

Hoberman, John. 2012. *Black and Blue: The Origins and Consequences of Medical Racism.* Berkeley: University of California Press.

Hoffman, Frederick L. 1896. "Race Traits and Tendencies of the American Negro." *American Economic Association* 11 (1–3): 1–329.

Hoffman, Kelly M., Sophie Trawalter, Jordan R. Axt, and M. Norman Oliver. 2016. "Racial Bias in Pain Assessment and Treatment Recommendations, and False Beliefs about Biological Differences between Blacks and Whites." *Proceedings of the National Academy of Sciences of the United States of America* 113 (6): 4296–4301.

"Honey Child." n.d. Central City Comprehensive Community Center. http://wheeler-a5cs.org.

Howell, Elizabeth A., Teresa Janevic, and Paul L. Herbert. 2018. "Differences in Morbidity and Mortality Rates in Black, White, and Hispanic Very Preterm Infants among New York City Hospitals." *JAMA Pediatrics* 172 (3): 269–77.

Hughes, Michelle M., Robert E. Black, and Joanne Katz. 2017. "2500-g Low Birth Weight Cutoff: History and Implications for Future Research and Policy." *Maternal and Child Health Journal* 21 (2): 283–89.

Hulsey, Thomas C., Greg R. Alexander, Pierre Yves Robillard, David J. Annibale, and Andrea Keenana. 1993. "Hyaline Membrane Disease: The Role of Ethnicity and Maternal Characteristics." *American Journal of Obstetrics and Gynecology* 168 (2): 572–76.

"Intergrowth 21st." n.d. Intergrowth 21st: The International Fetal and Newborn Growth Consortium. Accessed June 17, 2017. www.intergrowth21.org.

Ioanide, Paula. 2015. *The Emotional Politics of Racism: How Feelings Trump Facts in an Era of Colorblindness*. Stanford, CA: Stanford University Press.

Jackson, Antoinette T. 2016. "Exhuming the Dead and Talking to the Living: The 1914 Fire at the Florida Industrial School for Boys—Invoking the Uncanny as a Site of Analysis." *Anthropology and Humanism* 41 (2): 158–77.

Jackson, Fleda Mask. 2007. *Race, Stress, and Social Support: Addressing the Crisis in Black Infant Mortality*. Washington, DC: Joint Center for Political and Economic Studies.

Jackson, Fleda Mask, Sherman A. James, Tracy Curry Owens, and Alpha F. Bryan. 2017. "Anticipated Negative Police-Youth Encounters and Depressive Symptoms among Pregnant African American Women: A Brief Report." *Journal of Urban Health* 94 (2): 259–65.

Jacobs, Harriet. 1861. *Incidents in the Life of a Slave Girl*. New York: Oxford University Press.

Jain, S. Lochlann. 2013. *Malignant: How Cancer Becomes Us*. Berkeley: University of California Press.

James, C. L. R. 1989. *The Black Jacobins: Toussaint L'Ouverture and the San Domingo Revolution*. New York: Vintage Books.

Jo, Heui Seung. 2014. "Genetic Risk Factors Associated with Respiratory Distress Syndrome." *Korean Journal of Pediatrics* 56 (4): 157–63.

Jodicke, D., D. Maulik, P. Singh, P. Heitmann, and D. Maulik. 2012. "Role of Ultrasound in Pre-eclampsia." *Minerva Ginecologica: A Journal on Obstetrics and Gynecology* 64 (4): 293–308.

Jordan, June. 2002. *Some of Us Did Not Die: New and Selected Essays by June Jordan*. New York: Civitas Books.

Jorgensen, Anne M. 2010. "Born in the USA—The History of Neonatology in the United States: A Century of Caring." *NICU Currents*, June. http://static.abbottnutrition.com.

Kaiser Family Foundation. 2017. "Medicaid Enrollment by Race/Ethnicity. Timeframe FY 2011." www.kff.org.

Kanaaneh, Rhoda Ann. 2002. *Birthing the Nation: Strategies of Palestinian Women in Israel*. Berkeley: University of California Press.

Kemper, Michele Munro, and Jennifer Kemper Sinconis. 2010. *A Pound of Hope*. Issaquah, WA: PostScript Publications.

Kennedy, John F. 1962. "Special Message to the Congress on Health and Hospital Care. Feb. 9, 1961." Public Papers of the Presidents of the United States, John F. Kennedy. Washington, DC. https://quod.lib.umich.edu.

Kleinman, Daniel Lee. 2005. *Science and Technology in Society: From Biotechnology to the Internet*. Oxford: Blackwell.

Kluger, Jeffrey. 2014. "Saving Preemies." *Time*, June 2, 26–30.

Knight, Anna K., and Alicia K. Smith. 2016. "Epigenetic Biomarkers of Preterm Birth and Its Risk Factors." Edited by J. Craig and T. Mikeska. *Genes* 7 (4): 1–26. doi:10.3390/genes7040015.

Knight, Kelly Ray. 2015. *Addicted.Pregnant.Poor*. Durham, NC: Duke University Press.

Koudstaal, J., D. D. M. Braat, H. W. Bruinse, N. Naaktgeboren, J. P. W. Vermeiden, and G. H. A. Visser. 2000. "Obstetric Outcome of Singleton Pregnancies after IVF: A Matched Control Study in Four Dutch University Hospitals." *Human Reproduction* 15 (8): 1819–25.

Kozhimannil, Katy B., Rachel R. Hardeman, Fernando Alarid-Escudero, Carrie A. Vogelsang, Cori Blauer-Peterson, and Elizabeth A. Howell. 2016. "Modeling the Cost-Effectiveness of Doula Care Associated with Reductions in Preterm Birth and Cesarean Delivery." *Birth Issues in Perinatal Care* 43 (1): 20–27.

Kukla, Rebecca. 2005. *Mass Hysteria: Medicine, Culture, and Mothers' Bodies*. Lanham, MD: Rowman and Littlefield.

Ladd-Taylor, Molly. 1993. "Why Does Congress Wish Women and Children to Die? The Rise and Fall of Public Maternal and Infant Health Care in the United States, 1921–1929." In *Women and Children First: International Maternal and Infant Welfare 1870–1945*, edited by Valerie Fildes, Lara Marks, and Hilary Marland, 121–32. London: Routledge.

Lantos, John. 2010. "Cruel Calculus: Why Saving Premature Babies Is Better Business Than Helping Them Thrive." *Health Affairs* 29 (11): 2114–17.

Lathrop, Julia C. 1913. *Baby-Saving Campaigns: A Preliminary Report on What American Cities Are Doing to Prevent Infant Mortality*. Washington, DC: US Department of Labor, Children's Bureau.

Lea, Tess. 2008. *Bureaucrats and Bleeding Hearts: Indigenous Health in Northern Australia*. Sydney: University of New South Wales Press.

Leonard, Thomas C. 2016. *Illiberal Reformers: Race, Eugenics and American Economics in the Progressive Era*. Princeton, NJ: Princeton University Press.

Leroy, Justin. 2016. "Black History in Occupied Territory: On the Entanglements of Slavery and Settler Colonialism." *Theory and Event* 19 (4).

Levander, Caroline F. 2006. *Cradle of Liberty: Race, the Child, and National Belonging from Thomas Jefferson to W. E. B. Du Bois*. Durham, NC: Duke University Press.

Lewis, Carole Ione. n.d. "Whipper, Ionia Rollin (1872–1953)." *Black Past*. Accessed November 16, 2016. www.blackpast.org.

Lieberman, Ellice, Kenneth J. Ryan, Richard R. Monson, and Stephen C. Schoenbaum. 1987. "Risk Factors Accounting for Racial Differences in the Rate of Premature Birth." *New England Journal of Medicine* 317 (12): 743–48.

Lindenmeyer, Kriste. 1997. *"A Right to Childhood": The U.S. Children's Bureau and Child Welfare, 1912–1946*. Urbana: University of Illinois Press.

Lipsky, Michael. 1980. *Street-Level Bureaucracy: Dilemmas of the Individual in Public Services*. New York: Russell Sage Foundation.

Lorde, Audre. 1984. *Sister Outsider: Essays and Speeches*. Trumansburg, NY: Crossing Press.

Luker, Kristin. 1984. *Abortion and the Politics of Motherhood*. Berkeley: University of California Press.

———. 1996. *Dubious Conceptions: The Politics of Teenage Pregnancy*. Cambridge, MA: Harvard University Press.

Lyon, George M. 1941. "Epidemic Diarrhea of the Newborn. I. Clinicoepidemic Pathologic and Therapeutic Aspects." *American Journal of Diseases of Children* 61:427–44.

MacDorman, Marian F., and T. J. Mathews. 2011. "Understanding Racial and Ethnic Disparities in U.S. Infant Mortality Rates." National Center for Health Statistics. US Department of Health and Human Services, Centers for Disease Control and Prevention. NCHS Data Brief 74: 1–8.

Madan, Ashima, Sharon Holland, John E. Humbert, and William E. Benitz. 2002. "Racial Differences in Birth Weight of Term Infants in a Northern California Population." *Journal of Perinatology* 22 (3): 230–35.

Maddox-Whitehead, Lillian. 2008. "Birthing Project Nashville." Metro Davidson County Nashville Public Health Department.

Manton, W. P. 1910. "The Role of Obstetrics in Preventative Medicine." *JAMA* 55 (6): 159–75.

Marans, Daniel. 2015. "How a Prosecutor Managed to Blame a 12-Year-Old for Getting Killed by a Cop." *Huffington Post*, December 28. www.huffingtonpost.com.

Marantz, Andrew. 2015. "When an App Is Called Racist." *New Yorker*. July 29. www.newyorker.com.

March of Dimes. 2009. "Prematurity Campaign 2008 Progress Report." March of Dimes Foundation. www.marchofdimes.org.

———. 2011. "Special Care Nursery Admissions." March of Dimes Perinatal Data Center. www.marchofdimes.org.

———. 2016. "PeriStats." www.marchofdimes.org.

———. n.d. "Preterm Labor and Premature Birth: Are You at Risk?" Accessed January 23, 2017. www.marchofdimes.org.

Maron, Dina Fine. 2015. "Has Maternal Mortality Really Doubled in the U.S.?" *Scientific American*, June 8. www.scientificamerican.com.

Martin, Ashley E., Jo Ann D'Agostino, Molly Passarella, and Scott A. Lorch. 2016. "Racial Differences in Parental Satisfaction with Neonatal Intensive Care Unit Nursing Care." *Journal of Perinatology* 36 (11): 1001–7.

Martin, Emily. 1987. *The Woman in the Body: A Cultural Analysis of Reproduction*. Boston: Beacon Press.

Martin, Joyce A., Brady E. Hamilton, and Michelle J. K. Osterman. 2012. "Three Decades of Twin Births in the United States." NCHS Data Brief 80. National Center for Health Statistics. US Department of Health and Human Services, Centers for Disease Control and Prevention. www.cdc.gov.

Martin, Nina. 2017. "Black Mothers Keep Dying after Giving Birth: Shalon Irving's Story Explains Why." NPR. Accessed May 3, 2018. www.npr.org.

Mártir, Vanessa. 2017. "Can You See Me Now? The Fragility of Maternal Transition." *Bitch Media* (blog), August 31. www.bitchmedia.org.

Maternal Health Committee. 1942. "Selected Case Report of Maternal Death." *Virginia Medical Monthly* 61:35–37.

Mathews, Holly F. 1992. "Killing the Medical Self-Help Tradition among African Americans: The Case of Lay Midwifery in North Carolina, 1912–1983." In *African Americans in the South: Issues of Race, Class, and Gender*, edited by Hans Baer and Yvonne Jones. 60– 79. Athens: University of Georgia Press.

Mathews, Kasey. 2012. *Preemie: Lessons in Love, Life and Motherhood*. Hobart, NY: Hatherleigh Press.

Mathis, Dara. 2015. "It Takes a Village: Resources for Black Moms to Advocate for Healthy Childbirth." *BabyandBlog* (blog), December 10. http://babyandblog.com.

Mattingly, Cheryl. 2010. *The Paradox of Hope: Journeys through a Clinical Borderland*. Berkeley: University of California Press.

Mawdsley, Stephen E. 2010. "'Dancing on Eggs': Charles H. Bynum, Racial Politics, and the National Foundation for Infantile Paralysis, 1938–1954." *Bulletin of History and Medicine* 84 (2): 217–47.

———. 2016. *Selling Science: Polio and the Promise of Gamma Globulin*. New Brunswick, NJ: Rutgers University Press.

McClain, Dani. 2017. "What It's Like to Be Black and Pregnant When You Know How Dangerous That Can Be." *The Nation*, February 15.

McDonald, Katrina Bell. 2004. "Black Activist Mothering: A Historical Intersection of Race, Gender, and Class." PhD diss., Johns Hopkins University.

McGlotten, Shaka. 2016. "Black Data." In *No Tea, No Shade: New Writings in Black Queer Studies*, edited by E. Patrick Johnson, 262–86. Durham, NC: Duke University Press.

McGreevy, Patrick, and Phil Willon. 2013. "Female Inmate Surgery Broke Law." *Los Angeles Times*, July 14. http://articles.latimes.com.

Meckel, Richard A. 2015. *Save the Babies: American Public Health Reform and the Prevention of Infant Mortality, 1850–1929*. Reprint. Rochester, NY: University of Rochester Press.

Meijer, Miriam Claude. 2014. *Race and Aesthetics in the Anthropology of Petrus Camper (1722–1789)*. Reprint. Amsterdam: Rodopi.

Menzel, Annie. 2014. "The Political Life of Black Infant Mortality." PhD diss., University of Washington.

Meredith, Howard V. 1946. "Physical Growth from Birth to Two Years: II Head Circumference. Part I. A Review and Synthesis of North American Research on Groups of Infants." *Child Development* 17 (June): 1–61.

Meyer, Bruce A., Jane A. Arnold, and Debra Pascali-Bonaro. 2001. "Social Support by Doulas during Labor and the Early Postpartum Period." *Hospital Physician*, September, 57–65.

Miller, Annaick. 2015. "Using the 'War on Drugs' to Arrest Pregnant Women." *Political Research Associates* (blog), September 17. www.politicalresearch.org.

Minnesota VitalSigns. 2013. "Comparison of Births to Black/African American Women Born in the United States and Africa, Minnesota 2006–2010." Vital Signs. Minnesota Department of Health. www.health.state.mn.us.

Moehling, Carolyn, and Melissa Thomasson. 2012. "The Political Economy of Saving Mothers and Babies: The Politics of State Participation in the Sheppard-Towner Program." *Journal of Economic History* 72 (1): 75–103.

Mogul, Fred. 2017. "Black Mothers Face Higher Complication Rates When Delivering Babies in NYC." WNYC, January 9. www.wnyc.org.

Moraga, Cherríe. 1997. *Waiting in the Wings: Portrait of a Queer Motherhood.* Ithaca, NY: Firebrand Books.

Morbidity and Mortality Weekly Report. 1993. "Use of Race and Ethnicity in Public Health Surveillance. Summary of the CDC/ATSDF Workshop." Vol. 42 (RR-10). Atlanta, GA: US Department of Health and Human Services, Centers for Disease Control and Prevention.

Morgan, Jennifer L. 2004. *Laboring Women: Gender and Reproduction in New World Slavery.* Philadelphia: University of Pennsylvania Press.

Morgan, Lynn M. 2009. *Icons of Life: A Cultural History of Human Embryos.* Berkeley: University of California Press.

Morgan, Lynn M., and Meredith Wilson Michaels. 1999. *Fetal Subjects, Feminist Positions.* Philadelphia: University of Pennsylvania Press.

Morris, Theresa. 2013. *Cut It Out: The C-Section Epidemic in America.* New York: NYU Press.

Morris, Theresa, and M. Schulman. 2014. "Race Inequality in Epidural Use and Regional Anesthesia Failure in Labor and Birth: An Examination of Women's Experience." *Sexual and Reproductive Healthcare* 5 (4): 188–94.

Morrison, Toni. 1987. *Beloved: A Novel.* New York: Random House.

———. 1992. *Playing in the Dark: Whiteness and the Literary Imagination.* New York: Vintage.

Moynihan, Daniel Patrick. 1965. *The Negro Family: The Case for National Action.* Washington, DC: US Department of Labor.

Mullings, Leith. 1995. "Households Headed by Women: The Politics of Race, Class, and Gender." In *Conceiving the New World Order: The Global Politics of Reproduction,* edited by Faye D. Ginsburg and Rayna Rapp, 122–39. Berkeley: University of California Press.

———. 2000. "African-American Women Making Themselves: Notes on Black Feminist Research." *Souls* 2 (4): 18–29.

———. 2005a. "Interrogating Racism: Toward an Antiracist Anthropology." *Annual Review of Anthropology* 34:667–93.

———. 2005b. "Resistance and Resilience: The Sojourner Syndrome and the Social Context of Reproduction in Central Harlem." *Transforming Anthropology* 12 (2): 79–91.

Mullings, Leith, and Alaka Wali. 2001. *Stress and Resilience: The Social Context of Reproduction in Central Harlem.* New York: Kluwer Academic/Plenum.

Muraskas, Jonathan, and Kayhan Parsi. 2008. "The Cost of Saving the Tiniest Lives: NICUs versus Prevention." *Virtual Mentor. American Medical Association Journal of Ethics* 10 (10): 655–58.

Murphy, Eliza. 2013. "Photographer Creates Eye-Catching Images of Super Strong Babies." ABC News, September 9. http://abcnews.go.com.

Mwaria, Cheryl. 2001. "Biomedical Ethics, Gender and Ethnicity: Implications for Black Feminist Anthropology." In *Black Feminist Anthropology: Theory, Politics, Praxis and Poetics*, edited by Irma McClaurin, 187–210. New Brunswick, NJ: Rutgers University Press.

Nam, Ka Hyun, Ja Young Kwon, Young-Han Kim, and Yong-Won Park. 2010. "Pregnancy Outcome after Cervical Conization: Risk Factor for Preterm Delivery and the Efficacy of Prophylactic Cerclage." *Journal of Gynecologic Oncology* 21 (4): 225–29.

National Institute for Child Health and Human Development. 2016. October 27. www.nichd.nih.gov.

National Institutes of Health. n.d. "Ethel Collins Dunham: Celebrating America's Women Physicians." Accessed January 26, 2017. www.nlm.nih.gov.

National Perinatal Information System/Quality Analytic Services. n.d. www.npic.org.

Nelson, Alondra. 2011. *Body and Soul: The Black Panther Party and the Fight against Medical Discrimination*. Minneapolis: University of Minnesota Press.

Nelson, Charmaine A. 2010. *Representing the Black Female Subject*. New York: Routledge.

Nelson, Waldo E., ed. 1947. *Mitchell-Nelson Textbook of Pediatrics*. 4th ed. Philadelphia: W. B. Saunders.

New York City Department of Health and Mental Hygiene. 2016. *Severe Maternal Morbidity in New York City, 2008–2012*. New York.

New York State Department of Health. n.d. "Early Intervention Program." Accessed March 17, 2017. www.health.ny.gov.

Nivet, Marc A., and Laura Castillo-Page. 2014. "Diversity in the Physician Workforce: Facts and Figures 2014." Washington, DC: Association of American Medical Colleges.

Nordland, Rod. 2006. "Congo: More Vicious Than Rape." *Newsweek*, November 12. www.newsweek.com.

Oakley, Ann. 2016. "Interviewing Women Again: Power, Time, and the Gift." *Sociology* 50 (1): 195–213.

Oaks, Laury. 2015. *Giving Up Baby: Safe Haven Laws, Motherhood and Reproductive Justice*. New York: NYU Press.

O'Brien, Elizabeth, and Pratheek Rebala. 2017. "Find Out How Much It Costs to Give Birth in Every State." *Time*, October 30. http://time.com.

Omi, Michael, and Howard Winant. 1986. *Racial Formation in the United States: From the 1960s to the 1980s*. New York: Routledge.

O'Neil, Cathy. 2016. *Weapons of Math Destruction: How Big Data Increases Inequality and Threatens Democracy*. New York: Crown Books.

Ortiz, Ana Teresa, and Laura Briggs. 2003. "The Culture of Poverty, Crack Babies, and Welfare Cheats: The Making of the 'Healthy White Baby Crisis.'" *Social Text* 21 (3): 39–57.

O'Uhuru, Sakina. 2013. *Journey to Birth: The Story of a Midwife's Journey and a Reflection of the Heroic Women She Served along the Way*. Bloomington, IN: Author House.

Overfield, Theresa. 1995. *Biological Variations in Health and Illness: Race, Age, and Sex Differences*. Boca Raton, FL: CRC Press.

Paisley-Cleveland, Lisa. 2013. *Black Middle-Class Women and Pregnancy Loss: A Qualitative Inquiry*. Lanham, MD: Lexington Books.

Palmersheim, K. A. 2012. "Smoking during Pregnancy in Wisconsin and the United States: Trends and Patterns, 1990–2010." Milwaukee: University of Wisconsin–Milwaukee Center for Urban Initiatives and Research.

Patel, Roshni R., Philip Steer, Pat Doyle, Mark P. Little, and Paul Elliott. 2004. "Does Gestation Vary by Ethnic Group? A London-Based Study of Over 122,000 Pregnancies with Spontaneous Onset of Labour." *International Journal of Epidemiology* 33 (1): 107–13.

Patton, Stacey. 2014. "In America, Black Children Don't Get to Be Children." *Washington Post*, November 26.

Pérez, Miriam Zoila. 2016. "How Racism Harms Pregnant Women—And What Can Help." TED Talk. www.ted.com.

Perry, Joia Crear. 2016. "The Black Maternal Mortality Rate in the US Is an International Crisis." *The Root* (blog), September 30. www.theroot.com.

Petchesky, Rosalind Pollack. 1984. *Abortion and Woman's Choice: The State, Sexuality and Reproductive Freedom*. Lebanon, NH: University Press of New England.

———. 2003. "Fetal Images: The Power of Visual Culture in the Politics of Reproduction." *Feminist Studies* 13 (2): 263–92.

Petryna, Adriana. 2002. *Life Exposed: Biological Citizens after Chernobyl*. Princeton, NJ: Princeton University Press.

Phillips, Raylene. 2013. "Uninterrupted Skin-to-Skin Contact Immediately after Birth." *Newborn and Infant Nursing Review* 13 (2): 67–72.

Profit, Jochen, Jeffrey B. Gould, Mihoko Bennett, Benjamin A. Goldstein, David Draper, Ciaran S. Phibbs, and Henry C. Lee. 2017. "Racial/Ethnic Disparity in NICU Quality of Care Delivery." *Pediatrics* 140 (3): e20170918.

Rabinow, Paul, and Nikolas Rose. 2006. "Biopower Today." *Biosciences* 1 (2): 195–217.

Rahmanifar, Atossa. 2006. "Smoking during Pregnancy in Indiana, 1990–2004." Indiana State Department of Health October. www.in.gov.

Raju, T. N. K., B. M. Mercer, D. J. Burchfield, and G. F. Joseph. 2014. "Periviable Birth: Executive Summary of a Joint Workshop by the Eunice Kennedy Shriver National Institute for Child Health and Human Development, Society for Maternal-Fetal Medicine, American Academy of Pediatrics, and American College of Obstetricians and Gynecologists." *Journal of Perinatology* 34:333–42.

Raphael, Dana. 1969. "Uncle Rhesus, Auntie Pachyderm, and Mom: All Sons and Kinds of Mothering." *Perspectives in Biology and Medicine* 12 (2): 290–97.

———. 1973. *The Tender Gift: Breastfeeding*. New York: Schocken Books.

Rapp, Rayna. 1999. *Testing Women, Testing the Fetus: The Social Impact of Amniocentesis in America*. New York: Routledge.

Reagan, Leslie J. 2010. *Dangerous Pregnancies: Mothers, Disabilities, and Abortion in Modern America*. Berkeley: University of California Press.

Relman, Arnold S. 1980. "The New Medical-Industrial Complex." *New England Journal of Medicine* 303 (17): 963–70.

"Reproductive Justice: The Reproductive Justice Framework." n.d. Black Women for Reproductive Justice. Accessed March 15, 2014. https://bwrj.wordpress.com.

Riles, Annelise. 2013. "Market Collaboration: Finance, Culture, and Ethnography after Neoliberalism." *American Anthropologist* 115 (4): 555–69.

Rising, Sharon Schindler. 1998. "CenteringPregnancy: An Interdisciplinary Model of Empowerment." *Journal of Nurse-Midwifery* 43 (1): 46–54.

Rivoal, Isabelle, and Noel B. Salazar. 2013. "Contemporary Ethnographic Practice and the Value of Serendipity." *Social Anthropology* 21 (20): 178–85.

Roberts, Dorothy E. 1997. *Killing the Black Body: Race, Reproduction and the Meaning of Liberty*. New York: Vintage Books.

———. 2014. "Race, Gender, and Genetic Technologies: A New Reproductive Dystopia?" In *Women, Science, and Technology*, edited by Mary Wyer, Mary Barbercheck, Donna Cookmeyer, Hatice Örün Öztürk, and Marta Wayne, 318–33. 3rd ed. New York: Routledge.

Roberts, Elizabeth F. S. 2011. "Abandonment and Accumulation: Embryonic Futures in the United States and Ecuador." *Medical Anthropology Quarterly* 25 (2): 232–53.

———. 2012. *God's Laboratory: Assisted Reproduction in the Andes*. Berkeley: University of California Press.

Rogers, Naomi. 2007. "Race and the Politics of Polio: Warm Springs, Tuskegee, and the March of Dimes." *American Journal of Public Health* 97 (5): 784–95.

Rose, Nikolas. 2007. *The Politics of Life Itself: Biomedicine, Power and Subjectivity in the Twenty-First Century*. Princeton, NJ: Princeton University Press.

Ross, Loretta J., Lynn Roberts, Erika Derkas, Whitney Peoples, and Pamela Bridgewater Toure. 2017. *Radical Reproductive Justice: Foundations, Theory, Practice, Critique*. New York: Feminist Press.

Ross, Loretta J., and Rickie Solinger. 2017. *Reproductive Justice: An Introduction*. Berkeley: University of California Press.

Roth, Louise Marie, and Megan M. Henley. 2012. "Unequal Motherhood: Racial-Ethnic and Socioeconomic Disparities in Cesarean Sections in the United States." *Social Problems* 59 (2): 207–27.

Rothkopf, Joanna. 2014. "Ben Stein: Michael Brown Was Armed with His 'Strong, Scary Self.'" *Salon*, August 27. www.salon.com.

Rothman, Barbara Katz. 1993. *The Tentative Pregnancy: How Amniocentesis Changes the Experience of Motherhood*. New York: Norton.

———. 2016. *A Bun in the Oven: How the Food and Birth Movements Resist Industrialization*. New York: NYU Press.

Rusert, Britt. 2017. *Fugitive Science: Empiricism and Freedom in Early African American Culture*. New York: NYU Press.

Rushton, J. Philippe. 2000. *Race, Evolution, and Behavior*. 3rd ed. Port Huron, MI: Charles Darwin Research Institute.

Salihu, Hamisu M. n.d. "The Historic Origin of Prematurity/Low Birth Weight: Lessons from the Past." Delta Omega. Accessed April 4, 2017. www.deltaomega.org.

Scheper-Hughes, Nancy, and Margaret Lock. 1987. "The Mindful Body: A Prolegomenon to Future Work in Medical Anthropology." *Medical Anthropology Quarterly* 1 (1): 6–41.

Schiebinger, Londa. 2004. *Nature's Body: Gender and the Making of Modern Science*. New Brunswick, NJ: Rutgers University Press.

Schoendorf, Kenneth C., Carol J. R. Hogue, Joel C. Kleinman, and Diane Rowley. 1992. "Mortality among Infants of Black as Compared with White College-Educated Parents." *New England Journal of Medicine* 326 (23): 1522–26.

Schwartz, Marie Jenkins. 2006. *Birthing a Slave: Motherhood and Medicine in the Antebellum South*. Cambridge, MA: Harvard University Press.

Scott, James C. 1985. *Weapons of the Weak: Everyday Forms of Peasant Resistance*. New Haven, CT: Yale University Press.

Semple, Janet. 1993. *Bentham's Prison: A Study of the Panopticon Penitentiary*. Oxford: Clarendon Press.

Shamus, Kristen Jordan. 2016. "South Carolina Finds Innovative Way to Help First-Time Moms." *Detroit Free Press*, December 4. www.freep.com.

Shaw, Gary M., Paul H. Wise, Jonathan Mayo, Suzan L. Carmichael, Catherine Ley, Deirdre J. Lyell, Bat Zion Shachar, Kathry Melsop, Ciaran S. Phibbs, David K. Stevenson, Julie Parsonnet, and Jeffrey B. Gould. 2014. "Maternal Prepregnancy Body Mass Index and Risk of Spontaneous Preterm Birth." *Paediatric and Perinatal Epidemiology* 28:302–11.

Sims, J. Marion. 1853. *On the Treatment of Vesico-Vaginal Fistula*. Philadelphia: Blanchard and Lea.

Singhal, Astha, Yu-Yu Tien, and Renee Y. Hsia. 2016. "Racial-Ethnic Disparities in Opioid Prescriptions at Emergency Department Visits for Conditions Commonly Associated with Prescription Drug Abuse." Edited by Soraya Seedat. *PLOS One* 11 (8): e0159224.

"Sistersong: Women of Color Reproductive Justice Collective." n.d. http://sistersong.net.

Smart, Andrew, Richard Tutton, Paul Martin, George T. H. Ellison, and Richard Ashcroft. 2008. "The Standardization of Race and Ethnicity in Biomedical Science Editorials and UK Biobanks." *Social Studies of Science* 38 (3): 407–23.

Smith, Barbara, ed. 1983. *Home Girls: A Black Feminist Anthology*. New York: Kitchen Table: Women of Color Press.

Smith, Christen A. 2016. *Afro-Paradise: Blackness, Violence, and Performance in Brazil*. Urbana: University of Illinois Press.

Smith, Linda Tuhiwai. 2012. *Decolonizing Methodologies: Research and Indigenous Peoples*. 2nd ed. London: Zed Books.

Smith, Maureen Margaret. 2006. *Wilma Rudolph: A Biography*. Westport, CT: Greenwood Press.

Smith, Susan L. 1995. *Sick and Tired of Being Sick and Tired: Black Women's Health Activism in America*. Philadelphia: University of Pennsylvania Press.

Smith-Oka, Vania. 2013. "Managing Labor and Delivery among Impoverished Populations in Mexico: Cervical Examinations as Bureaucratic Practice." *American Anthropologist* 114 (4): 595–607.

Somashekhar, Sandhya. 2016. "The Disturbing Reason Some African American Patients May Be Undertreated for Pain." *Washington Post*, April 4. www.washingtonpost.com.

Spillers, Hortense J. 1987. "Mama's Baby, Papa's Maybe: An American Grammar Book." *Diacritics* 17 (2): 65–81.

Stacey, Judith. 1988. "Can There Be a Feminist Ethnography?" *Women's Studies International Forum* 11 (1): 21–27.

Staton, Lisa J., Mukta Panda, Ian Chen, Inginia Genao, James Kurz, Mark Pasanen, Alex J. Mechaber, Madhusudan Menon, Jane O'Rorke, JoAnn Wood, Eric Rosenberg, Charles Faeslis, Tim Carey, Diane Calleson, and Sam Cykert. 2007. "When Race Matters: Disagreement in Pain Perception between Patients and Their Physicians in Primary Care." *Journal of the National Medical Association* 99 (5): 532–38.

Steckel, Richard H. 1986a. "Birth Weights and Infant Mortality among American Slaves." *Explorations in Economic History* 23 (2): 173–98.

———. 1986b. "A Dreadful Childhood: The Excess Mortality of American Slaves." *Social Science History* 10 (4): 427–65.

Stevenson, Alexa. 2010. *Half Baked: The Story of My Nerves, My Newborn, and How We Both Learned to Breathe*. Philadelphia: Running Press.

Stevenson, Lisa. 2014. *Life beside Itself: Imagining Care in the Canadian Arctic*. Berkeley: University of California Press.

Stovall, Maya, and Alex B. Hill. 2015. "Blackness in Post-bankruptcy Detroit: Racial Politics and Public Discourse." *North American Dialogue* 19 (2): 117–27.

Strain, Tracy Heather. 2008. *Unnatural Causes . . . Is Inequality Making Us Sick: When the Bough Breaks*. California Newsreel.

Suite, Derek H., Robert La Bril, Annelle Primm, and Phyllis Harrison-Ross. 2007. "Beyond Misdiagnosis, Misunderstanding, and Mistrust: Relevance of the Historical Perspective in the Medical and Mental Health Treatment of People of Color." *Journal of the National Medical Association* 99 (8): 879–85.

Tandy, Elizabeth C. 1937. "Infant and Maternal Mortality among Negroes." *Journal of Negro Education* 6 (3): 322–49.

Terrell, Mary Church. 2005. *A Colored Woman in a White World*. Amherst, NY: Humanity Books.

Theilein, Kathleen. 2012. "Exploring the Group Prenatal Care Model: A Critical Review of the Literature." *Journal of Perinatal Education* 21 (4): 209–81.

Thomas, Patricia E. 2011. "Do Racial Disparities Persist in Infant Mortality from Respiratory Distress Syndrome?" *Journal of Obstetric, Gynecologic and Neonatal Nursing* 40 (1): 47–51.

Thompson, Charis. 2005. *Making Parents: The Ontological Choreography of Reproductive Technologies*. Cambridge, MA: MIT Press.

Trawalter, Sophie, Kelly M. Hoffman, and Adam Waytz. 2012. "Racial Bias in Perceptions of Others' Pain." *PLOS One* 7 (11): e48546.

Tsing, Anna Lowenhaupt. 1990. "Monster Stories: Women Charged with Perinatal Endangerment." In *Uncertain Terms: Negotiating Gender in American Culture*, edited by Faye Ginsburg and Anna Lowenhaupt Tsing, 282–99. Boston: Beacon Press.

Turner, Timothy. 2012. "Development of the Polio Vaccine: A Historical Perspective of Tuskegee University's Role in Mass Production and Distribution of HeLa Cells." *Journal of Health Care for the Poor and Underserved* 23 (4): 5–10.

Twine, France Winddance. 2011. *Outsourcing the Womb: Race, Class and Gestational Surrogacy in a Global Market*. 2nd ed. New York: Routledge.

US Children's Bureau. n.d. *The Hygiene of Maternity and Childhood: Outlines for Study*. Separate No. 1 Child Care and Child Welfare Bureau Publication No. 90. Washington, DC: US Government Printing Office.

US Congress. 1963. "Civil Rights Hearings Before Subcommittee No. 5." Washington, DC: US Government Printing Office.

US Department of Health, Education, and Welfare, Public Health Service. 1986. "Vital and Health Statistics: Data from the National Survey of Family Growth." National Center for Health Statistics, 1986.

Valdez, Natali. 2018. "The Redistribution of Reproductive Responsibility: On the Epigenetics of 'Environment' in Prenatal Interventions." *Medical Anthropology Quarterly 32 (3): 425–42.*

Virey, Julien-Joseph. 1837. *Natural History of the Negro Race*. Translated by J. H. Guinebault. Charleston, SC: D. J. Dowling.

Wadman, Meredith. 2017. *The Vaccine Race: Science, Politics, and the Human Costs of Defeating Disease*. New York: Viking Press.

Wailoo, Keith. 2001. *Dying in the City of the Blues: Sickle Cell Anemia and the Politics of Race and Health*. Chapel Hill: University of North Carolina Press.

Wall, L. Lewis. 2006. "The Medical Ethics of Dr. J Marion Sims: A Fresh Look at the Historical Record." *Journal of Medical Ethics* 32 (6): 346–50.

Walters, Suzana Danuta, and Laura Harrison. 2014. "Not Ready to Make Nice: Aberrant Mothers in Contemporary Culture." *Feminist Media Studies* 14 (1): 38–55.

Ware, Harry. 1936. "Cesarean Section in Richmond, Virginia." *Virginia Medical Monthly* 68:82–86.

Washington, Harriet. 2006. *Medical Apartheid: The Dark History of Medical Experimentation on Black Americans from Colonial Times to the Present*. New York: Anchor Books.

Webb, Jamilla H. 2016. "Why Black Birth Matters." *Mamablack* (blog), October 13. www.mamablack.org.

Weheliye, Alexander G. 2014. *Habeas Viscus: Racializing Assemblages, Biopolitics and Black Feminist Theories of the Human*. Durham, NC: Duke University Press.

Weinbaum, Alys Eve. 2013. "The Afterlife of Slavery and the Problem of Reproductive Freedom." *Social Text* 31 (2): 49–68.

White, Michael. 2011. "The End at the Beginning." *Ochser Journal* 11 (4): 309–11.

Wies, Jennifer R., and Hillary J. Haldane. 2015. *Applying Anthropology to Gender-Based Violence: Global Responses, Local Practices.* Lanham, MD: Lexington Books.

Womack, Autumn. 2017. "Visuality, Surveillance, and the Afterlife of Slavery." *American Literary History* 29 (1): 191–204.

Woodbury, Robert Morse. 1925. *Causal Factors in Infant Mortality: A Statistical Study Based on Investigations in Eight Cities.* Publication no. 142. Washington, DC: US Department of Labor, Children's Bureau.

Woods, Simon. 2016. "Big Data Governance: Solidarity and the Patient Voice." In *The Ethics of Biomedical Big Data*, edited by B. Mittelstadt and L. Floridi, 221–38. Switzerland: Springer.

Wun, Connie. 2015. "Against Captivity: Black Girls and School Discipline Policies in the Afterlife of Slavery." *Educational Policy* 30 (1): 1–26.

Yin, X. A., and Y. S. Liu. 2015. "Association between Placenta Previa and Risk of Hypertensive Disorders of Pregnancy: A Meta-analysis Based on 7 Cohort Studies." *European Review for Medical and Pharmacological Sciences* 19 (12): 2146–52.

Ylppö, Arvo. 1919. "Pathologisch-Anatomische Studien Bei Frühgeborenen Makroskopische Und Mikroskopische Untersuchungen Mit Hinweisen Auf Die Klinik Und Mit Besonderer Berücksichtigung Der Hämorrhagien." *European Journal of Pediatrics* 20 (1): 212–431.

Zelizer, Viviana A. 1994. *Pricing the Priceless Child: The Changing Social Value of Children.* Princeton, NJ: Princeton University Press.

INDEX

Page numbers in italics indicate an illustration. Page numbers followed by a "t" indicate a table.

ABOUT THE AUTHOR

Dána-Ain Davis is Professor of Urban Studies at Queens College. Davis is also on the faculty of the PhD Program in Anthropology and Director of the Center for the Study of Women and Society at the Graduate Center, CUNY.